FACE-TO-FACE

The Cinema of Adoor Gopalakrishnan

PARTHAJIT BARUAH did his postgraduation in English literature from Pune University. He later joined the film appreciation course at the Film and Television Institute of India (FTII), Pune. He received the 2010 Prag Channel Film Critic Award for *Chalachitraor Taranga,* a book on film theory, while his documentary on an abused young tribal woman, *Laxmi Orang: Rising from the Grave*, won him multiple awards at the Darbhanga International Film Festival. His second documentary, *The Dhemaji Tragedy*, won awards at the Delhi International Film Festival, the Film-North East Festival 2016, the 4th Kolkata Short International Film Festival 2015, the 3rd Indian Cine Film Festival 2015 and the 4th Delhi International Short Film Festival 2015. The Nehru Yuva Kendra, Assam, has conferred on him the Youth Icon Award 2016. He presented his paper 'Shakespeare and Assamese Cinema' at the Indian Shakespeares on Screen conference in London recently. He teaches English and cinema at the Renaissance Junior College in Nagaon, Assam.

FACE-TO-FACE

The Cinema of Adoor Gopalakrishnan

PARTHAJIT BARUAH

HarperCollins *Publishers* India

First published in 2016 by
HarperCollins *Publishers* India

Building 10, Tower A, 4th Floor, DLF Cyber City, Phase II,
Gurugram Haryana – 122002, India
www.harpercollins.co.in

P-ISBN: 978-93-5136-195-4
E-ISBN: 978-93-5136-196-1

2 4 6 8 10 9 7 5 3 1

Typeset in 10.5/13.5 Minion Pro at SURYA, New Delhi

Printed and bound at
MicroPrints India, New Delhi

Dedicated to my wife Ananya
who taught me how to live and love life

Contents

Foreword

A Question of Rephrasing

'You have been in the business of film-making for so long, yet why such few films?' This is a question I am asked very frequently. Little do these well-meaning souls know that it has been no easy path that I have traversed in making my eleven feature films in a career spanning forty years. One can hardly blame the curious questioner because he knows of many prolific directors capable of producing one film after another with no intervals between. While I salute the faith and capacity of directors who can deliver such products, I must add here that I do not appreciate those films which are made in the name of entertainment for the masses and designed solely to suit the market.

In India, where the so-called film industry prides itself on the fact that we churn out the largest number of films in so many languages, the term 'cinema' automatically refers to commercial cinema. Everything other than the standard products is an aberration and hence untouchable. They get no financing, no distribution, and so no exhibition either. The committed film-maker must have indefatigable faith and a strong will to struggle against all odds and still sustain his sanity in the face of various hostilities. Even if such a film-maker manages to make a film on his own, there is little chance of its getting shown in the theatres. And a national or international award for a film becomes a sure indication for the common man to avoid it!

In a bleak and hopeless scenario like this, the question, in all fairness, should have been, 'How did you manage to make those eleven films?'

In all probability the next question would be, 'So you make art movies?' To which, invariably, my humble answer is, 'No, I just make films the way I like to.'

My young friend Parthajit Baruah has single-mindedly and tirelessly studied my work before venturing to write this book. His detailed research on the background as well as the foreground of my film career, I believe, has paid off. I hope this book will contribute substantially to the understanding and appreciation of my work.

—*Adoor Gopalakrishnan*

Preface

Adoor Gopalakrishnan: Pathfinder

Beyond the admiration and gratitude any cinephile – or I should rather say, any viewer – is likely to feel for Adoor Gopalakrishnan and his films, what does a foreign observer like me have to say about him, and them? Certainly unable to achieve the precise and knowledgeable understanding of his work that Parthajit Baruah shares in this book, I can only point out a few significant aspects of Adoor's cinema, and the way it appealed to me, and, I assume, to many non-Indian film lovers. Seen from afar, his films stand in a very specific place inside the huge modern current that vigorously swept cinema all over the world since the 1950s, from Italian Neo-realism and the French New Wave onward.

On that level, the specificity of Adoor's input was mostly noticeable with his second feature film, *Kodiyettam*, that is, more than the more explicitly neo-realist *Swayamvaram*. Schematically, I'd characterize this by the almost impossible fusion of two qualities which are so often separate, if not antagonistic: a subtle mix of deep humanity, empathy for the body and soul of humans as they are, and, at the same time, a stylized organization of storytelling, defying the usual rules of narration, choosing time and space instead of action and plot whenever needed, boldly affirming the abilities of cinema to open up the viewer's spirit, and to enhance and interrogate its relation with the world. It is most unusual that such an affirmed aesthetic option would cohabit with such a heartfelt relation with characters. Parthajit Baruah talks about Adoor's work as 'a voice of humanity who believes in the Gandhian principle'. I confess I don't know much about Gandhian principles beyond superficial common knowledge, but obviously one from a different cultural background can relate with such an attitude towards mankind, social relations, and the world as a whole – including what westerners call 'nature' in a questionable separation of the cultural and social.

Adoor's very rare ability to associate stylistic elements with emotional empathy reaches an unparalleled peak with his masterpiece *Elippathayam*. Though effective with all characters, it is even more true with the depiction of Unni, the childish landlord. In terms of finding the fusion between stylization and sentiment, the only acceptable comparison I can think of is with Chekov stage plays, though with extremely different components. But, and this leads us far away from stage theatre, it is unfair to talk only about the human characters, though they are unforgettably moving, specially thanks to the clever lack of psychological explanation. Unfair because one should also mention the house, the landscape, even the light and the sky of Kerala. Adoor's cinema is deeply rooted in a geographical and climatic setting, which is much more than a film set: elements of a world as active protagonists of happenings around.

As a foreigner who, at the time, had never been in Kerala – and, I should admit, was hardly aware of the existence of this state, not to speak about the ability to locate it on a map – there was the immediate discovery of a certain quality of green and blue, that is, of a certain relation between heat and rain, clouds and trees, and a certain tonality in a language, which, I learned only later, is called Malayalam. It is only at the end of this book, in the chapter dedicated to *Nizhalkkuthu*, that Parthajit Baruah has this subtle insight about the meaning of palmyra trees as witnesses. But, at least for foreign viewers raised and living where no palmyra tree naturally grows, it seems obvious that these trees, as well as the elevated paths circulating between the fields, the shadows in the traditional houses, all testify to the reality and the specificity of a certain world, or a certain state of our common world.

Ignorant as I was – as I am still, but a little less though, and ignorant as most Western viewers were and are – 'Indian cinema' meant either Satyajit Ray or Bollywood (with, hopefully, the discovery of one Guru Dutt and one Ritwik Ghatak movie). Now, with these Gopalakrishnan movies, we were elsewhere. The atmosphere had changed, the physical aspect of men, women and children had changed, the rules of the game had changed. And though not quite lost, the immense humanity of Adoor's point of view was opening access to this other world.

This is probably not obvious to Indian viewers, who are of course aware of all this, but one has to underline how mind-opening it was to discover such wonderful films, so different to what we used to call 'Indian films' – certainly even beyond Adoor's consciousness of the phenomenon. Later on, we were able to discover yet more Kerala creations among the great cinema of the world.

These qualities also relate, and maybe in an even more important way, to another aspect. Worldwide, the modern cinema of the 1960s and '70s belongs to a time of intense political activity. Almost always, in western as well as eastern Europe, in Japan, in Latin America, in the US, it related to liberation movements, youth uprisings, new forms of criticism of the dominant regimes and social organizations. This was part of the energy of the 'new cinemas' from all over the world but, as well, it became very often a limit, when the militant agenda prevailed upon cinema itself.

Hopefully, many among the greatest directors played with this threat in various creative ways, from Jean-Luc Godard to Oshima Nagisa, Glauber Rocha to Milos Forman or Bernardo Bertolucci. But very rare were those who managed to openly, frontally, acknowledge the complexity and the urge of the political issues in their countries, and invent a cinematic form that would, again, open up the understanding of the medium. This is what Adoor Gopalakrishnan did, the most explicit example being the amazing *Kathapurushan*.

Kathapurushan is a quite unique case of a political film which moves forward with the hopes and promises of activist action, and, at the same time, is able to display the contradiction and dead ends of what it stands for without despising or betraying it. A film that not only relates with human characters on a personal level and shares the emotion of generous engagement, but also shows up some of its ridiculous facets. A film which finds its way to ultimately laugh about all of it, in a way that does not dismiss what was previously done and seen, but on the contrary enriches it, bringing a larger understanding of the complexity of a social, political and individual situation, in a simultaneously heartfelt and light way. For an ignorant foreigner like me, it was also the discovery of the astonishing political history of Kerala, its very specific blend of utopia, progress towards democracy, corruption, traditionalism (in itself and as part of the larger Indian historical process) both before and since Independence.

At the time, we did not know about *Mukhamukham* which, to a certain extent, anticipates what *Kathapurushan* fully accomplishes, in terms of giving access to the specificity of Kerala's political history – a specificity which it is very possible to relate to, despite its local aspects.

If *Elippathayam* and *Kathapurushan* are probably the most significant and obvious achievements of this ability to bring together the life and depiction of real persons and the metaphoric parable, to articulate the individual and the collective with a proud sense of the emotional and intellectual effects of original formal choices, these characteristics also infuse each of Adoor's films.

In the chapter dedicated to *Kathapurushan*, Parthajit Baruah quotes Adoor saying, 'I am talking of things I know intimately.' The director refers to the historical background, the factual events that happened and affected India, or more specifically Kerala, during the period of time covered by the film. But this sentence is appropriate for all of Adoor's works, sometimes in some unexpected ways: though he did not personally experience the position of all his characters, he always engages with the viewer from a deeply felt inner approach – this is, for instance, very clear and remarkable in case of his feminine characters, who are so important in many of his films even before *Naalu Pennugal*.

Once again, in the twilight parable *Nizhalkkuthu*, the 'Adoor blend' does not only achieve a unique level of artistic and humanist triumph, it also turns out to be the base to elaborate the depth of meanings and questions contained in this astonishingly delicate, though violent, film. Adoor once said that the only thing he hates is violence. I figure that what he meant was brutality. Because, in their apparently soft tones, his films deal with the reality of violence, the violence of the world, but without taking advantage of it, without capitalizing on violence, even under the excuse of denouncing it, as so many films do. Which is paramount to an ethical work of art. In the chapter dedicated to *Nizhalkkuthu*, Parthajit Baruah appropriately underlines that 'Adoor breaks the conventional and stereotyped notion of a hangman and makes an effort to show that the hangman is a normal human being who leads a family life.' This is one of the many ways, but one of the most significant, through which a director with an open spirit is likely to reconstruct the perception of humans mechanically associated with one facet of their complex being.

Even more than a mark of respect for the character, and eventually for the real persons this character refers to, it is a mark of respect for the viewers.

Visually magnificent but always in a non-self-imposing way, inventing creative use of the musical score (and of the absence of it), redefining the relation between the camera and the bodies of actors as a resource field so rarely exploited, understanding the meaning and the efficiency of the films' pace, and especially of the long take, Adoor's mise en scène makes use of an extraordinarily large array of cinematic tools. With both his deep understanding of cinema language and his immense knowledge in various cultural fields (as many of his documentaries testify) this film-maker proves that the mise en scène itself can capture high spiritual values, and can help share them. In this sense, Adoor Gopalakrishnan's films not only proclaim his own achievement, but serve as a kind of anthem for the very nature of film-making at its best.

Jean-Michel Frodon

Introduction

From Kerala to the World

Adoor Gopalakrishnan has brought about a renaissance in the narrative technique of Indian cinema. This technique grew increasingly elaborate as he went on to become not only a staunch practitioner of India's alternative cinema but also one of the foremost film-makers on the map of world cinema.

Adoor is not handcuffed to the ethos of the twentieth and twenty-first centuries; rather, he observes, probes and reflects upon the changes effected in the period his story springs from, giving it new shape and colour. The sense of belonging, of identity, of responsibility, the quest for selfhood, dreams and enchantments, the thirst and lust for power, identity crisis, spiritual progress or regression – are all themes that he explores and develops melodically in his films.

Adoor portrays the common man and his struggles to find his footing in a world ridden by political and social upheavals. His foremost concern is the capability of this man/woman to sustain and survive in such a world, to stand up against adversity, yet hold on to human values and moralities. But his visions can be optimistic: in spite of the harsh and bleak world that Sita (the female protagonist in *Swayamvaram*) faces after her husband's demise, she is not decimated by her circumstances – life doesn't come to a standstill for her. Rather, the film impresses on the viewer how Sita's strength of character helps her overcome adversities.

Renowned director Shyam Benegal observes in the Foreword to the book, *A Door to Adoor*:

> Adoor's films are meditations on the human condition. He has an extraordinary ability to delve into the complexities of human existence:

> compulsions forced by history and tradition, and by the dynamics of social and political change. His narrative appears simple enough but as the stories unfold, nothing is simple any more. Moral ambiguities, multiple realities, spin their web around the protagonists who are driven by forces that are as much released by individual volition as they are by social, environmental or historical factors.

Adoor's strength is the strength of his principles and convictions. He never compromises on these whatever be the marked (or market) trends of cinema. When Indian cinema was infected by cheap populist formulae (Malayalam cinema being no exception), Adoor, committed to the cause of pure cinema, never yielded. (On some film-makers who had fallen into the popular formula trap, Adoor noted, in an interview with Prem Panicker, 'Moviemaking has become a gamble, not a creative endeavour.') Adoor, for his part, continued to voice the predicament and angst of human existence through his creations.

Adoor Gopalakrishnan is always aware that change is inevitable. Nothing in this world is permanent. But an artist can through timeless works of art inspire posterity. Adoor has witnessed the hopes and dreams of Indians since Independence, their disillusionment at the failures, split of the Communist Party of India, the Naxal uprising, economic crises, the Emergency, the alarming rise of communal politics. The change in the socio-economic and political sectors in Kerala is a running theme through his films. Never giving in to commercialism, never compromising with his creativity, Adoor continues to draw and flesh out pictures of human beings caught in combative conditions.

Nandita Das is an established name in serious Indian cinema, and has received national/international awards for her brilliant performances in films both in Hindi and several other languages (four in Malayalam, including Adoor's *Naalu Pennungal*) and won a national award too for the first film she directed. She candidly remarks, 'He is one of the very few eminent film-makers who have really stuck to their commitment to good cinema. So it was an honour to have been asked to work with him.'

Another way of putting it is: Adoor is born and lives for good cinema. He once said to me, 'Cinema is my profession and I treasure it. You do many things in your life. But cinema has given meaning to my life.'

Every time he ventures into cinema, he looks for a new grammar, a new language. He deals with ongoing problems that have universal meaning. He does not limit himself to any specific period, but rather the quality of timelessness of his works makes the film always contemporary and relevant. That is why he has a large number of viewers worldwide who wait eagerly for his explorations into untrodden zones. And while he is well aware and keeps abreast of changing technology, his cinema always employs a fresh language that is unhindered by the new technology.

Adoor's films start from the 1940s and invariably focus on the traditions, history and aesthetics of Kerala. The eminent French film critic Jean-Michel Frodon, while discussing the thematic dynamics of Adoor's works, states:

> Adoor's films are unique since they articulate stories of human and social issues that work universally but simultaneously have a very local base, form and setting. For me, it is very impressive to find an original answer to a very general question of how you translate local, social and historical questions to a global level and, at the same time, discover a new world. I do not know at all about the people of Kerala, the language of Kerala and the landscape of Kerala. But you experience it in his films so strongly along with the locale and its concerns.

In his forty-year journey across the cinematic map, Adoor has given us eleven thought-provoking films that transcend the linguistic, cultural and geographic confines of regional scenarios. Adoor's own original, inimitable stories were visualized in works such as *Swayamvaram, Kodiyettam, Elippathayam, Mukhamukham, Anantaram, Kathapurushan* and *Nizhalkkuthu*. His adapted works are *Mathilukal*, based on a story by Vaikom Muhammad Basheer, *Vidheyan* (Paul Zacharia), *Naalu Pennungal* and *Oru Pennum Randaanum* (Thakazhi Sivasankara Pillai).

In a personal email communication with me, film scholar Anil Zankar writes:

> Over the years he has depicted a variety of subjects. If one considers films like *Elippathayam, Mukhamukham, Kathapurushan* and *Anantaram*, we find that he wants to explore the world within an individual living in a certain historical context. His protagonists are not men of action, who will drive the narrative forward. In fact, sometimes an intriguing stasis and ambiguity define them. In *Elippathayam*, the main character is confined to his own self and the limited space around

> him. He is completely frozen in time. In *Mukhamukham*, in the earlier part of the film, the hero is a leader, an organizer of workers. Then he goes underground for many years. After his emergence, he has changed irreversibly. He maintains a most intriguing silence from then on till the end of the film. *Kathapurushan* is a journey and growth of a person who has to overcome many obstacles. *Anantaram* gives us the delightful experience of discovering the introvert as well as the extrovert within the same person. It also is one of the rare experiences in Indian cinema of non-linear time created with multiple dimensions.
>
> His concerns and the fact that his films are not plot-driven has shaped his mise en scène in some way. His mise en scène is quiet, contemplative, observing human beings in landscapes or in the architecture of their habitat and borders on the minimalist. The courtyards, the interiors of the homes, the various properties therein gain an eloquent presence in Adoor's films. He has been an explorer, who has stuck to the difficult task of depicting ambivalence and multivalence of human life through his film narratives.

It was during the 1970s, when Kerala was experiencing severe economic crisis and the Emergency (the darkest period in Indian history) that Adoor emerged and evolved as a film-maker, his seminal works being *Swayamvaram* (1972) and *Kodiyettam* (1977). There followed *Elippathayam* (1981), *Mukhamukham* (1984), *Anantaram* (1987), *Mathilukal* (1990), *Vidheyan* (1993), *Kathapurushan* (1995), *Nizhalkkuthu* (2002), *Naalu Pennungal* (2007) and *Oru Pennum Randaanum* (2008).

Swayamvaram (One's Own Choice), dealing with life's choices and the consequences thereof, exposes the moral and spiritual crisis of the middle class through the protagonist of the film, Viswanathan. *Kodiyettam* (Ascent) describes the metaphoric journey of Sankarankutty from his waywardness to the realization that he is a responsible member of society. Sankarankutty is the epitome of the common man who is good at heart but is unaware that he has a duty towards family and society. *Elippathayam* (The Rat-trap) tells the tragedy of Unnikunju who has a feudal past and is trapped within himself and his claustrophobic ancestral house, unable to grasp the changes that are taking place around him. The film weaves in the theme of how women are caught in the web of the feudal system. *Elippathayam*, for which Adoor received the British Film Institute Award in 1982 – classing him with such world masters like

R.W. Fassbinder, Alain Resnais and Bernardo Bertolucci – established Adoor as a director of international stature. He is the only Indian director, other than Satyajit Ray, who has been honoured with this award.

Mukhamukham (Face-to-Face) is set against the backdrop of the political scenario of Kerala around the time of the great split in the Communist Party of India. People often prefer a myth to the reality as we see from the life and career of Sreedharan, the protagonist. *Anantaram* (Monologue) deals with the duality of reality. The film advances through a monologue by Ajayan as he seeks to find as well reveal the routes his life has taken to bring him to his present predicament. *Mathilukal* (The Walls) is a unique love story: Confined within the precincts of a jail in the pre-Independence era, Basheer falls in love with Narayani, a woman prisoner on the other side of the high prison wall. They cannot see each other but love blossoms regardless. *Vidheyan* (The Servile) probes the master–slave relationship through the story of Bhaskara Patelar and Thommi in a south Karnataka setting. *Kathapurushan* (Man of the Story) documents the emotional journey of Kunjunni, a young sensitive middle-class man who hopes to change a society into a more just and equitable one and in the process himself undergoes a change. *Nizhalkkuthu* (Shadow Kill) looks at the last hangman in Travancore who cannot deal with death any more. *Naalu Pennungal* (Four Women) records the journey, in a male-dominated social set-up, of four Indian women from different classes in the period from the 1940s to the 1960s. The four stories are adapted from works by the famous Thakazhi Sivasankara Pillai. *Oru Pennum Randaanum* (A Climate for Crime) has four separate stories, again not directly connected with one another but all dealing with crime in different contexts and social situations.

Adoor is regarded by many as the heir to Satyajit Ray. British film critic Derek Malcolm wrote to me:

> Adoor Gopalakrishnan is generally considered as the one Indian director able to take over the mantle of the great Satyajit Ray. His films come from as deep within the culture of Kerala as Ray's come from within Bengal. But, like Ray, his work easily transcends those boundaries and thus becomes international in appeal. He is as strict with himself as Ray, refusing any compromise for the sake of popularity, and his films not only have an acute sensibility but a force of expression

> that underlines the nature of what he wants to say. Few other directors combine cinematic skill with such a keen feeling for people, places and the social and political culture of the land he knows so well. We should cherish such a film-maker. He is a rare example of total integrity in an age where even some of the best directors play the game of compromise for the sake of gaining increased appeal.

What differentiates Adoor from Ray is his approach and representation of human problems – his films are more complex and metaphorical than Ray's. He makes ordinary day-to-day occurrences extraordinary through the power of his observation, research, creative imagination and cinematic technique. 'The power of silence, the quasi-Japanese sense of space, the stolidity of the steady image, the force of repetition are all his,' film scholar Chidananda Dasgupta wrote in his thought-provoking book of essays, *Seeing Is Believing*.[1]

Adoor's films are replete with autobiographical elements: for example, Adoor was a follower of Gandhi's principle of non-violence and the Gandhian value of dignity of labour. Gandhi figures prominently in the masterly *Nizhalkkuthu*: we see the protagonist's son, Muthu, a faithful follower of Gandhi's idealism, forced by circumstances to accompany his father to execute a convict. Adoor's entire family, including himself as a child, completely broke down at the news of the assassination of Gandhi. This situation is picturized in *Kathapurushan*. In the same film, the story of estranged parents and the breech delivery of the child and the astrologer's prediction for the baby's future are all drawn from Adoor's own life.

Today, Adoor has been honoured round the world with numerous awards and recognition for his contributions to the art of cinema. These include Lifetime Achievement Awards at the Mumbai, New Jersey and Cairo International Film Festivals (2009), and the Denver Film Festival in 1996, and retrospectives at major festivals and museums, including the Munich Film Museum (2010), Ljubljana (Slovenia, 2009), the Smithsonian Institution in Washington DC (2002), Lincoln Centre, New York (1998), the Cinematheque in Paris (1995), more screenings in New York and in Figuera da Fos in Portugal (1994), Munich (1992), Nantes (1989), La Rochelle (1987), Pesaro (in Italy), and Helsinki (1985). Recent honours include the Deshikottama award (DLitt) from the Viswa Bharati University in Santiniketan, earlier given to Satyajit Ray. Adoor has also been conferred the 2015 Biswaratna Dr Bhupen Hazarika International Solidarity Award, instituted by Assam's premier literary organization, Asam Sahitya Sabha. He is the second to receive this prestigious biennial award, the first going to a well-known dancer and writer from Bangladesh. Adoor has also served as jury president at various international film festivals, including those at Valladolid (Spain) and Goa in India (both 2011), Dubai (2010), and Cairo and Fribourg (2009), the Alexandria Film Festival in Egypt (1996), and Singapore (1991). The Adoor Gopalakrishnan Film Archive and Research Fund was inaugurated at the University of Wisconsin in April 2013, the first such fund to be set up in honour of an Indian film-maker.

Through this book it is my endeavour to convey to the reader an understanding of the films of this master and an insight to his life and cinema, which seem inseparable.

1
Three Cs
Culture, Custom, Communism

Cinema has become an integral part of the culture of Kerala and its people revel in film festivals as much as any religious festival in the state. Cinema, culture and Kerala are inextricably intertwined and the meaning of one cannot be comprehended in isolation.

At the opening ceremony of the fifteenth International Film Festival of Kerala, 2010, at Nishagandhi, I was impressed by the speech of M.A. Baby, the then minister for education and cultural affairs, Government of Kerala, who said, 'Along with culture, education also should have film components ... we, as part of the new curriculum, tried to introduce great cinema to students, even to those who are studying in schools, and the impact has been amazing. Of course, taking advantage of the availability of technology, now many school students are not only making short films but even short features.'

And in understanding the cinema of Adoor Gopalakrishnan, it is necessary to look at the major political, social and cultural landscapes that inform his films.

Kerala's scenic beauty, its lush greenery, mountains and hills, the sea, flora and fauna and its geographical position, have been celebrated by poets and authors, for example, in the following poetic picture that Mahakavi Vallathol paints: 'Mother Kerala sleeps with her head on the lap of the Sahyadri, clad in green, and her feet pillowed on the crystal ocean sand, Kumari on the one hand and the Lord of Gokarna on the other.'[2]

According to a legend on the formation of ancient Kerala, the land was a gift of the Arabian Sea to Parasurama, one of the ten avatars of Lord Vishnu. Parasurama threw his parasu or axe across the sea from Gokarnam to Kanyakumari and the waters receded right up to the spot where the axe fell. The tract of territory so thrown up is said to have constituted the land of Kerala, otherwise called Parasuramakshetram.[3] This mythical description on the formation of Kerala can be found in Kalidasa's *Raghuvamsa*.[4]

As French film critic Jean-Michel Frodon points out, Kerala's wealth of culture, folk arts and classical dance forms can be learnt from the cinema of Adoor and other well-known film-makers of Kerala. Kerala is known worldwide for its vibrant and spectacular traditional forms of art which are practised to this day.

The ancient visual art form 'Tholppavakkoothu' (leather puppetry) anticipates cinema in its technique of presentation. The shows are generally arranged at temple festivals in villages. A large, long white screen is set up before the viewers and the leather puppets are positioned behind the screen. Unlike a simple puppet show where the puppets are moved with threads held in the fingers of human hands, here they are moved with the help of sticks having flexible joints. The shadows of the puppets, created with the help of a light source (normally an oil lamp) kept behind, fall on the screen. The viewers, instead of looking at the puppets directly, are treated to the shadows of the puppets moving, dancing and talking, as if they were human beings. Songs are always used with the Tholppavakkuthu to lively dramatic effect.

'Koothu', 'Koodiyattam' and 'Kathakali' are some of the traditional performances of Kerala which have greatly enriched its art down the ages. Older forms like 'Mudiyettu' and 'Kalarippayattu' have had an impact on the evolution of Kathakali which is, unarguably, one of the superlative dance forms of the world and, of course, very popular among the people of the state. The subject matter of Kathakali is derived from the myths and the great Indian epics like the Ramayana, the Mahabharata and the *Bhagavata Purana*.

Kathakali is a preponderantly pantomimic dance form with rich gestural codes. With great ease, it employs abhinayas or 'modes of conveying the performance to the spectator'. According to Bharata, author of the *Natya Shastra*, the most ancient Indian text on stagecraft, there are four kinds of abhinayas, namely, sattvika, or expression of feelings through concentration of the mind; angika, or conveyance of ideas through movements of the various parts of the body; vacika, or use of spoken words, songs and sounds of various kinds; and aharya or costumes and make-up.[5]

What attracts people to the Kathakali form is its elaborate make-up, bright costumes, unique emotional expressions, strong dance form and instrumental accompaniments. 'The basic postures, steps and body movements can be found in the martial arts of Kerala ... The costumes, make-up and the external appearance of the characters are refined versions of the ritual art forms of both Aryan and Dravidian cultures.'[6] (The Malayalis are said to be descendants of the original Dravidian inhabitants and the Aryans who arrived later.)

The legacy of Kerala's rich dance and drama traditions and distinctive styles inspires Kerala's film-makers too. Adoor Gopalakrishnan was born in a family that patronized Kathakali and had its own repertory. Growing up watching these performances at home, Adoor too learnt Kathakali. 'Usually, on Sundays and holidays, all the family members would gather in our house and enjoy watching Kathakali at close quarters. I was a small kid then. I used to sit on my mother's lap and watch the troupe perform.'

'The cinema of Adoor Gopalakrishnan is deeply rooted in the culture of Kerala,' says P.K. Nair, founder director of the National Film Archive of India, and a fellow Malayali, in a conversation with me at the Film and Television Institute, Pune.

Fading Away of the Matrilineal System

Kerala and Meghalaya are the two Indian states where a matrilineal society is prevalent. How deep-rooted is the matrilineal system in Kerala society?

In Kerala, the Hindu matrilineal joint-family tradition is followed mainly by the Nair community. According to this system, a husband must reside in his wife's house where the children are taken care of by the maternal uncles. Descent is traced through the female line. To keep the family property undivided, the sister's son has traditionally married the maternal uncle's daughter. These consanguineous forms of marriages did play a key role in keeping the ancestral property within the family circle, with the women in the family inheriting the property. Property is transmitted through the woman and whatever a male member of the family earns belongs to his family, either going to his mother or is inherited by his sister and her female descendants.[7]

Anthropologist K.M. Kapadia points out that as descent is traced through the female side, only the children of the females of the family can become members of the family. The birth of a daughter was thus always welcomed in Kerala. The children of the male child cannot be members of his mother's family as they cannot take the family name of the father, but will take the name of their own mothers.[8]

But with modernization and political awakening, and later state legislation bringing about radical sociocultural changes in Kerala, the matrilineal system in the state disintegrated and matrilineal communities had to accept changes that came their way. Maternal uncles began to show more concern for their own children rather than bothering about their nephews and nieces, and fathers began to take charge of the family and pay interest to the well-being of their sons and daughters. As a result, the matrilineal tradition began to disappear from society and by 1940, the tharavads (or the matrilineal joint families) were being relegated to the past.

Though it was the Nairs who mainly kept up the matrilineal joint-family tradition, some of the other communities in Kerala, like the Namboothiris, the Ezhavas, the Christians and the Muslims too, also called ancestral homes tharavad. The senior maternal uncle who ruled the tharavad was known as the karnavar. He took most of the major decisions with the consent of the eldest female member of the family. (Even after the decline of the matrilineal system, the word karnavar is used in an extended sense to signify the authority of an elderly person.)

With the decline of the tharavad in Kerala society, the nalukettu – or the traditional homestead where several generations of a matrilineal family could live with comparative ease – became rare too. The nalukettu (literally meaning buildings on all four sides), a rectangular structure with four halls joined by a central courtyard that is open to the sky, is an architectural wonder. This traditional architecture is symbolic of Kerala's traditional family structure and constructed so that the large families of the tharavad (as many as fifty to eighty persons and even more) could live under one roof and share the belongings within. A nalukettu is designed so that sunlight reaches every nook and corner of the rooms and the cross-ventilation subdues even the scorching heat of summer. But today these images have merged with the shadows of the past.

As far as Malayalam cinema is concerned, many film-makers have showcased the severe psychological shock experienced by individuals as well as society on the decline of the matrilineal joint-family tradition in Kerala. For instance, A. Vincent's *Murapennu* (1965) – a National Certificate of Merit winner – was an adaptation of a short story on the subject by celebrated Malayalam novelist M.T. Vasudevan Nair. The role of the karnavar in the film was enacted by P.J. Antony, who later went on to become the first actor from Kerala to receive a National Film Award (for Vasudevan Nair's *Nirmalyam*).

Time to Rise

In terms of social structure, the Namboothiris, the Kshatriyas and the Nairs belong to the upper castes and were the feudal lords, while the Ezhavas and the Mappilas were farmers and tenants who were treated as slaves. The tenants were deprived of basic human amenities and fundamental rights. Some of the backward communities (Avarnas) were prohibited from going near the temples, schools and other social institutions. Untouchability was widely prevalent in Kerala and those of the lower castes had to maintain a certain distance from those of the upper castes, so as to prevent 'pollution'. Indeed, the extent of untouchability practised in Kerala provoked saint philosopher Swami Vivekananda to label it 'the lunatic house of India'.

The first decade of the twentieth century, however, saw the dawning of several social reform movements. If Bengal and Assam can boast of Raja Ram Mohan Roy and Mahapurush Sankardeva as the fathers of the Bengal and Assamese renaissances respectively, Kerala claims Sree Narayana Guru, himself of the Ezhava untouchable caste, as the father of its renaissance. Narayana Guru was blessed with a rational, scientific and secular mindset, and single-handedly initiated attempts for the eradication of untouchability among society's downtrodden.

Chattampi Swamikal (1853–1924), another powerful social reformer, emphasized the emancipation of women and inspired them to come to the forefront. Another stalwart was V.T. Bhattathiripad who launched an attack on the social evils prevalent in the Namboothiri community:

> Under his leadership, Namboothiri youths openly started to flout established customs and practices. They cut the *kudumas* (tuft of hair at the centre of a shaven head) and flaunted cropped hair. They cut the sacred threads worn over their chests. They took to inter-caste dining and practised inter-caste marriage … V.T., as he was lovingly called, also promoted the idea of widow re-marriage…[9]

The Vaikom Satyagraha, a historic movement, was launched on 30 March 1924, under the leadership of Madhavan, K. Kelappan and K.P. Kesava Menon. It was the first organized agitation against the orthodox society of Kerala, its chief aim being to create a social order where untouchables were given equal social status or, at least, enjoyed the fundamental rights due to every human being in a society. The Vaikom Satyagraha proved to be a very successful mass movement which attracted the attention of the people of the whole country.

Vaikom was, in fact, a small town situated in central Travancore, known for its Shiva temple. The townspeople belonging to lower castes (the Avarnas) were prohibited from entering the temple and even restricted from using the public roads around the temple. A glorious chapter was scripted in the history of Kerala – and indeed, the whole nation – when, on 12 November 1936, Chitra Thirunal Maharaja of Travancore passed the Temple Entry Proclamation abolishing the ban on Avarnas entering Hindu temples. Gandhiji wrote in praise of the reform and exhorted others to follow this example. Today the day is celebrated by the Kerala government as 'Social Reformation Day'.

World's First Elected Communist Government

Kerala has a turbulent socio-political history. Before India's independence, Kerala was composed of two princely states, and the district of Malabar. Travancore in southern Kerala and Cochin in the central part were 'princely states', governed indirectly with the help of local rulers. These rulers were, however, more in the nature of caretakers with little freedom to apply their policies or exercise power over their subjects. Malabar in the north was caught directly in the web of British power, and life in the villages of Malabar, their traditions and customs were gradually eroded. Many tried tirelessly to unite the divided parts of the state, the first attempt dating to 1928 when a resolution was passed on 'Aikya Kerala' (United Kerala) at the State People's Conference held at Ernakulam.

The Indian National Congress (INC), established in 1885, led the struggle against the British and soon captured the interest of the Malayalis. Malabar being under direct British rule, the Congress sited the protest there rather than in Travancore Cochin, and set fire to all foreign goods. In 1921, the Kerala Provincial Congress Committee (KPCC) held the first All Kerala Provincial Conference at Ottappalam. This was unsuccessful as the police unleashed violence against the Congress members:

> The Congress workers in Malabar were enraged when the government declared the INC unlawful and resorted to a series of repressive measures. The withdrawal of the Civil Disobedience Movement in 1934 saw a realignment of forces within the Congress on ideological basis. The younger sections of the Congressmen accepted the socialist ideology. They felt that the Gandhian method of non-cooperation would not help. They wanted to bring peasants and workers into the movement for which they formed the Kerala Congress Socialist Party within the INC on 12 May 1934...[10]

The year 1938 was significant in the history of the peasant struggle in Kerala. A large procession of peasants, led by Chandroth and E.P. Gopalan, both KPCC leaders, headed for the collector's office to submit a petition demanding changes in tenancy laws. The numbers made the feudal lords realize they were on the brink of losing their feudal powers and, in a last-ditch effort, with the help of the police, registered false cases against the hard-core activists in the peasant movement. They were arrested and subjected to inhuman torture in the prisons.

The emergence of the leftists in Kerala was a significant socio-political phenomenon. The members of the leftist movement were directly or indirectly associated with peasant movements and wanted to mobilize the people politically. The following passage narrates the developments in working-class peasant struggles held in Malabar during the period 1934–47:

> A.K.G. [A.K. Gopalan] strongly believed that the civil disobedience and non-cooperation struggles conducted by the INC and the KPCC on Gandhian lines failed because they could not mobilise the exploited and the downtrodden classes of small peasants, tenants, landless labourers and factory workers. The Congress Socialists, kindled by the Marxist-Leninist ideology, and the experience of the Soviet Union in building a socialist state, wanted to build up a similar society in the country.[11]

After long years of struggle with the British colonial power for freedom and selfhood, India emerged victorious on 15 August 1947. On 1 July 1949, the rulers of both Travancore and Cochin signed a Covenant of Integration. Trivandrum was selected as the capital of the new state and a high court was set up at Ernakulam. But internal chaos and disagreement among leaders of the Congress ministry resulted in the imposition of president's rule in Travancore–Cochin.

Nine years after Independence, Kerala was declared a full state as against a B-category state by the 1956 State Reorganization Act, which significantly redrew the boundaries and governance of India's states and territories on the basis of language:

> Under the State Reorganisation Act of 1956, the four southern taluks of Tovala, Agatiswaram, Kalkulam and Vilavancode and a part of the Shencottah taluks were separated from Travancore-Cochin and included in Madras State. The district of Malabar and the Kasaragod taluk of South Canara district were added to the remaining portions of Travancore-Cochin to constitute the new State of Kerala. The State of Kerala came into existence on 1 November 1956 with a Governor as the head of the State. The last vestiges of princely rule in Kerala also disappeared with the end of the institution of *Rajapramukh* (akin to a governor) consequent upon the formation of the new State.[12]

The first general elections after the formation of the state were held in February–March of 1957. Of the 126 seats in the Kerala state legislature, sixty seats were won by the Communist Party of India (CPI). With the support of five independent candidates, the CPI, under the leadership of E.M.S. Namboodiripad, formed the government in Kerala, creating history as the first communist government in the world elected through democratic means rather than armed struggle.

Namboodiripad was appointed chief minister on 5 April 1957. With the reins of power in hand, the communist government introduced the Land Reform Ordinance and the Education Bill for the uplift of the downtrodden in society:

> The Communist victory has been seen as a continuation of the several renaissance movements that were blowing through Keralan society since the beginning of the 20th century. In the wake of colonialist interventions in the economy and polity, several socio-religious reform movements took shape in different parts. Such a resurgence was both a response of the Malayali society to its confrontation with western modernity and also a deep critique of itself and the status quo. The coming to power of the Communist Government in turn led to the implementation of land reforms and some radical initiatives in the education, health and other public service sectors. This historical backdrop has been hailed as one of the major reasons for the later emergence of the much-adulated 'Keralan Model' of development that lays great emphasis on social justice and economic distribution though without equal emphasis on production.[13]

The Land Reforms Ordinance that brought about radical changes in the socio-economic set-up, paved the way for the end of feudalism in Kerala despite strong opposition from the landlords. The reforms curbed the extent of land one could possess and ensured fixity of tenure and protection from eviction. 'Land for the tillers' was the slogan raised by the socialists that sent shockwaves through the landlord community. Further, the ordinance stated that the tenants and those deprived could claim the excess land. Landless farmers and those evicted from the lands on which they had so long and so tirelessly laboured for the feudal lords at last had the opportunity to have their grievances redressed.

Paul Zacharia, recipient of the Sahitya Akademi Award and known for writing on radical themes, has written on how the Land Reforms Ordinance had a tremendous impact on the social set-up of Kerala. According to him, it was a major – perhaps the most significant – step taken by the government because for the first time the average agriculture labourer (or kudiyan) became the owner of the particular plot of land on which he had toiled for years together.

Stability followed in the wake of changes effected in social equations.

Casteism was more or less wiped out. With the coming of communism and the left movement, no one could support the caste system. On the other hand, the system underwent a kind of reverse transformation, with the so-called lower castes emerging as more powerful than those above them in the social order.

The land and other associated reforms literally created a new society which can be seen even today. Professor Joseph Mundasseri, Kerala's first education minister in the EMS ministry, was instrumental in introducing the Education Bill which aimed at improving prevailing conditions and uprooting malpractices prevalent in the sector of private education.

In 1946, under the British Raj, Kerala's communists had sought to give voice to the voiceless and fought for freedom against the oppression of the dewan (or chief minister). The popular Punnapra–Vayalar uprising in the princely state of Travancore demanded a socialist society. When the communist regime came to power in 1957, they introduced measures and policies to improve the condition of the proletariat, farmers and labourers, but when these went to extremes, the rulers were vehemently opposed by the Congress, the Praja Socialist Party and the Muslim League. With the agitation – later referred to as the 'liberation struggle' – having almost broken down the state's administration, the Central government brought down the EMS government in 1959. The president of India took over the administration of the state under the controversial Article 356 of the Indian Constitution allowing such takeovers in case of failure of constitutional machinery.

Two years before this, at an international meeting of communist parties held in Russia in 1957, the CPI had been roundly criticized for forming a government in Kerala. By 1962, ideological differences among members of the CPI had surfaced, and in 1964 the party split countrywide into the CPI and the CPI-Marxist (CPM).

In 1967, eight tumultous years after he was unseated, EMS came back to power as chief minister, heading a coalition of seven political parties including the CPI and the Muslim League. This stint too did not last long because the CPI walked out of the coalition. However, it is widely acknowledged that it was EMS's wisdom and vision that were instrumental in shaping Kerala society and politics of that time and after.

The cinema of Kerala – with the exception of those who opted for the commercial formula – took up social issues and became an alternative mode of documenting history. Adoor Gopalakrishnan, skilfully employing the cinematic medium and a poetic narrative, familiarized viewers with the socio-political and cultural history of Kerala.

Gopalakrishnan's *Elippathayam* (1981), for instance, is an excellent example of how, after the decline of the matrilineal joint-family structure, the male ego encounters and is unable to cope with the changed times. The political backdrop to *Mukhamukham* (1984) is the people's disenchantment with the government's failure to deliver on its promises. *Kathapurushan* (1995), which covers a period of almost forty-five years from the period before Independence, can undoubtedly be considered the best story of socio-political developments in Kerala told in the language of cinema.

2
Society on Celluloid
From Children's Rights to Tribal Rites

While early Malayalam cinema made social and filial issues its focal points right from its inception, these were wrapped in melodramatic elements and artificiality, highly manipulated plots, slapstick comedy and song-and-dance sequences to attract all sections of the people irrespective of class, caste and gender. Indeed, the first talkie in the Malayalam language, *Balan*, released in 1938, deals with a social issue – the ill-treatment of children. *Balan*, directed by S. Nottani, has twenty-three songs and portrays the trials and tribulations of two orphaned children, Balan and his younger sister. It narrates convincingly, if melodramatically, how the two orphans are exploited by their stepmother till they are rescued from her clutches by a kindly lawyer.

In the 1950s, some film-makers took up class and caste as themes of their films. One such film that made a humble attempt to deal with this serious social issue was *Neelakuyil* (1954), directed by P. Bhaskaran and Ramu Kariat. Though once again a melodrama, it cleared a new path, away from stereotype Tamil/Hindi films and their poorer imitations. The storyline focuses on the romance between Sreedharan Nair, a married upper-class schoolmaster, and Neeli, an untouchable peasant girl, a relationship that seems to be made in heaven but challenges all codes of social conduct, caste and class. When Neeli becomes pregnant, Sreedharan Nair, however refuses to marry her, fearful that he will face protests from the conservative society. Frustrated by her lover's betrayal, Neeli leaves the illegitimate child beside the railway track and commits suicide. Sankaran Nair, a kind-hearted village postman, wants to adopt the baby in spite of the risk of being ostracized by the villagers. He is married to a young woman belonging to an upper caste, but their childlessness wrecks their relationship. Belatedly, Sreedharan confesses his feelings of guilt to his wife and both decide to bring up the child as their own.

Newspaper Boy (1955), written and directed by P. Ramadas, was a starkly realistic drama on the life of Appu, the young protagonist of the film, and the members of his impoverished family. After the death of Appu's parents, he takes on the responsibility of looking after his brother and sister and is employed as a newspaper boy. The films of the 1950s sought to arouse social consciousness and instil a new sensibility in the cinema-going audience.

Drawing on Literature

In the 1960s, film-makers, instead of borrowing theatrical and overtly sentimental themes from Tamil, Telugu and Hindi cinema, based their films on Malayalam literature:

> The 1960s were marked by a deeper interaction between literature and films with many a successful novel becoming a popular screenplay and with many recognised writers displaying their skills as powerful scriptwriters as well. M.T. Vasudevan Nair's screenplays were hailed as guarantors of a film's success at the box office...[14]

Malayalam cinema made an aesthetic leap with Ramu Kariat's *Chemmeen* (1965), which was the first Malayalam film to receive the President's Gold Medal for Best Film. Adapted from a critically acclaimed novel of the same name written by Thakazhi Sivasankara Pillai, it deals with a tragic love affair between Karuthamma, daughter of an ambitious Hindu fisherman, and Pareekutty, a young Muslim fish trader. In fact, *Chemmeen* is based on a myth popular among the fishermen's community according to which the chastity of a fisherman's wife can protect the life of her husband during his fishing expeditions at sea. On the other hand, her infidelity will result in her husband being swallowed by the Sea Goddess – his death indicating to the community that his wife was unfaithful.

Another significant film during this decade was *Olavum Theeravum*

(1969), based on a story by Vasudevan Nair, that sought to escape the confinement of staged dramas. Directed by P.N. Menon, whose films played a pivotal role in bringing about a change in the attitude of audiences to cinema, *Olavum Theeravum* eschewed the usual artificial studio sets and was shot on many outdoor locations. It portrays the love story of Bapputti, a Muslim trader, and Nabisa, both poor, which is jeopardized by the entry of the prosperous Kunjali to their village. The film ends on a tragic note with Nabisa refusing to marry Kunjali, and committing suicide. The cinema of the 1960s did touch upon social issues, thus opening the door to realism in Malayalam cinema – but a realism that was mixed with elements of melodrama so as to capture the hearts of millions of film watchers.

Onwards the Film Society!

With the arrival of the film society movement in the late 1960s, Malayalam cinema took a revolutionary step forward. It opened up new vistas for the people of Kerala by bringing world cinema to their doorstep and making them realize the significance of cinema as a work of art.

A younger generation of film-makers like Adoor Gopalakrishnan, who passed out of film schools with dreams in their eyes, was already well acquainted with the great works of world cinema. Rebelling against the rigid traditions of film-making and the highly sentimental and melodramatic fare audiences were accustomed to, they set out to replace these with new artistic and aesthetic films.

In this charged and challenging milieu, under the aegis of the young Adoor Gopalakrishnan and Kulathoor Bhaskaran Nair, his close friend, the Chitralekha Film Society – the first film society in Kerala – was formed in July 1965 in Trivandrum. Chitralekha laid the foundation for educating people in cinema and introduced film societies in universities and colleges.

As Gopalakrishnan says in Gautaman Bhaskaran's *Adoor Gopalakrishnan – A Life in Cinema*:

> There were two important reasons why we started the society. One, I wanted to continue watching the best of international movies. Two, I wanted to introduce the audience to a different kind of cinema. And tell them, 'Look, it is not the song and dance kind of cinema alone that

> is being produced. There are many other kinds of cinema being made elsewhere in the world...'

Adoor and his friends were overjoyed when, within a short span of time, the number of film societies in Kerala rose to above one hundred.

Just six months after its formation, Chitralekha, with the support of the Fifth All India Writers' Conference, organized the first-ever film festival in Kerala that screened films of world-class film-makers like Roman Polanski, Georges Clouzot, Lindsay Anderson, Ritwik Ghatak and Satyajit Ray, who had by then become a strong and influential force in world cinema.

The Chitralekha Film Cooperative – first of its kind in the country – was set up the same year for production and distribution of quality films.

Bengal was already familiar with the film society movement: the Calcutta Film Society had been formed on 5 October 1947 by young enthusiastic cinephiles such as Satyajit Ray, Chidananda Dasgupta and Hari S. Dasgupta. It screened world classics considered to be outside the commercial circuit. Such classics fired Satyajit Ray with the desire to make films. In 1948, Ray shared his dream with close friend Chidananda Dasgupta – some day, he said, he would make a great film. That dream came true in 1955 with the release of his epoch-making film *Pather Panchali*. At the Cannes Film Festival the following year, it was honoured as the Best Human Document and became the first Indian film to receive major international recognition. Of course, the film society movement went on to give birth to many other stalwarts in Indian cinema.

In Kerala, the film movement acquired real momentum in the 1970s. Socio-political narratives on celluloid underwent a radical change, so much so, that it was a major turning point for Malayalam cinema. The familiar domestic themes, the melodramatic plots, the song and dance and comedy sequences that were considered to be essential ingredients in films at the time, were tossed aside by the new-wave Malayalam cinema. It was Adoor Gopalakrishnan's seminal work *Swayamvaram* (1972) that heralded the arrival of this alternative or new mode of Malayalam cinema. Shooting on actual locations, outdoor settings, with synchronized sound, were new to Kerala's cinema, though it would be wrong to assume that people were unaware of these aspects.

Even more, what was new in *Swayamvaram* was the radical theme, its treatment and ideas. Unlike Satyajit Ray's *Pather Panchali*, where the setting is the remote village of Nischindipur in Bengal of the 1920s, and the theme is the grim face of poverty and human predicament, Gopalakrishnan's *Swayamvaram* deals with the moral crisis of the bourgeoisie in an urban setting. It focuses on the struggle of a couple, Viswanathan and Sita, who run away to the small town of Trivandrum, to begin life anew. Defying their parents and society, they decide to stay together without going through the formal ritual of marriage – which is a real challenge for the young couple besides being a daring theme for the film-maker. The ending of the film (what is known as an 'open ending') was new, even puzzling, to many in the audience: Sita stares into the camera, that is, the audience, as if posing her predicament to them.

> Adoor Gopalakrishnan's *Swayamvaram*, considered to be a turning point in Malayalam film history, focused on a runaway couple facing the insecurities of life ... *Swayamvaram* exploded the myth of family happiness in an urban India riddled with unemployment and poverty. This total disillusionment with the family became an indictment of a new nation that had failed to deliver its promises of social security and support structures. The most powerful image of this failure was the closing shot of the young widow Sita...[15]

Swayamvaram marked a change in the aesthetics of cinema because, through a seemingly ordinary love story, Adoor made an uncommon departure from the conventional mode of cinema. The use of sound effects as a leitmotif offered viewers a new experience: 'The impulses aroused by *Swayamvaram* were more important than the film itself. It helped filmgoers acquire a new awareness about the art of cinema.'[16] As Shyam Benegal, himself a stalwart of the New Indian Cinema of the 1970s, has observed: '*Swayamvaram* was a seminal film in terms of the ideas and themes that would eventually take centre stage in practically all his later works.'[17]

Initially this group of young professionals, to which Adoor belonged, was not accepted by senior film-makers. Indeed, they treated the newest entrants with contempt and suspicion. Reminiscing about those difficult times, Adoor says the so-called film industry, ignorant of what was taught in film school, perceived these young and 'different' film-makers from the film society movement as a threat: 'They felt that this group of young people running the film society and showing all kinds of films in Kerala would intrude into their empire. They were scared of these so-called aliens invading their system.'

The Middle-stream Moviemakers

Even as the new film-makers made their mark, 'good cinema' in Kerala meant 'middle-stream cinema', otherwise known as the 'meaningful' mainstream cinema, at the forefront of which were directors Padmarajan and Bharathan. This form of cinema followed a middle path, amalgamating the popular and the parallel cinema, taking evocative subjects but adopting commercial formulae for presentation. Padmarajan, a writer of note, secured his place as a leading proponent of the middle-stream cinema with his very first film, *Peruvazhiyambalam* (1979), about an innocent boy who becomes a hero by accident; and Bharathan with *Prayanam* (1977), which dealt with the realities of the Brahmin community of the day. These films addressed real issues, real problems and real people, but incorporated elements of entertainment. These films, however, boasted only moderate success at the box office.

By the end of the 1970s, there were a number of film-makers who added new concepts and colour to the canvas of Malayalam cinema. One of them was Govindan Aravindan (1935–91) who, coming up in Adoor's wake, made *Uttarayanam* (1974). Aravindan was a dynamic artist and cartoonist and a connoisseur of Indian classical and folk music. *Uttarayanam* portrays the struggle of an unemployed boy, Ravi, and is set against the backdrop of the freedom struggle. His second film, *Kanchana Sita* (1977), narrates a story taken from the 'Uttara Kanda' of the Ramayana, when Rama leaves wife Sita in the jungle so as to satisfy those who doubted her chastity after her capture by Ravana. What is fascinating is that though the name of Sita resounds again and again in the film, and her presence is strongly felt throughout, she is never seen in person. The film is, in fact, a retelling of the epic from a feminist perspective.

Malayalam cinema, transcending its cultural and geographic space, marked out its place on the world map in the 1980s – and did not look back thereafter. The landmark film of the era that gained international recognition was Adoor Gopalakrishnan's *Elippathayam* (The Rat-trap, 1981) which was honoured with the prestigious British Film Institute Award for the Most Original and Imaginative film shown at the National Film Theatre in 1982. Adoor's film was the second Indian film to be so awarded after Satyajit Ray's *Apur Sansar* in 1959. *Elippathayam* is a dexterously crafted work set against the backdrop of post-feudal Kerala and portrays the life of the middle-aged Unni, last descendant of an erstwhile landowning family. He is trapped in the web of tradition, and unwilling to open his eyes to the changes taking place all around him.

John Abraham was yet another stalwart of Malayalam cinema, an avant-garde film director who fought all his life against the establishment. Also a graduate of the Film and Television Institute of India (FTII) and greatly influenced by his teacher Ritwik Ghatak, he believed passionately in using the power of cinema to transform society.

His masterpiece, *Amma Ariyan* (For the Information of My Mother, 1986), a complex work with multiple layers of meaning, depicts incidents following the death of a young Naxalite and the journey of his friends to the village to inform his mother of the death of her only son. Another film, *Cheriyachante Kroorakrithyangal* (Wicked Deeds of Cheriyachan, 1979), portrays the oppressive attitude of the landlords and the police towards the poor peasants during the feudal era in Kerala, and the peasants' movement against the feudal system.

Another soldier of the new cinema was P.A. Backer (1940–93), who made *Kabani Nadi Chuvannappol* (When the River Kabani Turned Red, 1975). The film, which centres on a love affair between a young woman and a radical political activist, was released during the Emergency (1975–77), considered to be one of the darkest periods in the annals of post-Independence India.

The premature death of talented film-makers like G. Aravindan, John Abraham and P. A. Backer, each with his distinctive way of making films and all of whom fought heart and soul to establish good cinema, left an indelible mark on the world of Malayalam cinema – as also a great void.

There followed a host of talented film-makers who took Malayalam cinema to new heights of artistic experience: P.N. Menon, K.G. George, K.R. Mohanan, Shaji N. Karun, M.P. Sukumaran Nair, among others.

But Adoor Gopalakrishnan occupies a place apart. On his role in revolutionizing the form of cinema, eminent Malayalam writer Paul Zacharia comments:

> Malayalam cinema, with the arrival of Adoor Gopalakrishnan, who took cinema to the international arena, has a different momentum. When G. Aravindan and John Abraham were there, they were powerful forces. Except Gopalakrishnan, there is hardly anyone who is making such kind of films – films of artistic value that impress audiences internationally.

Social Issues to Soft Porn

The 1990s were another turning point – for the worse – in Malayalam cinema as serious social issues visibly gave way to soft porn and hackneyed themes. A star-centric and spectacle-seeking film culture was rolling along – with digital technology oiling its wheels. So much so, that it was said: 'Outside the state of Kerala, Malayalam cinema is known mostly for the art cinema of Adoor Gopalakrishnan, G. Aravindan, Shaji N. Karun et al. – but also for soft porn!'[18]

The fear is that Malayalam cinema is on the verge of losing its identity as an art form in the face of audience indifference. Mohanlal and Mammootty continue to be the reigning superstars that they have been for the last two decades and more. Nevertheless, in the face of commercial cinema's domination, a section of middle-stream film-makers like Srinivasan, Jayaraj, Kamal and Lohitadas – following in the footsteps of Padmarajan and Bharathan – continue to deal with social issues though spiked with a heavy dose of humour.

Film critic C.S. Venkiteswaran has this to say of the grave concerns of the new generation film-makers of Kerala in the twenty-first century: 'The saddest thing is that there is no fraternity among the new film-makers as in the seventies or eighties. You had film-makers who fought against mainstream, there was a brotherhood. Now, there is none.'

In a 2002 article, 'Contemporary Malayalam Cinema', written for the British Film Institute, Venkiteswaran comments:

> Working within limited economies of scale, unable to compete technically and with no substantial outlet outside the State, Malayalam

> cinema of the 1990s retreated to slapstick and sleaze – the only areas where the indigenous had an assured market and could not be combated ... In recent years, the Malayalam cinema industry has been dominated by two kinds of films – one, a number of low-budget, full-length comedies, and the other, soft-porn films with second-line stars and shoestring budgets. The comedies are all dialogue-based and depend entirely upon mimicry artists who are making a beeline to films. And, at the crest of the soft porn wave that is lapping the shores of Kerala at present, is an uncrowned super star – Shakeela. In 2001, about a third of the films released in the state were of the Shakeela genre.

The inclusion of the Bollywood kind of masala has become necessary to ensure commercial success, which means social issues get thrust aside. Award-winning film director Shaji N. Karun (*Piravi*, 1989; *Vanaprastham*, 1999; and *Kutty Srank*, 2010) laments:

> Kerala is going away from the old ways of telling stories. Now they are, more or less, in tune with Tamil films or the Bollywood kind of fare. Moreover, after the entry of the world television into the entertainment industry, I think Malayalam cinema has forgotten its tradition of storytelling and of addressing common people, filming stories related to social development and the growth of the society.

Adoor Gopalakrishnan's mastery of the art of cinema continues to be a guiding light for young film-makers. One of these promising new-generation film-makers is Sherry, director of the much acclaimed and award-winning *Aadimadhyantham* (The Beginning, the Middle and the End), which tells the story of a speech-and-hearing-impaired tribal boy from northern Kerala who has to perform tribal rites to carry forward his family tradition in Theyyam worship, but fears death and loneliness. Says Sherry:

> Definitely, no other film-maker in Malayalam has been able to inspire as much as the newer film-makers who came well after him. We salute Adoor ... But what our predecessors say is that what they created should be cast aside and replaced with new norms and forms. What Adoor says is that you have to find your own path. But unfortunately, we are just following our masters without creating something new.

Vipin Vijay, Salim Ahmed, Sherry, K.R. Manoj, Suveeran are but some of the names fighting against odds to give a new dimension to Malayalam films today. Some of these new-generation film-makers I met gave me hope that the golden days of the 1970s and '80s will return because while they are aware of the tradition lying behind them, they are also familiar with the psychology of the new-generation audiences. Film critic C.S. Venkiteswaran has this to say: 'For contemporary film-makers, the challenge is to relate to the new environment as also to connect to the past or to tradition. This is a huge challenge. I am hopeful that some of these youngsters will succeed in creating sensible cinema.'

3

Deconstructing Cinema Stereotypes

Beyond the Wife-to-Vamp Circuit

In the Biblical tale of creation, the story of Eve tempted by the duplicitous snake underscores how easily a woman can be made a victim. She is identified as the source of original human sin and made to shoulder the blame for the downfall of Man (Genesis 3, St James version). In Hindu mythology, epic characters like Sita and Sati Savitri are painted as women of untainted purity, love and sacrifice. The image of woman as an archetype wife or mother in the Indian cultural space is placed in the shadow of the male identity. Against this stream of images, the deities of learning and wealth in the Hindu religion are feminine – the goddesses Saraswati and Lakshmi.

India is a largely conservative country with many taboos and prejudices against the imaging of woman. In the first-ever Indian silent feature film, *Raja Harishchandra* (1913), directed and produced by Dadasaheb Phalke and based on the legend of the ever-truthful King Harishchandra, the roles of women were performed by male actors since women considered it unrespectable to appear on screen. In the film, the lead role of King Harishchandra was played by D.D. Dabke, while the part of Queen Taramati was performed by A. Salunke.

Regarding the discovery of Salunke, Erik Barnouw and S. Krishnaswamy describe how Phalke spotted a young man with delicate features and slender hands working as a cook in a restaurant. He asked the young man what he was earning. When he said ten rupees a month, Phalke offered fifteen to work in his films. Salunke agreed to join Phalke's company and was cast as the first heroine in India's first feature.

> In a later Phalke work, *Lanka Dahan* (The Burning of Lanka), based on a portion of the Ramayana, Salunke was to play both hero and heroine. He was the beautiful Sita, held by the ten-headed demon-king Ravana on the island of Lanka; and he was also Rama on the mainland, organising the invasion with an army of men and monkeys. The film, Phalke's greatest success, made Salunke, at one time, indisputably the most popular film actor and actress in India.[19]

Directors had a tough time casting female characters. Regarding the position of women in Kerala society, Meena T. Pillai notes that it is significant that until the beginning of the 1950s, there were no female stars in Malayalam cinema. Back in 1928, J.C. Daniel, the director of the first Malayalam movie, had to search far and wide for nearly six months before he could get a woman to play the lead role in *Vigathakumaran* (The Lost Boy). He finally had to make do with an Anglo-Indian lady playing the role of a Malayali woman.[20]

And travelling to another corner of the country, Assam, Aideu Nilambar Handique, the first heroine of the first Assamese talkie, *Joymoti*, of 1935 vintage, was ostracized from her village till her death – she died in 2002 – for playing a role in the film. Because not only was cinema considered forbidden territory for women, social prejudices prevented her from even watching one. On many an occasion, Jyoti Prasad Agarwala, the director of *Joymoti* and the father of Assamese cinema, was driven away by locals who abused him as a 'thief of girls' as he went from village to village in search of girls to act in his debut film.

One of Indian cinema's groundbreaking (in more ways than one) woman characters had actor Nargis playing a poor farmer's wife/widow in the epoch-making *Mother India* (1957) directed by Mehboob Khan. Made just over a decade after Independence, the title character evoked a strong sense of nationalism in the nation taking its first steps towards selfhood. The role of Radha in *Mother India* is ambivalent as, for some critics, she represents older traditional values, but for some others she is an emblem of empowered woman. The film depicts the poor village widow Radha who, inspite of the hardships she faces, fights hard to bring up her two sons, Birju and Ramu. She struggles to escape the clutches of the malevolent village moneylender, Sukhilala. Virtually a destitute, she emerges as the emblem of the ideal Indian mother, even sacrificing her son Birju at the end in the cause of justice.

> *Mother India* is an enormously powerful cultural signifier, gaining strength not only from atavistic memories from the Hindu epics – Sita, Sati Savitri, Draupadi – but also its use in moments of national (typically conflated with Hindu) cultural resurgence. The symbol of woman/mother as the nation also suggests another of the sustaining analogies of the myth of nation...[21]

In the socio-political-cultural space of India, the responsibility of woman as a part of society was from the start confined to the social and familial context. However, in fast-changing cinematic discourse, the image of women went on to be transformed to vamps and dancers, heady objects of the male gaze.

In narrative cinema, the woman plays a traditional exhibitionistic role – her body is held up as a passive erotic object for the gaze of male spectators so that they can project their fantasies on to her. She connotes 'to be looked-at-ness'. The men on screen, on the other hand, are agents of the look with whom spectators identify to enjoy a vicarious control and possession of the woman. We can see in almost any classic Hollywood film that the heroine is an object to be looked at: she is filmed in soft focus, coded for strong visual and erotic impact...[22]

> The German philosopher Hegel argued that each conscious being enters into a struggle for recognition with every other conscious being, and each concludes that he or she is the essential subject (the self), whilst all others are the inessential objects (the Other). This is how we achieve a sense of identity. Simone de Beauvoir, however, argued that woman is always situated as the other to man. The man is always the subject-self – the 'I' – whilst the woman is always the object – the Other. This belief, she continued, permeates human history and informs the whole of Western philosophical thought.
>
> It is, for example, central to the work of the famous psychoanalyst, Sigmund Freud, who based his theory of sexuality on the possession of

> the phallus/penis. A man is a man because he possesses the phallus, a woman is, simply, not a man. Therefore, a woman is a lack, a negative – she lacks the phallus that confers subjectivity. This lack of the female self can also be detected in art and literature, where women frequently appear as objects of men's desires or fears...[23]

In the West, with changing times, literature as well as other art forms rejected the stereotyped representation of woman as someone gullible, as too dependent on the male of the species. Both in Western and Indian films, consideration of woman as the Other has gradually changed to seeing her as her own person. The portrayal of woman in films as the object of male desire gave way over time to women characters who are emotionally stronger than men and more dominating, for example, Alfred Hitchcock's *Rebecca* (1940). As Shohini Chaudhuri points out in her book, *Feminist Film Theorists*: 'Rebecca's beauty, wit and breeding embody the image of Woman. But this image does not only figure as an object of desire for men. More crucially, it marks the place and object of an active female desire – not only the heroine's but also that of the housekeeper, Mrs Danvers, who adored Rebecca and is jealous of the heroine who takes her place...'

As for Indian films, Shyam Benegal's *Ankur* (Seedling, 1973), tracing the self-empowerment of a young woman in the face of patriarchal, feudal oppression; Jabbar Patel's *Umbartha* (Threshold, 1982) dealing with an educated middle-class housewife who defies convention to work with traumatized womenfolk in a reformatory; and Assamese director Dr Bhabendranath Saikia's *Agnisnan* (Trial by Fire, 1985) portraying a housewife's direct protest against her bigamous husband, stand out. Film-makers like Satyajit Ray, Ritwik Ghatak, Shyam Benegal and Mrinal Sen have represented women in different ways and in ways that marked a refreshing change to the dominant discourse in mainstream movies.

> Sacramental and sociological ideals cruelly trap and imprison the Ray woman who has to undertake a long and painful *yatra* (journey) to break out of the Sita-Savitri mould and to fight for what are her rights as a woman. These stages are precisely what Ray succeeds in establishing in his women-centred films. By implementing them, Ray exposes a host of prejudices and customs governing many of the 'roles' an Indian woman is expected to perform in her quotidian existence.

> Her instinctive fight, therefore, is to reassert her position as 'woman' over and above all roles. Ray becomes the perfect spokesperson on behalf of all the Ratans, Charulatas, Bimalas, Aratis, Sutapas, Aditis and Karunas of India ... Ray's analysis of the Indian woman's struggle also arises out of the historical situations in which they find themselves. Their struggle necessitates a variety of determined responses carved out of the historical changes taking place in Indian society...[24]

Shyam Benegal made his stance clear from his very first feature, the widely acclaimed *Ankur*:

> *Ankur* visually preserves traditional rural life in Andhra Pradesh, far outside the range of highway traffic, where ox carts still take care of the transportation and the arrival of certain birds is the way to mark the calendar. But this script could be transplanted to rural Mississippi, or any other plantation in the world. It's surprisingly accessible ... Azmi's performance is the secret to the film's success. Rather than being the helpless woman of the soap opera, forced into a fate worse than death, her relationship with the worthless young master is always complex and always changing. There's some sort of attraction to his power, perhaps some physical attraction; perhaps there's even some belief that she can use her influence to make a good man out of him. That hope can never distract Lakshmi from the knowledge that she will starve if she falls out of his favour. The mix of emotions is suggested behind Azmi's pose of mask-like subservience ... Living in a country where the men are gods and women are expected to touch their feet in submission would make any woman ironic. As a feminist film-maker and as a film-maker far more comfortable with matters of attraction and sex than even Satyajit Ray ever was, Benegal distinguished himself right out of the gate...[25]

A much revered film-maker of Assam is Dr Bhabendranath Saikia whose films were screened at international film festivals held the world over, from Cannes to Karlovy Vary to Korea. His film *Agnisnan*, which received the National Awards for the Best Regional Film and Best Screenplay, speaks of the angst of a married woman, Menaka. In spite of fathering four children with her, her zamindar husband, Mohikanta, takes a second wife. This results in a psychological upheaval in Menaka's life; as a sign of protest against her lecherous husband, she begins a clandestine relationship with a man of the village who, otherwise respectable, is constrained to rob because of his poverty. She conceives a baby. When Mohikanta grows suspicious of her affair, Menaka says to her husband, 'If you want your wife to be like Sita, the husband should also be like Ram.'

Challenging Patriarchal Power

Adoor Gopalakrishnan deconstructs the image of the typical Indian woman and paints her anew on his cinematic canvas. The voice of protest of Adoor's female characters against the patriarchal system is not to be seen in other Indian New Wave films. The position of women was deplorable in the feudal system of Kerala, where they lived in the shadow of the chauvinistic males of the household. Adoor's *Elippathayam* creatively brings to the fore how women in a dying feudal society had to survive under the power of patriarchy. As if the ancestral house is a trap, and the women within it, rats.

Gopalakrishnan explores the world of women to understand their position within the socio-economic set-up; his women are an amalgamation of tradition and modernity, independent-minded beings who are at the same time deeply rooted in society's norms. Adoor's women characters are not objects of the male gaze nor do they evoke voyeuristic feelings in the spectator.

Adoor, who was deprived of paternal care and warmth in his childhood, was brought up by his mother who was the epitome of courage, endurance and love. For Adoor, 'The woman is a permanent institution, while the male is a transient figure. The most important figure in nature is the woman, the female who also has the responsibility of nurturing a child, bringing it up, even when the man is not around. The woman will take care of the child right from the womb up to the time when he/she can stand on his/her own.'

Adoor's women characters are of three kinds, the first being those who are eager to break social prejudices and customs. Characters like Sita, Janaki and Kalyani in *Swayamvaram*, Kunju Pennu and Kamakshi in *Naalu Pennungal*, Sridevi in *Elippathayam*, Narayani in *Mathilukal*, represent the struggle of women to survive in conservative Indian society.

The second group of women is socially and traditionally bound, drawn in the conventional image of the ideal Indian woman and ready to sacrifice and suffer for others – characters like Santhamma in

Kodiyettam, Rajamma in *Elippathayam*, Chinnu Amma and Kumari in *Naalu Pennungal*, and Saroja in *Vidheyan*.

The third category is the ultimate victim of male exploitation – characters like the widow Kamalamma in *Kodiyettam* who is spurned by her lover, the hypocritical schoolmaster, when she reveals she is pregnant. Also, Omana in *Vidheyan*, who suffers at the hands of the men she is associated with.

In Search of Independence

In *Swayamvaram*, Sita, who is educated, opts to live a life of her own. By defying social prejudices and taboos, and her parents too, she flees with her partner, Viswanathan, to a distant place of hope. But when hard realities surface, Viswanathan (representative of the inadequate male) gets frustrated and, finding it difficult to face the world, gives in to death. Sita is left in a difficult situation with a newborn child. A sympathetic old man, who worked in the sawmill with her husband, offers her a home with his family – but Sita declines firmly. On a different occasion, Janaki, a sympathetic neighbour, advises her to return to her parents' home. Again Sita refuses. At the same time, Adoor Gopalakrishnan makes it clear that she will not follow the path of Kalyani who has taken up prostitution, as hinted by repeated images of her room's bolted door. Sita is aware that choices once made cannot easily be undone. She decides to fight and to hold on to her self-respect and dignity regardless of the arduous circumstances. I asked Adoor if he would call Sita a feminist since she seems strong enough to lead her life all alone. He clarifies:

> Sita represents the ordinary middle-class woman. There is no scope for feminism. Basically, it is a human problem whether it is a man or a woman. So she has to face it, but it is very difficult for a woman when she is alone. Every working woman is not a feminist in the sense of the negative connotations that are stereotypically assigned to the word. It's common for people to describe the stereotype feminist as hairy-legged, lesbian, man-hater, etc. Sita works because she has self-respect and she thinks that she is capable of earning and making a living.

Another independent woman who has a minor role in the film is Janaki. She sells her goods in the market, returns home and leads a life of her own. Then there is the prostitute Kalyani who is candidly open about her profession and whose alcoholic husband only wants money from his wife for drink.

Sridevi in *Elippathayam* is a rebel in pursuit of an independent life, an escape from the suffocation and entrapment of the feudal system. *Elippathayam* focuses on the landlord Unni and his three sisters. Janamma, his elder sister who is married, fights for her share of the property, while the middle sister, Rajamma, is submissive and servile. The youngest, Sridevi, dreaming of a life outside the four walls of the ancestral house, finally elopes with her lover.

Standing by Your Man

Characters of the second type – Rajamma, Saroja, Santhamma, Chinnu Amma and Kumari – are the voices of all those Indian women who sacrifice their own identity in the interests of the male's satisfaction/ fulfilment. In *Elippathayam*, Rajamma works for Unni like a human machine, her aim in life being to keep her brother contented. If she has a hidden desire to fly out of the trap, her sense of duty restrains her. In *Vidheyan*, Saroja, wife of the aggressive landlord, Bhaskara Patelar, is a traditional woman who once in a long while cautions her husband about his misdeeds – but her protests are not strong enough to dissuade him. In fact, she is like a weak-voiced conscience of Patelar, only to be ignored, even violated, till she falls victim to her husband's violence.

Santhamma in *Kodiyettam* finds that her husband Sankarankutty does not understand the concept of family bonds. She goes back to her mother's home but continues to yearn for her husband. Finally, when he gains maturity and understands the meaning of married life, he arrives to take Santhamma home. Glad to be back with him, she cries with joy when her husband presents her with new clothes.

In *Naalu Pennungal*, Chinnu Amma, in spite of being childless, leads a happy conjugal life with her husband, Raman Pillai. The sudden arrival of her classmate, Nara Pillai, in her life poses a dilemma as he tries to talk her into bed with the added lure of an offspring. She vacillates for a while, but finally rejects Nara Pillai's amorous advances. In another episode in the same film, Kumari, the farm girl, is married to Narayanan who has no interest in sex and one day, without any reason, leaves her at her parents' house and never returns. Rumours of her infidelity spread. Her story symbolizes the notion that in the event of failure of a marriage, it is the woman who is usually considered to be at fault.

Victimized Sex?

Yet another category is of those unhappy women who become victims of the male sex – of which the widow Kamalamma in *Kodiyettam* is a perfect example. In *Kodiyettam*, the most respected individual in the village is the schoolmaster, who is having a secret affair with a widow in the village, Kamalamma, mother of a nine-year-old son. But when she reveals she is pregnant, to her utter shock she finds that the schoolmaster lacks the guts to accept her and the child to be. To escape social disgrace, she commits suicide. Meanwhile, the schoolmaster continues to hold on to his revered position.

In *Vidheyan*, Omana, wife of Thommi, is sexually abused by the landlord Bhaskara Patelar and yet does not protest or object. Initially, Thommi is inclined to retaliate and asks Omana whether they should leave the place. But she understands that if she and her husband are to survive in the new home, she must compromise. Her submission to the landlord is nothing but survival strategy.

Adoor Gopalakrishnan never presents woman in a titillating way in his films, or promotes voyeurism. He creates sensuous images, yes, but these are artistic and beautiful pictures. In *Swayamvaram*, Kalyani plays a prostitute who leads a carefree life, unmindful of community opinion, and whose husband has no objection to her ways as long as she pays for his booze. Street prostitute Kunji Pennu in *Naalu Pennungal*, having resolved to lead a decent life and give up prostitution, marries Pappukutty, a labourer. But they get punished for the offence of prostitution regardless, since they cannot prove that they are legally husband and wife. Characters like Kunji Pennu and Kalyani are sex workers but with minds of their own. Adoor never brings into focus the theme of prostitution, rather shows the unsympathetic attitude of the middle class to prostitution as a way of life.

In *Kodiyettam*, Gopalakrishnan depicts the clandestine relationship between the village schoolmaster and the widow:

> The sexual affair between the widow and the teacher is handled subtly and with dignity. We see 'meetings' between them. On a ridge that cuts across a vast rice field, he sees the man and the woman walk towards each other. But do they stop to exchange a word or two? (Hero) Sankarankutty misses the moment because he is momentarily distracted by the boys fishing in the rivulet. By the time he turns around, they have crossed each other and are walking in different directions. Another time, he sees them in a temple, but they disappear behind a stone pillar. Yet another time, he hears them talk behind the high wall. It is not very clear what she is telling him, but she is weeping. Sankarankutty is perplexed. He suspects there is something going on between them, but is not quite sure.[26]

In Adoor's *Mathilukal*, the character of Narayani is never shown in the film, but her alluring and powerful voice indicates her close physical presence to Basheer and the conversation between the two over the prison wall is marked by intensity and sensuousness. When Narayani asks Basheer how broad his chest is, Basheer describes it as huge and elephantine. She retorts that her chest too is broad like his! These conversations between Narayani and Basheer over the wall spark off sensuous images in our minds. Erotic, yes; vulgar? No.

Adoor Gopalakrishnan's attempt is not to present women in a radical avatar, but to provide historical, psychological, sociocultural images of women which position them as the bearers and the preservers of our cultural ethos. His women characters, while existing within the social framework and its codes, have the power to mould their own lives. They remind us of the women of the two epics, the Ramayana and the Mahabharata, who with their strength of character shape their own destinies and are truthful delineations of the Indian woman.

4

The Adoorian Approach

Cinema, for Adoor, is a form of spiritual meditation – and the process of film-making, a religion. His films, made at prolonged intervals, are products of long periods of contemplation and analysis. They look upon contemporary life and contemporary issues, and while they are made in the Malayalam language and are deeply rooted in the sociocultural milieu of Kerala, they speak a universal language – of human emotions and human psychology. This is what differentiates him from other film-makers in India.

In an interview published in *The Maharashtra Herald* on 17 January 1986, Adoor explains his preference for making films in Malayalam: 'True Indian cinema is represented by films made in different regional languages. It is through these languages that true life and reality in society are portrayed.'

Again, in the same paper, on 31 May 1992: 'Language is not the problem – there are many countries where one can regularly release films with subtitles. But if one were to make films in English, what happens to the film in France, Germany or Spain? When a film shows a Punjabi, a Malayali or a Tamilian, living the kind of life he does live and speaking in English, it would look very artificial.'

What is more, since Adoor believes in the language of images rather than dialogue, his richly composed visuals transcend geographical and cultural barriers. As Bina Paul, the director of the International Film Festival of Kerala, told me, 'Adoor is completely committed to the idea and art of cinema. Viewers should look for his innovative ideas and the artistic play of images rather than judge a film of his as good or bad in a conventional sense.

Actor and film-maker Nandita Das, a well-known name in the story of serious Indian cinema, says:

> Adoor Gopalakrishnan is one of the most respected directors in this country. He is one of the few truly independent film-makers – someone who never compromises on his creative vision. It was a real honour to work with him … Adoor's involvement in his work is 200 per cent and to see that level of dedication and perfectionism is a real pleasure.

Many aspects of Adoor's works have made his name a revered one in world cinema: his cinematic aesthetics, thematic and narrative elegance, poetic sensibilities, and his merging of modernity and tradition.

His is a voice of humanity, focusing on the individual but illuminating the complexities of the larger community of the world. His protagonists like Viswanathan in *Swayamvaram*, Sankarankutty in *Kodiyettam*, Unni in *Elippathayam*, Sreedharan in *Mukhamukham*, are ordinary human beings with ordinary human emotions and passions but given ethical and allegorical dimensions by the director. His many-layered cinematic themes can give rise to many interpretations. Viewers from different strata of society ranging from laymen to intellectuals can feel a sense of oneness with the subject though each may interpret it from his or her own angle. Using elliptical techniques in presenting scenes, he leaves it to the viewers to complete with their own imagination what is left unexpressed. Adoor said in an interview with Khalid Mohamed (*Filmfare*, 1–15 February 1982): 'Ellipses are the basis of my work, the inspiration for this device, of course, has been poetry. If I mention T.S. Eliot's *The Waste Land*, it would be stating the obvious.'

His narration that usually develops in linear form is thematically and stylistically organized. The logical development of music, the use of leitmotifs, varied kinds of juxtaposition and, as already mentioned, the use of rich visuals rather than dialogue are the general features of his technique. Regarding his style, Adoor said in an interview that, in fact, he had no fixed style: 'Maybe there is a style evident to others in my work, but I am not conscious of that. Each cinema of mine has a form of its own. I do not believe in gimmicks. For instance, I will use a crane shot only if the situation demands it.'

Adoor believes that a film must contribute to the audience's aesthetic satisfaction – not that he does not believe in entertainment but that it should be at a deeper level. He once said to me:

> My films have to be entertaining, otherwise there is no sense in making them. The idea is not to take the audience for granted. If the audience cannot be entertained, why do they come to see the cinema? The only problem is that usually people take inanities happening on the screen for entertainment. For me, it is very nonsensical when a boy and a girl are in love and you introduce one hundred extras in the background and make them do all kinds of odd things in the name of dance. The whole idea of beauty in romance is vulgarized. Whereas every art has as its ultimate aim the intellectual and emotional entertainment of its viewer and perceiver. Then it remains with you – becomes part of your cultural make-up.

As a film-maker, Adoor understands his responsibility towards society. His cinema is not just storytelling, but its impact goes beyond to provide a sense of awareness of the society one lives in.

He uses satire as a potent weapon and satirizes social maladies very subtly. As has been said, 'Satire is a literary genre that uses irony and wit to expose the world's vices and foibles, giving impetus to change or reform through ridicule. The satirist reduces the vaunted worth of someone or something to its essence.'[27]

William Shakespeare's immortal creations like Falstaff and Malvolio are represented as comic characters to provide the audience a kind of entertainment, but a satiric tone underlies the humour. Adoor Gopalakrishnan exposes the middle-class mindset in *Swayamvaram*, the mask-wearing and hypocritical people in society like the village schoolmaster in *Kodiyettam*, the changing face of politics in Kerala in *Mukhamukham*, the exploitation of weaker sections of society including women by feudal lords in *Vidheyan*, the male's lecherous attitude towards the woman in the third story, *The Housewife* (in *Naalu Pennungal*), as also in *Two Men and a Woman* (in *Oru Pennum Randaanum*). But the satire in his films is subtle and hinted at, never going into gross elaboration.

One of the best ironical scenes Adoor Gopalakrishnan has created features in his brilliantly constructed *Kathapurushan*, when Veluchar, the estate manager and father figure, pleads for Kunjunni's release so that he may meet his ailing grandmother. But the police officer responds, 'Let her die. Then we will see.' On the wall just behind the police officer hangs a portrait of Mahatma Gandhi, the epitome of non-violence and peace. The intention of this particular frame is crystal clear: Adoor wants to show how the system makes a mockery of the image of Gandhi. The police officer, rather than being sympathetic towards Veluchar, is very rude. Later, Kunjunni is allowed to attend the funeral rites of his grandmother. His pronounced limp suggests the atrocities he was subjected to by the police.

Adoor Gopalakrishnan's films are strong weapons that question the system or the establishment. In *Mukhamukham*, Adoor looks at the leftist mindset through the eyes of the protagonist Sreedharan: 'Personal relationships, pleasures, selfish gains, have to be given up by a communist. Individual achievement is not our goal. On the contrary, it can only be a hindrance to overall social progress. Individuals are only the leaves on the tree of society.'

But when Sreedharan returns home, a broken man after a lapse of ten years, he finds that his leftist friends have utterly changed, have abandoned their one-time ideology. Some have ended up alcoholic, others have turned opportunists. The thirst for power has turned some into self-seeking politicians.

Silence Bracketed by Sound

The use of silence as a dramatic element in the structure of a film takes the art form to a different level. For instance, one of the most poignant scenes in Satyajit Ray's path-breaking *Pather Panchali* is when Harihar returns from Varanasi and is shocked to see that his home has been shattered in a storm. He advances, shouting for his children, 'Apu, Durga.' Silence is used in this entire sequence to great emotional effect and artistic beauty.

Adoor too employs silence to paint the emotions of the characters on his filmic canvas. Says Adoor, 'Silence is always bracketed by sounds on both sides. In fact, silence is an integral element of sound.'

In *Kodiyettam*, the village wastrel Sankarankutty is shocked to hear from a girl of the neighbourhood that his wife Santhamma has left his house for good. In a top-angle shot, Adoor shows Sankaran sitting dumbfounded on the porch of his house. The silence is only emphasized by the ambient sounds of a dog whining and two crows in the courtyard chasing each other. In *Swayamvaram*, as the principal of the tutorial college regrets that he can no longer keep Viswanathan as a lecturer because of financial problems, we notice the silent pauses in their conversation. During one such pause, we can hear the voice of a teacher in a neighbouring classroom. Adoor's use of ambient sounds heightens the scene's emotional content. According to him:

> I was shooting the bar scene in *Swayamvaram* with Viswanathan (Madhu) and the principal of a tutorial college as well as his manager (Karamana). There are long silences in their conversations. Through these silences, the characters continued to eat and drink, making noises: the clink of glasses and the sound of drink being poured and dishes being laid out on the table produced a rhythmic pattern. I preserved all this while editing the scene, and later found that these sounds between the talk actually complemented the dialogue and the mood.[28]

Ritwik Ghatak (in *Ajantrik*) uses sound effects that oddly evoke science fiction, probably to express his amusement with Bimal talking to and treating his 1920 Chevrolet – named Jagaddal – as if it were a living creature, an extension of his own personality. And off-screen as well as on-screen, the sounds that Ghatak uses to characterize this vehicle through various stages of health and fitness are a major aspect of this film's tragicomic tone – as important as the music, or the sound of Bimal's weeping when Jagaddal finally breaks down. The sound of the wreck being pulled away is especially harsh and poignant, yet the sound of the detached car horn still wheezing and honking when an infant squeezes it allows the hero some sense of triumph and joy in the film's final shot.[29]

Regarding the use of silence in his masterpiece *Elippathayam*, Gopalakrishnan said in an interview that the large swathes of silence play a vital part in the movie, with the camera lingering on the characters and following them through the scene patiently.

Leitmotifs to Reinforce Themes

'Leitmotif', a musical term used for a recurring theme, was invented by Friedrich Jähns, a German music scholar, but it was the German composer known for his operas, Richard Wagner, who gave leitmotif a new musical form. According to *Grove's Dictionary*, 'Leitmotif is a theme, or other coherent idea, clearly defined so as to retain its identity if modified on subsequent appearances, and whose purpose is to represent or symbolize a person, object, place, idea, state of mind, supernatural force or any other ingredient in a dramatic work, usually operatic but also vocal, choral or instrumental.' In cinema, leitmotif is used to conjoin events, images, character traits, or other elements of the mise en scène.

One of the first uses of leitmotif was in Fritz Lang's *M* (1931), an application that opened up new possibilities. Leitmotif is presented at the very beginning in the title sequence. While we see a large M covering the screen, we listen to a fragment of Edward Grieg's '*Peer Gynt*'. The simple, repetitive and effective rhythmic theme is immediately retained in auditory memory, making it very easy to associate with the mysterious murderer. This example is interesting because, despite its simplicity, it introduces the idea of identifying or labelling a character by means of sound.[30]

About using music in his films as a leitmotif, Adoor says:

> The leitmotif music is not intended to heighten or underline individual scenes. There will be the main score for the central theme. Then there are sub-themes. Here the music composed will bring to mind the sub-themes. That means the background music in my films follows the themes, not individual scenes. The purpose of the theme music is to impact audience attention at a subconscious level.

In the closing scene of his debut film *Swayamvaram*, instead of using dialogue to convey the emotions of his protagonist Sita, Adoor uses visuals accompanied by music. The resonance of the ragas of the male and the female voices suggest metaphorically Sita's strength and the lifeforce that impels her.

In *Elippathayam*, Adoor uses theme music to draw a parallel between a rat and the inmates of the house who are trapped in a time warp. Adoor uses a special kind of ritualistic music on three occasions: the first when the youngest sister Sridevi traps the rat and sets out to drown it in the village pond; the second when another sister, the sick Rajamma, is carried away on a makeshift stretcher; and on the third occasion when Unni is chased, caught and taken away to be thrown into the village pond. Adoor says: 'There is an equation drawn between the rats and the humans. The music, in fact, signifies the cruelty of the situation and evokes sacrificial ritual. Unni is thrown into the pond, but he emerges from it. Then only is the full score of the theme music played.'

And in an interview with Khalid Mohamed (*Filmfare*, 1–15 February 1982) he confirms: 'Technically, I have attempted to make the background score more effective by mixing in unusual sounds. When the rats are being dumped in the pond, that sharp music is achieved by distorting the sound of ghungroos.'

Adoor's second film, *Kodiyettam*, heralded a new element in Indian cinema – the first Indian film not to use background music. The judicious use of a variety of ambient sounds like the chatter of people, chirping of birds, fire crackers from the village temple, barking of dogs, cawing of crows was such that viewers never noticed the absence of background music. When Satyajit Ray saw the film, his immediate reaction was to ask whether Adoor planned to do away with the background score in future works. He also suggested that, if sparingly used, music could enhance the effect of the film. Adoor's decision not to use any background music in the film remains a landmark innovation in the narrative of Indian cinema.

Aesthetics of Colour

Adoor uses colour as an aesthetic code that lends a new dimension to the development of his characters. The notion of colour is different in different cultural contexts of the world. For example, white is a symbol of peace and purity in India, but at the same time, in both Indian and Chinese contexts, it also implies grief and sadness. In the Western context, black is always associated with a sense of sorrow.

In *Edward Scissorhands*, the primary colours used for the suburban houses would normally communicate optimism and well-being; yet a slight excess in their brightness, coupled with the fact that no darker or mixed hues are visible anywhere, alerts the spectator to a critique of suburban blandness and conformity. In the animated *Corpse Bride* (2005), Tim Burton uses vivid primary colours to suggest the vibrancy of the underworld as against the oppressive world above ground...[31]

In *Elippathayam*, his first colour film, Adoor typically uses colour to shed light on the hidden recesses of the character. The film revolves around four persons, namely, Unni, Janamma, Rajamma and Sridevi. Janamma, who is married and has children and lives outside her ancestral house, is given a green blouse that implies fruition, cleverness, practicability and earthiness. (The lower garment for both men and women is white.) Sridevi, the youngest sister, wears red which implies revolt, vitality and energy. She yearns to fly out of the confining cage. Rajamma, the middle sister, is given the colour blue. Blue is the colour of the sky and the sea which signifies her generosity and gentleness and, at the same time, self-effacement and submissiveness. If the three colours are mixed, one gets the colour white. Unni's shirts are white with vertical stripes which psychologically indicate restlessness. On the other hand, horizontal lines signify repose, calm and a quiet nature. The entire drama of the family is played out against the background of the grey colour of the ancestral wooden house. When Unni is chased, caught and taken to the pond, it is the dead of night and the colours of objects are non-existent. It is the same journey that the rats have earlier made, but now all is dark shadow. The use of colour to manifest the nature of the characters elevates the film to another level.

The Evocative Camera

Adoor grew up watching Kathakali dance dramas performed at his ancestral home and patronized by his family. He absorbed its culture and aesthetics which in turn subtly influenced his art. In *Elippathayam*, Adoor uses slow and steady camera movement, allowing concentration on details. One of several such scenes is when Unni, getting ready to attend a marriage ceremony, snips slowly and concentratedly at a white hair in his moustache. In extreme close-up, Adoor shows Unni's index finger reaching for the snipped whisker, then his sorrow to find it is black in colour. So he takes up his scissors again. This lengthy shot serves to convey Unni's sloth and lethargy.

The slow panning in the depiction of religious rituals for Mallika's maturation in *Nizhalkkuthu*, or the swift camera movements in the kite sequence in *Kodiyettam* are perfect examples of how the pace of movement of the camera can evoke different meanings in different contexts.

Adoor uses camera movements very sparingly; the bedrock of his filming is the steady shot, more often than not at eye level. It is very different from those who resort to the tracking shot as soon as movement within the frame ceases so as to keep things moving and, thus, keep the spectator's eye engaged. Adoor's objective is to keep the screen full of realistic detail and yet eliminate all minor movements, demanding from his audience complete concentration on the central action.[32]

Adoor Gopalakrishnan is often regarded as heir to Satyajit Ray's legacy, but the Adoorian approach to unfolding the narrative and his filmic techniques are distinctive. He is a true pioneer of Indian New Wave cinema, a master craftsman who is highly original and innovative. The language of his cinema speaks subtly, yet is charged with intense implications. He revolts against the flat storytelling technique, preferring the complexity of tropes.

The themes of his cinema are culled from the evolutionary process of a changing Kerala. He is a believer in Gandhian principles and indeed studied at the Gandhigram Rural Institute. His *Nizhalkkuthu* speaks volumes against capital punishment. As Adoor says, 'Some of my films do reflect on Gandhian principles. The image of Gandhi, who teaches us dignity of labour, non-violence and integrity, is ever imprinted on my mind.'

What is distinctive about Adoor as a film-maker is his treatment of themes and his catholic attitude towards the world and the characters that populate his films. He has the sensibility of a writer, the craftsmanship of a playwright and the artistry to paint the world and its figures on the canvas of the cinema screen. All these are part and parcel of what one may call the 'Adoorian Approach'.

5

Back Story

Pallickal to Pune and Farther

In the early years of the twentieth century, education was a distant dream for the vast majority of the people of India, particularly for those living in remote Indian villages. Indeed, those who completed even their matriculation were considered brilliant. Take Madhavan Unnithan, for instance. He was born in 1898 and graduated from university in the second decade of the twentieth century. As a bright and dedicated student, he immersed himself in his studies, exploring through books the world that lay beyond his own. After graduation, he got a job in the forest department as forest ranger and over time could have been promoted to a much higher rank had he not been a principled man who disdained dishonest means to better his position. So he remained a forest ranger. After retirement, realizing a long-cherished dream, he taught English to poor children who were deprived of education. Soon he earned a reputation as a good teacher and was also very popular with his students. He breathed his last at age eighty-six.

Gouri Kunjamma, his wife, belonged to a conservative, cultured family that patronized the culture and traditions of Kerala. Musicians, artists, dancers, and magicians regularly flocked to their house. Gouri Kunjamma's eldest brother, Mouttathu Gopalan Unnithan, continuing the tradition of his parents and ancestors, patronized Kathakali and many other performing arts. An interesting initiative of his was the setting up of the first cinema house in Adoor town and in a couple of nearby places. Gouri Kunjamma's third elder brother was Mouttathu Madhavan

Unnithan, a lawyer and in later life, an MLA. Gouri Kunjamma's younger brother, Mouttathu Raman Unnithan, was a painter, playwright and cartoonist with a keen interest in photography. He was the most artistically inclined among the siblings. Kunjamma's eldest sister, Kutty Kunjamma, was a writer who boasted a library of choice books. And Gouri Kunjamma herself could play the violin very well. Love for music ran in the family.

Coming from two entirely different backgrounds, Madhavan Unnithan and Gouri Kunjamma were married. In all, they had seven children. Gopalakrishnan, sixth child of the family, was born on 3 July 1941 in a small village called Pallickal, situated on the fringes of Adoor town. His three sisters and three brothers were Savitri, Sukumari, Vamadevan, Sarojini, Ramachandran and the youngest, Ayyappan. Having five or six children was considered usual in Indian society in those days. Ritwik Ghatak (b.1925) had nine siblings, while Mrinal Sen (b.1923) had five sisters and seven brothers. Of Adoor's siblings, Ramachandran Unnithan was a voracious reader and lover of books. He wrote short stories and even acted in some amateur plays. Ramachandran was Gopalakrishnan's role model.

Pallickal village, serene and covered in thick greenery, was far removed from everything modern. It was here that Gopalakrishnan's maternal grandfather built a two-storey home named 'Medayil' which simply means a large two-storey house – the house where Adoor Gopalakrishnan was born. This two-storey building reflected the status of his family. They were landlords and they owned bullock carts, the only means of transport for the fortunate few.

Gopalakrishnan's maternal grandmother was a visionary and understood that Pallickal would not be able to provide her family with the kind of education she wished for them. It was also too far from hospitals, government offices and the like. Adoor town, on the other hand, had all the amenities she desired. After the death of her husbands (she was married to two brothers according to the then prevailing custom), she shifted with her entire family from the Pallickal mansion to Mouttathu Tharavadu (a large joint family), her own ancestral home at Adoor. This was indeed a far-sighted decision. According to the matrilineal custom in Kerala, a woman after her marriage stays in her own parents' house and her children are brought up by the maternal uncle. Her husband too stays at his wife's house. Moreover, the daughters inherit the ancestral property. The family newly residing at Mouttathu Tharavadu was almost thirty members strong.

It was a time when joint families had started breaking up due to successive legislations as well as the degeneration of the matrilineal system. Nuclear families had started forming as members of the joint families took their individual shares of the property. Gopalakrishnan's parents built a new house not far from the Tharavadu and named it 'Kaniyarethu'.

Onset of Independence

The decade of the 1940s is significant for the socio-political temper of the times. The freedom movement climaxing in Partition of the country, the riots that marked the Partition, and the assassination of Mahatma Gandhi soon after left deep and enduring scars on the psyche of the inhabitants of the subcontinent.

In the first half of the decade, Adoor joined Kottara Government Primary School, his first formal school. Set up by Adoor's mother's family, it was initially named the Hindu Mission School, but was later taken over by the government. The school, unlike some of today's sophisticated private institutions, could provide only the basic amenities like a bare hall with benches and blackboards. There was an endless cacophony of sound produced by both the teachers and the students from adjoining classes. But Adoor's early schooling was miserable not so much on account of the environment as the poor marks he scored and for which he earned the nickname of 'dud' ('Mantan' in Malayalam). Adoor says:

> The primary school was quite miserable. I always fared poorly in the exams. It was not the fault of my teachers. They did their best, I believe. But I was not focused on studies. I was interested in everything else. So, during my primary schooldays, both the teachers and the elders at home took me for a dud.

Somehow, he managed to get through primary school. But when he joined Vadakkedathu Kaavu Middle School, the pathetic marks he got at the primary level and the schoolteacher's harsh words fired him to do his best.

Indeed, taking these as a challenge, he emerged as one of the top-ranking students in the class. Sheer determination, strong character, an ability to work hard – all these became part of his new persona. Adoor says:

> I got tired of being treated as a dud and made a good effort on my own to improve my performance in middle school. And it worked! I started scoring good marks in every subject except mathematics in which I had no proper base. But somehow I managed to scrape through my maths exam as well.

He went on to pass his matriculation exam from Adoor High School with flying colours. It was during his Intermediate course at the Nair Service Society College at Pandalam (a small town near Adoor) that he secured high marks in Malayalam and discovered he had a talent for literary writing. For a while he dreamt of completing his bachelor's degree in Malayalam literature but following suggestions from his family members, he took up zoology instead as a short cut to medical studies. But just a couple of months into zoology classes, he came upon an advertisement for admission to the Gandhigram Rural Institute located near Dindigul, Madurai (Tamil Nadu). Gopalakrishnan had been a great admirer of Gandhi from his early schooldays and it was the lure of social service which attracted him to the course in Gandhigram.

Gandhian Ways, Pillai's Plays

Gopalakrishnan studied public administration, economics and political science at Gandhigram from 1957 to 1959. The Gandhigram Rural Institute had a deep impact on his mind, attitude and behaviour. Founded in 1956, the institute propagated the philosophy of Gandhi and Tagore who believed knowledge and work should go together, and that education must be made available to people of every caste and religion and class of society. One of the aims of the institute was to enlighten villagers deprived of knowledge in various fields.

Besides Gandhian ideology, at this point Adoor came into contact with G. Sankara Pillai who was one of Kerala's pioneer playwrights. The encounter was to prove significant in shaping Adoor's world view. Pillai was a major force in theatre, known for his originality, experimentalism and creativity, whose dramatic techniques came to be known as the

'Sankara Pillai style'. Some distinctive features of his plays are the use of rich images, symbols, metaphors, and a Western-style surrealistic approach. He is also known for his ability to amalgamate traditional and modern elements. He was in touch with all the new trends in world theatre and most major playwrights were his close friends. All the same, his works are deeply rooted in the rich soil of Malayalam culture, two of the best-known being *Snehadutan* (Messenger of Compassion, 1956) and *Sabarmati Dooreyaanu* (Sabarmati Is Far Away, 1958). In the latter part of his life, Pillai, to foster creativity in the minds of the new generation, set up a School of Drama at the Calicut University in 1977 and was its first director. This great man passed away in 1989, leaving a huge void in the world of theatre.

Adoor was fortunate to know Sankara Pillai personally. When Adoor was a student at the Gandhigram Rural Institute, the playwright joined the faculty. Adoor's deep love for theatre brought him very close to Pillai. 'It must have made Gopalakrishnan extremely proud when Pillai gave him his manuscripts to read and comment on. Pillai also added to the Gandhigram library, stocking it up with innumerable books on plays, playwrights and production. Gopalakrishnan read all that Pillai had collected and acquired for Gandhigram...'[33]

During his stint at the institute, Adoor penned a few plays such as *Ninte Rajyam Varunnu* (Thy Kingdom Cometh) and *Vaiki Vanna Velicham* (The Light That Came Too Late), which brought him recognition as a promising writer. In 1974, Adoor directed Samuel Beckett's *Waiting for Godot* which had been translated into Malayalam by the celebrated poet Kadammanitta Ramakrishnan.

Starting Early

Adoor was no stranger to the theatre. He was brought up in a family devoted to the arts. His maternal uncle was a patron of Kathakali and as a boy he was a rapt viewer of these performances. According to him:

> Since my young days, I have been drawn to this classical art form. It was part of our daily life. Birthdays in the family were special occasions, for there invariably used to be a Kathakali performance. We even had a Kaliyogam (Kathakali troupe) in the family. But somewhere along the way, I neglected it, believing that Western theatre was superior.[34]

When Adoor was just eight years old, he played the role of Siddhartha, the Indian prince who gave up material pleasures to seek the true meaning of life. He enacted the role so brilliantly that everyone was awestruck. Before completing his tenth year, he had earned a reputation as a versatile actor – and, what's more, as the young playwright, having surprised his family by writing a play titled *Kapatayogi* (Malayalam for 'The Fake Yogi'). Writing plays, poems and stories in the company of his cousins, particularly Ravindran and Narayanan, was part of his growing-up experience. The young gang got together on Sundays and other holidays, developing their creativity as they immersed themselves in such activities. They enacted their plays before the family members and elders.

In an interview to Khalid Mohamed (*Filmfare*, 1–15 February 1982), Adoor says:

> I started writing plays myself, some of which have been published. One of these is called *The Green Room* (1958) which is about an audience waiting for the show to begin but there are problems backstage among the cast and the performance is never held – a sort of play within a play...

During his schooldays, Gopalakrishnan, with the help of friends and relatives, set up a library in their village. His playwright aunt, Kutty Kunjamma, had a big library. She encouraged Adoor to go through her collection of books – Adoor, of course, needed no urging. His maternal uncle Raman Unnithan, the most artistic of the older siblings, who recognized both Adoor's intense interest in theatre and his latent talent, asked his nephew to read the plays he wrote. Every family member seemed to have deep faith in Gopalakrishnan's competence, particularly in theatre. Adoor confides in a whisper: 'In fact, I wanted to go into theatre. Basically I am a theatre man. It was by sheer accident that I landed up in cinema.'

After the course at Gandhigram, Adoor began looking for a job. His application for the post of investigator at the Agriculture University in Gwalior being rejected for some untold reason, he was dejected at not being able to supplement the family income. However, he did get a job in the Bharat Sevak Samaj in a slum service project for a couple of months, then shifted to the National Sample Survey as a statistical investigator in

Trivandrum. He was diligent and honest in discharging his duties but job satisfaction still eluded him. Nevertheless, it gained him new experiences:

> It was a very rewarding period of my life. As an officer in the Department of Statistics and connected with the National Sample Survey, I had to travel throughout Kerala collecting all kinds of samples from various strata of the population. Often, in areas where there were no proper roads, particularly in the Malabar region, I was forced to stay back in the villages at the end of a day's work. I lived with the local people, shared their food with them. Thus, my earlier profession which provided me with a good opportunity to observe human behaviour closely has helped me as a film-maker…[35]

His dream in those days was to do a course in play production at the National School of Drama in Delhi. But he was unaware that a good command over Hindi – which he lacked – was a necessary qualification. Though he had to drop that idea for the moment, he never gave up the search for a formal training school for drama. Then, in 1961, the Pune Film Institute published an advertisement inviting applications for courses in screenplay writing and direction which would start in 1962. Grasping the value of such a course, he instantly applied. Happily, Adoor was not only selected but given a merit scholarship as he topped the list of the successful candidates at the written examination and viva voce. Tragedy, however, struck during early days at the institute: his mother died of cancer in 1962, and Adoor was able to reach home only two days after her death.

From Play to Screenplay

Embarking on the course, Adoor thought that screenplay writing would not be very different from playwriting. So when he got admission into the film institute, he continued his study of theatre, spending all his spare time in the library which had a great collection of books on theatre. It was only in the second year that Adoor realized the differences between playwriting and screenplay writing. As he explains, 'I had not watched many Hindi films or world cinema before, and it was only after I joined the institute that I came into contact with important films in Hindi and languages other than Malayalam.'

Classmates like John Sankaramangalam and Sound Engineer Devdas were also from Kerala. Their professor R.S. Pruthi, Adoor recalls, was both austere and a man of principles. He told his students to submit typed screenplays. When Adoor got his scripts typed by professional typists, he found them full of errors – and after corrections they came back with even more! Since this was a regular exercise, a frustrated Adoor purchased a JK typewriter and a guide titled *Teach Yourself Typewriting* by Pitman, and proceeded to educate himself.

The film institute in Pune opened up a whole new world, as Adoor understood the vast potential of cinema as a visual medium. A nonconformist teacher at the institute those days was Ritwik Ghatak who was vice principal and professor in the direction department. Adoor reminisces:

> Ritwik Ghatak taught us invaluable lessons in directing. Watching his films and then listening to him – why and how he did it in a particular way – was great learning for us. Some of my juniors like Mani Kaul would meet him outside after class. But maybe because I was too shy, I did not make any attempt to get close to my teachers.
>
> Ghatak was a great influence on all of us. He was very well read and always took a stand which was unconventional. He was an excellent teacher and his love and passion for cinema always came through whether he was talking about his own works or some other masters like Bunuel. He seemed to like Bunuel a lot but did not share the same enthusiasm for Bergman.
>
> Another teacher who left a lasting impact on us was Prof. Satish Bahadur who taught us film appreciation. He joined the institute halfway through the first year. Film appreciation was a subject of study prescribed in the syllabus but there was little understanding of what it constituted. I remember the guest lecturer who screened a documentary titled *A Portrait of Madam Ga* for us and then started appreciating it in terms of how beautiful Madam Ga's fingers were and how delicately she opened the chocolate packing and so on! We intuitively knew this was not film appreciation! Later, when Satish Bahadur took over, he sparked off a whole range of discoveries and discussions on how to read a film, analyse, and appreciate it.
>
> There were also other important teachers on our faculty like Prof. R.K. Ramachandran (editing), Prof. S.B. Thakar (sound), Prof. G.B.

> Kulkarni (cinematography), Prof. L.P. Shah (production) and some others to whom we owe a lot.

No wonder *The Indian Magazine*, August 1984, quoted Adoor as saying: 'The New Indian Cinema owes its newness to the film institute. It is a fact which cannot be denied or questioned.'

As part of the course, Adoor made two student films, namely, *Light*, a dialogue exercise with a serious story, and *A Great Day*, a comedy. *Light* focuses on the hardships faced by a poor family of a father, mother and sickly daughter, while *A Great Day* is about a lethargic young man faced with meeting his prospective father-in-law.

After completing his direction course in 1964–65, Adoor, instead of heading for Bombay, the usual Mecca of young aspiring film-makers, returned to his home state.

In the 1960s, most audiences being unaware of world cinema, Adoor made it his first mission to make people cinema-literate. Supported by his Gandhigram batchmate Kulathoor Bhaskaran Nair, Adoor launched Chitralekha – the first film society in Kerala – in July 1965. This was part of a strategy to propagate film culture in the state through the establishment of film societies, publication of film literature, and production and distribution of quality cinema. Adoor and Nair travelled extensively to screen good films. The Fifth All India Writers' Conference held in Kerala in January 1966 provided the right venue for Adoor and his friends to hold the first international film festival in the state. Encouraged by literary stalwarts like M. Govindan, the festival, held over seven days and simultaneously in ten district headquarters, was a huge success. Subsequently, the Chitralekha Film Cooperative expanded to establish a studio of its own with facilities for shooting, processing, recording and editing, priding itself on being the first institution of its kind in the country. Chitralekha had a great influence in bringing about a change in the consciousness of Kerala's cinephiles.

Adoor describes the early years of film-making to Gautaman Bhaskaran in *Adoor Gopalakrishnan: A Life in Cinema:* 'I struggled not one or two, but seven years. I never waited for something to happen, but kept working, not necessarily on a feature or a documentary, but on other things. I kept the film society going, visited universities and colleges, screened movies, and gave lectures on cinema to students.'

Adoor and His Cinema World

Adoor's short film *The Myth* was made for the competition section at the 1967 Montreal Expo, the theme being 'Man and His World'. It was awarded a merit certificate. Another 1967 film was a twenty-minute documentary for the Kerala State Lottery Department, *A Millionaire Is Born*.

His documentary on the Idukki Hydroelectric Project covered the entire eight-year construction of the dam; his 1968 films were *A Mission of Love*, on the Christian Missionary Service; *Danger at Your Doorstep*, for the Government of India's Films Division (FD) on Life Insurance; *And Man Created*, on handicrafts; and *Manntharikal*, on family planning. In the next couple of years, he made *Towards National STD* for the FD; *Pratisandhi*, a docu-drama on family planning; and *Romance of Rubber*, for the Rubber Board.

In 1972, Adoor made his first feature film *Swayamvaram* and has never looked back. In 1984, the Government of India conferred on him the Padma Shri, followed in 2006 by the Padma Vibhushan, India's second-highest civilian award. In 2005, he became the youngest film-maker to receive the prestigious Dadasaheb Phalke Award, conferred annually by the government on those who have made an outstanding contribution to Indian cinema. That same year, the Mahatma Gandhi University, Kottayam, conferred an honorary DLitt (Doctor of Letters) on Adoor, followed by another doctorate from the University of Kerala in 2011. His alma mater, of course, did not lag behind in recognizing his contributions: Adoor served two terms as chairman of the FTII Governing Council – 1987 to 1989 and 1992 to 1995.

His collection of essays, *Cinemayude Lokam* (The World of Cinema), was honoured with the National Award for the Best Book on Cinema in 1984, while his *Cinema Anubhavam* (The Experience of Cinema), a collection of articles dealing with the art and practice of cinema, won the Kerala State Award for Best Book on Cinema in 2004. His third book, *Cinema, Sahityam, Jeevitham* (Film, Literature and Life) was published in 2005, and his next, *Cinema Samskaran* (Film Culture) in 2011. It would seem Adoor Gopalakrishnan was no less an artist on the written page than on celluloid.

On 15 April 2013, the University of Wisconsin in Milwaukee (US) formally inaugurated The Adoor Gopalakrishnan Film Archive and

Research Fund to preserve his films and to encourage and promote study and research of his work. Adoor is the first Indian film-maker to be honoured thus by a university outside India.

Life at Darsanam

It was on 10 September 1972 that Adoor married Sunanda. It was an arranged marriage. Sunanda, born of Keralite parents, was brought up in Malaysia and came to Kerala for her university education. They have a daughter Aswati, now serving as a senior IPS officer in Mumbai.

Soft-spoken and charming, Sunanda welcomed me and my wife Ananya with a bright smile when we visited them in Thiruvananthapuram. We stopped to admire the small, rectangular courtyard in their home which lets in the sunlight and in season – how wonderful! – the monsoon rains. As we enjoyed the delicious breakfast of idlis, appams and tea that she offered us that fine Sunday morning, looking out at the lush garden (which Adoor helps tend) I noticed a cart leaning against the wall. 'Sir, isn't that the same cart which carries the hangman and his son to the jail in *Nizhalkkuthu*?' I asked. Sunanda grinned as Adoor replied, 'Yes … we parked it here because the bullock cart has now become a rarity and today's young generation has not seen one!'

Adoor built his dream house named 'Darsanam' (meaning 'vision') in Thiruvananthapuram in 1977. Wrote K.G. Kumar in his article 'Celluloid Magic' published in *The Indian Magazine*, August 1984:

> The house in which Adoor Gopalakrishnan lives seems to exude something of the man himself. To the stranger climbing up the road there is nothing to announce the existence of the house on the crest of the hill above Akulam lake. He would be more likely to pause and soak in the view of the Arabian Sea glinting in the distance. It is only past the little shops and past the Chitralekha Film Studio that the gate slides into the visitor's line of vision. It appears ensconced in a world quite its own. The curved tile roof, so beautifully characteristic of traditional Kerala architecture and the unhurried profusion of woodwork, add to the ambience of Adoor Gopalakrishnan's house, an anachronism that is surprisingly not grating … At the door the visitor's finger searches for the button of the bell. In vain – electric bells are somehow not congruous with the sense of time gone by that

> the place is imbued with. Chastened by this awareness, he is quick to tug at the string of the temple bell that hangs above the wooden door … Sonorous chimes waft through.

Adoor bought the wood from an almost 200-year-old house which belonged to a Travancore palace official, then single-mindedly trained his artistic vision upon it. Gautaman Bhaskaran writes in *A Life in Cinema:*

> The process was laborious, because the wood had been painted several times over and was done to death with nails, and finding master craftsmen who knew the intricacies of erecting a traditional Kerala wooden house – which Gopalakrishnan planned – was difficult. It took eight months of struggle, supervision and several changes of craftsmen before Darsanam emerged, wood with wood, plank with plank, all blended into a harmonious whole…

Sounds familiar? Shot by shot, scene by scene, the way Adoor builds his films into a unique and harmonious whole…

Swayamvaram *(Courtesy: Kerala State Chalachithra Academy)*

6

Swayamvaram (One's Own Choice)

Romance in a Real World

Adoor Gopalakrishnan's *Swayamvaram* (1972) – which made a landmark departure from the conventional mode of narrating a story – depicts the shift of Kerala's bourgeois society to a modern one, its predicaments and struggles. *Swayamvaram* focuses on bourgeois anguish in post-Nehruvian times, and the question of survival in a society undergoing economic, social, political and moral crises. The conflict between the individual and the society is presented through the narrative of the two young lovers, Viswanathan and Sita, who, defying social norms, go away to the town and struggle to build a life of their own on the foundation of their hopes and dreams.

Swayamvaram has a seemingly simple plot which could even be – mistakenly – considered commonplace. But the simplicity is on the exterior. The more we ponder over the film, the deeper it draws us into itself, revealing new visions and layers not discernible at first gaze. It is not just a love story but a journey from the world of expectancy and dreams to the hard realities of the world. The American poet Robert Frost writes in one of his finest poems, 'Road Not Taken', about the difficulties of making a correct choice at critical junctures in life. The poet, walking in the deep and dark woods, comes to a bifurcated road and is utterly confused about which direction he should take. After deep consideration, he chooses the road that is less trodden but is still not sure whether he has made the right choice. The young man in our story, like Frost, is not too sure of the choice he and his lover have made – but the two are happy enough that they are together.

'Swayamvaram' is a Sanskrit word, literally meaning 'one's own choice' (*swayam* meaning 'self' and *vara*, 'choice'). Some choices are irrevocable. At the start, Sita, the protagonist, has to make a choice between staying with her parents and running away with her lover to a distant town. It is a tug of war between two alternatives, that is, between parental care and one's life companion – between certainty and uncertainty. She settles for her lover, Viswanathan, an educated but unemployed youth, an aspiring writer whose future is uncertain. Sita's choice indicates her strong and positive nature. She is able to 'accept reality and defy convention' at a critical time in her life.

Swayamvaram begins with shots of a bus journey against which the opening titles are displayed. The opening shots, the driver of the bus, the backs of the passengers, some napping, some reading a newspaper or talking, establish the day-to-day reality of a bus journey. In the midst of these everyday passengers, sit the young couple, Viswanathan and Sita. Adoor never spotlights the couple with his camera; the two are introduced very casually. Such couples are to be found everywhere – the camera passes from one corner of the bus to the other, capturing the movements and conduct of all the passengers, including Sita and Viswanathan. The close-up shot of Sita's smiling face indicates her sense of fulfilment and joy at having realized her dreams. Visuals, not words, are Adoor's pointers to indicate another layer of meaning. Conversations among the bus passengers are largely in the form of inaudible dialogue. Suddenly, the bus brakes to a halt at a signal, followed by a jump cut to a hotel room. Says Adoor:

> We are describing a journey, a long journey. First of all, when you see a vehicle in motion, normally, it is conceived as only a device to show that so-and-so is travelling from one place to another. But here, it is very different because without explaining anything and just by the way they look at each other and whisper to each other, it is suggested they are a new couple and what the relationship is between them. They are unfamiliar with the town they are entering.The film is about a trip from illusion to reality. You see the 'Stop' sign – it is a signal indicating the end of the dream. Then life proper starts…

The three-storey building where the couple initially stays is itself a metaphor – a metaphor for high-flying dreams and illusions. In a top-angle shot, Adoor shows Sita watching a religious procession through the window. The devotees, using musical instruments like drums and gongs, sing, '*Hare Rama, Hare Rama, Rama Rama Hare Hare, Hare Krishna, Hare Krishna, Krishna Krishna Hare Hare*'. Adoor uses the chanting of the devotees as a background score while Viswanathan and Sita are making love. I was reminded of the metaphysical poet John Donne, who philosophized that the body and the soul are two distinct entities but related aspects of the totality of love, with the amalgamation of two souls being the purest and the sublimest form of love. His poem, 'Extasie', implies that love is a religious experience, just as 'To His Mistress Going to Bed' looks upon sex as a religious experience. The physical communion of Viswanathan and Sita is not merely one of love-making, but a spiritual and metaphysical experience.

There follows a dream sequence where they act out their love for each other, which combines a mockery of what the popular cinema has passed on to viewers as romancing (singing and dancing and prancing around) with powerful metaphorical visuals – of sea waves, railway tracks and forests. There are three segments to this sequence, each of which ends in Sita losing Viswanathan.

At the end of the dream sequence, Sita is shown running breathlessly through dense forest in search of Viswanathan. The images are, in fact, encapsulating the story as a whole. As soon as the dream visuals fade, we see a gloomy and melancholic Viswanathan smoking. The reason for his grimness becomes clear when Sita asks Viswanathan, 'Why brood over it? We can as well move into a cheaper hotel.' Viswanathan replies, 'Do you regret all this, Sita?'

The End of a Dream

From the bus journey to the dream visuals and after, we travel the gamut from fantasy to actuality. The second part of the story, beginning from their shift to a cheaper hotel and thereon to a rented house and to the film's end, is about their continuous struggle as they keep encountering bitter realities and disenchantment.

The couple comes to stay in a cheaper hotel which is dingy and squalid, full of drunkards and people of dubious character. Stinking surroundings, wine bottles on the floor, ragged mattresses and soiled bedsheets indicate the dilapidated state of the hotel – but Viswanathan's pathetic financial condition rules out any better accommodation. They clean up the room and somehow manage to stay on. They are married but not in the eyes of society, since Sita does not wear a mangalsutra – the symbol of a married Hindu woman. She is aware of the situation but does not complain. One day, however, she gives Viswanathan her bangles to sell and buy a mangalsutra instead. She considers it necessary, not because she wishes to conform to society's traditions and customs which she has already defied, but to stop others from pointing a finger at the two of them.

Viswanathan goes to see the editor of a literary magazine to get his novel serialized. A couple of elderly writers at the editor's office are discussing the younger and older generations of writers. Viswanathan remains a silent listener. One of the older writers comments, 'Oh these modern writers! They put form above content. They have not seen life yet. What is literature without life's experience? Whatever one writes is printed these days. Look at this, just half a page makes a short story! Can you make head or tail of it?' A young writer sitting by them replies, 'Should the work be condemned for that? The old never accommodates the new!' Later, the editor picks up Viswanathan's novel and asks him to meet him the following Sunday.

In the meantime, the unpleasant and suffocating atmosphere of the hotel compels the couple to shift to a new abode which happens to be a small cottage with a tiny verandah and courtyard, on the outskirts of the town. Just opposite lives a prostitute named Kalyani whose customers range from smugglers to daily wage earners. Her husband, perpetually drunk, simply ignores the 'visitors'. What he wants from his wife is just money for his drinks. Kalyani candidly admits her profession and carries on, unaffected. One of Kalyani's regulars is Vasu, a known smuggler. Another neighbour is the middle-aged lady, Janaki, who is helpful and sympathetic. Viswanathan and Sita now find themselves in a strange new environment.

Viswanathan meets the editor as scheduled, but returns frustrated at his refusal to serialize the novel which he dismisses as 'too sentimental'.

The editor's rejection shatters his dream of becoming a writer. Sita sympathizes deeply with Viswanathan. He lands a job as a lecturer in zoology in a private tutorial college, which brings a ray of hope into their lives. Alas, their happiness is short-lived – the principal reveals that he is terribly in debt and is going to shut down the college. The principal instructs the clerk to settle Viswanathan's dues. Sita and Viswanathan's hopes and aspirations are going up in smoke…

Circumstances force Viswanathan to accept the job of a clerk in a sawmill. This job brings some solace to their lives, but again it is short-lived. One day, when he emerges from the sawmill, he is approached by a stranger who pleads, 'I worked here for twelve years. They sacked me without an explanation and drove me out into the street. You took my place. Do you think it is fair?' This disclosure weighs heavily on Viswanathan's heart. He is haunted by a sense of guilt for having robbed someone else of his job. Viswanathan's mental equilibrium begins to wobble. Meanwhile, Sita gives birth to a baby girl. Although Viswanathan feels sympathy for the sacked employee, how can he afford to give up his only source of sustenance? He is torn between feelings of guilt and helplessness. The conflict between his inner self and his own inability to act shatters him, affecting his health. Finally, he dies – leaving Sita all alone.

When I asked Adoor Gopalakrishnan if at all it was necessary for Viswanathan to die, he says, 'Actually, it is a fact of life. From the time the retrenched worker accosts him, his conscience hounds him and ultimately he succumbs. His spiritual death occurs much earlier than his physical one – which follows naturally as a matter of course.'

Images, juxtapositions and metaphors all come into play, to underline, to intensify the end of the couple's dream. Sita is sitting, heartbroken in a corner of her house. A kind old man, Viswanathan's colleague in the sawmill, seeing her misery, invites her, 'Listen to me, come and live with us. We'll share whatever we have.' But Sita refuses. On another occasion, her neighbour Janaki advises, 'My dear child, go home to your parents. If only they knew of this, they would surely come for you.' Sita says, 'No, I won't.' It is clear that she is not going to stay with either of them. Neither will she take the path that Kalyani has – suggested by repeated shots of the bolted door of her room, signifying that outsiders cannot trespass.

There is an earlier indication too when Vasu, the smuggler, gazes at Sita and Kalyani tells him, 'You are aiming for the impossible.'

Adoor does not use dialogue in the opening and closing sequences of the film but powerful images and music which together suggest much more than dialogue would have conveyed. With the resonance of the tanpura and Carnatic ragas on the soundtrack, Sita is seen boiling milk and feeding her baby. The tanpura which serves as a prelude to the ragas seems to underline Sita's unyielding spirit and determination, while the ragas and raginis evoke not only Sita's loneliness in the absence of her husband but also their one-time loving togetherness. Outside the house, lightning flashes and there are heavy showers. The picture of the divine Sita's swayamvaram pasted on the wall is being drenched in rainwater leaking through the thatched roof and contrasts with the plight of the heroine's own swayamvaram. She is aware that choices once made cannot be altered. But she has decided to fight and not yield her self-respect and dignity whatever the circumstances. The film ends with an extreme close-up of Sita's face looking at the viewers, querying them perhaps. The narrative comes back to where it began, to the realm of uncertainty…

The Other Sita

Is Sita, the protagonist of the film, a metaphorical representation of the mythological Sita?

Various incidents define the film heroine for us. Defying her parents, Sita chooses the unemployed Viswanathan, though she is aware of the uncertain future ahead. Adoor establishes this through a dream which Sita narrates to Viswanathan, 'I dreamt of my father. The temple pond is full of lotuses. I climbed down and reached for flowers. But I began to sink deeper and deeper. Someone was pulling me down. Was it father? Yes, it was him. I struggled hard. But I could not move. I shouted for you. You were nowhere. Then I was running and running through dense forest. Father almost caught me … I could not run any longer.'

On another occasion, Viswanathan asks, 'You read the novel?' Sita replies, 'I like the title' ('*Nirvrity*', ecstasy). 'How about my heroine?' Viswanathan persists. Sita replies, 'She should not have died.' Viswanathan says, 'Should she have married and lived happily after – like in the old movies?'

Sita does not ever complain. To support the family she seeks a job. 'I saw your ad for salesgirls,' she tells the lady official. Says the lady, 'Yes, we need matriculates.' Sita says, 'I have a BA degree.' The lady says, 'Can you remit a security deposit of Rs 1,000?' Sita, utterly disappointed, questions, 'Deposit?' The lady affirms, 'The deposit is compulsory. It is the board's decision.'

Sita is supportive of Viswanathan. After losing his job at the tutorial college, Viswanathan, lying on his bed, asks Sita, 'Did we do wrong?' By 'wrong', Viswanathan probably refers to their running away or defying their families. Well into their married life, Viswanathan appears still in confusion over the choice they have made. In contrast, Sita is a symbol of courage and optimism and believes they have done nothing wrong. While Viswanathan is kind, loving and morally strong, he is also diffident. He meets a double death, one spiritual and the other, physical. His moral crisis takes root from the time financial constraints force them to shift from the sophisticated hotel to cheap accommodation.

Madhavan Nair, commonly known by his stage name Madhu, who plays Viswanathan, said to me, 'There was a particular scene when the headmaster in the film says to me (Viswanathan) that he cannot afford to keep me on as a teacher and so I have to leave the job. At this point I have to register despair on my face. As an actor, I always want to do my best – and I thought I managed that. Adoor explained to me very clearly what he wanted from me and from the character and I understood it clearly. I am glad to say he was satisfied. Adoor is better than almost all the directors with whom I have worked. He is sincerely devoted to the art of cinema and does his homework thoroughly before coming to the sets – which not all directors do. But Adoor is a man you can trust.'

Picturing Kerala in the 1970s

Swayamvaram is a social document that reflects the socio-political and economic picture of Kerala in the 1970s. Corruption, hypocrisy, anti-social activities like smuggling, prostitution, political unrest, uprising of the working classes against the government, unemployment, the attitude of the old writers against the young and upcoming – all these features of Indian society in general and in Kerala in particular are hinted at and implied in the film rather than elaborated in detail.

The owner of the rented house tells Viswanathan and Sita, 'Govind Pillai, the head clerk, was staying here. When he moved in, he was only a lower division clerk. Lucky man. All his daughters are happily married. He used to take bribes, of course...'

Or in case of workers' uprisings, Viswanathan hears the radical labour leader hold forth, 'The working class of this country is being misled. Maybe these parties have some influence over some workers. But on close scrutiny one thing becomes clear. Their operations are not different from that of the bourgeoisie. To obstruct the liberation of the proletariat, they all use the same means.'

Unemployment was one of the major problems of the 1970s in Kerala. Many people migrated to different places in pursuit of jobs. Viswanathan is representative of the educated unemployed youth through whom Adoor presents the socio-economic condition of Kerala. Says Adoor:

> Trivandrum is the place where the story happens. It is just a small town. But the town itself reflects the social situation prevailing at that time as regards employment, political turmoil, the kind of people inhabiting the place and the value systems of the society. Does the society of the time allow two young people, bereft of any support from their parents, to live on their own?

According to Madhu, 'I belong to the realistic school of acting and hence liked the character of Viswanathan. It was more real and more natural compared to other characters I have played in my life. He is a human being, not a film hero.' In one of the most poignant scenes of the film, Viswanathan observes a rally in progress, protesting, 'Reinstate retrenched workers! Long live revolution! Long live workers' unity! You came to power with promises to the people. Have you fulfilled them? Answer us now!' But he never shows the slightest inclination to join. Rather he looks upon the rally as a simple spectator though the protest reflects the grim reality of the middle class too. However, his awareness and feelings of sympathy for the retrenched workers take shape in his mind. The question of his not joining the workers' protest also became a topic of debate. In an interview published in *Filmfare*, 1–15 February 1982, Adoor said to Khalid Mohamed,

> ... the workers take out a procession but Viswanathan does not join it because although he has genuine sympathy for them, he does not

> consider himself one of them – that is the moral crisis of the middle class. His not joining the political procession came in for criticism at the Moscow Film Festival where it was world premiered. They seem to have missed the point that the film is about his *not* joining the protest march.

Bhasi-less? Songless?

Adoor Bhasi was the most popular comedian of the times – considered an indispensable element of Malayalam cinema. Unfortunately, Adoor had no place for him in this debut film. As Adoor tells me:

> The Kerala audience was content with the kind of faces they saw routinely on the screens at the time. But we were confident that we were making the right kind of cinema and we thought people would like it. That was our approach. When we went to book theatres for the release, many of the theatre managers said, 'How come you made a film without Adoor Bhasi?' 'How come there are no songs?' When the film was running in cinema halls, some managers regretted that if only we had introduced songs in the film, it would have proved a big hit. They just could not imagine that a film could be made without these ingredients.

It is not as if the film only manifests grim social and individual realities – there are also light moments. There is the scene, for instance, in which little Sukumaran, a likeable eight-year-old, makes acquaintance with Sita. Not only is it light-hearted, it augments the socio-economic picture of the times. The desire of the lower middle class to send their children to a good school and their inability to afford to continue their studies give us a glimpse of the social conditions of those times. Sita, who is washing clothes in the courtyard of her rented house, notices the boy at her gate. When she asks his name, he readily answers, 'Sukumaran.' When she asks why he has not gone to school, he says, 'Mother asked me not to go.' Sita smiles and requests, 'Can you run up to the store and get a pack of indigo powder?' Sukumaran collects the money, reverses his imaginary car, negotiates a curve and speeds away. (This kind of game is very popular among village children.) When Sukumaran returns quickly with the purchase, a pleased Sita engages him in conversation:

Sita: Which class are you studying in?

Sukumaran: Standard three.

Sita: Only three?

Sukumaran (*shyly*): This is my second year in the third standard.

Sita: Do you like your teacher?

Sukumaran: She is very strict and beat me once.

Sita: Why?

Sukumaran: For bursting crackers in the classroom!

Writing a New Cinematic Language

Today *Swayamvaram* is undoubtedly recognized as Kerala's pioneering, path-breaking New Wave film in which Adoor introduced a new cinematic language. Famed critic Iqbal Masud wrote, '*Swayamvaram* depicted the sensuousness of love depleted and destroyed by a dehumanising environment. The mastery of the cinematic medium was evident in the slow conjuring up of an ambience and the almost precisely measured rhythm of the denouement.'[36]

But at the time of its making, its FTII-trained director went against all the stereotyped conventions of the commercial success formula. The film was shot at actual locations in a natural ambience with direct recording of sound. It was the first-ever film in south India to record sound with the help of the Nagra recorder. There are no songs or comic elements, no actor or actress whose voice is dubbed (except Sarada who is from Andhra Pradesh). The conscious use of sound, economy of expression, meaningful framing and sharp visuals distinguished the film from others. This was altogether new cinematic language for the people of Kerala.

Wrote C.T. Venkiteswaran in *A Door to Adoor*:

> *Swayamvaram* begins with a journey that marks a departure from the prevalent notions about cinema and announces the arrival of New Wave cinema in Malayalam. It is one of the finest works of the period that several critics have identified as heralding a new age in Malayalam cinema. It was produced by a film cooperative, Chitralekha, and its audience comprised mainly middle-class intellectuals, students and film-society buffs. Its theme and style are formally self-conscious,

> intense, slow and ponderous. The absence of songs, stunts and buffoonery, are typically New Wave and markedly distinct from the commercial fare.[37]

Before *Swayamvaram*, Adoor Gopalakrishnan submitted a script for a feature film to the then Film Finance Corporation. It was titled *Kamuki* and was based on a story and script penned by a well-known Malayali playwright. To his utter disappointment, it was rejected. Later, when he inquired of one of the officers as to the reason, he was told, 'Why do you want to make a film about love? Our country has so many big problems.' Adoor reminisces about those early frustrations: 'When we approached the Department of Cooperatives for funds they said, "Our main aim is to finance farmers, we don't think films are loan-worthy and sorry, we don't deal with gamblers."'[38]

But later on, *Swayamvaram*, written by Adoor himself, was granted a loan by the Film Finance Corporation. The total cost of production of the film was Rs 2.5 lakh. The Film Finance Cooperation sanctioned a loan of Rs 1.5 lakh. The rest was raised from the Chitralekha Film Cooperative.

Initially, Adoor Gopalakrishnan thought of casting non-professional actors for the lead characters, particularly for the leading female role. He searched for new faces for some months and wrote letters to colleges, inviting aspiring girls. But there was no response at all. In the Indian context, getting a female actor for a film was like looking for a blade of grass in the desert! In Assam (where I come from), when the first Assamese talkie *Joymoti* was made in 1935, director Jyoti Prasad Agarwala, the father of Assamese cinema, had to face numerous hurdles in his search for the lead actress. Somehow he managed to get a young lady named Aideu Nilambar Handique to play the role of Joymoti. But when she returned home after the shooting, the villagers and even her parents ostracized her. She remained unmarried all her life and lived on her own till her death.

Adoor, not finding a suitable actress, approached the popular and glamorous actress Sarada. She readily consented. Adoor decided to cast his long-time friend Madhu opposite her. The release of the film on 24 November1972 stunned the people of Kerala. There were no songs to sing along with, no Adoor Bhasi to make you laugh out loud. Without these elements, *Swayamvaram* was an instant flop. In most theatres the film did not run for more than a week. Most of the viewers who were familiar with films laced with songs, dance and comedy failed to grasp the deeper meaning of the film. Adoor recalled the general reaction, 'No distributor offered to take up the film, so we had to take on that work also, establishing contacts with the cinemas, but the film was not a success.'[39]

Initially, the regional selection committee simply did not consider the film fit for being sent up to the jury for the national awards. A frustrated Adoor sent a telegram to Romesh Thapar who headed the jury, appealing to him to view the film. Though Adoor did not get any response to his telegram, after a few days he heard the news on the radio that *Swayamvaram* had won National Film Awards for Best Film, Best Director, Best Actress and Best Cinematography – setting a record for the largest number of major awards won by a film by a debutant! This completely changed the attitude of people towards the film and, released again, the impact was totally different. The entire loan amount from the Film Finance Corporation was returned in record time.

To the question whether *Swayamvaram* was influenced by neo-realism, Adoor says:

> More than neo-realism, it is the French New Wave. Neo-realism was too old by that time but of course it had its influence. By then the French New Wave had already come into vogue – that was the immediate influence. In 1958, when the French New Wave was at its height, it swept away the majority of the awards at Cannes.

Swayamvaram, like *Pather Panchali* about two decades before, was condemned for displaying Indian poverty on the screen. Adoor Gopalakrishnan candidly says:

> Nargis Dutt was famously quoted as making a statement in Parliament that *Pather Panchali* was 'selling India's poverty' abroad. They are ill-informed. That's all. M.G. Ramachandran, who was the chief minister of Tamil Nadu at that time, also made a similar comment about *Swayamvaram*. Instead of feeling ashamed of our backwardness which is a reality, these people do not realize that they are also responsible for it. Instead of working towards achieving better standards of life for our people, they wish to cover up poverty by falsifying the life we live as they do in those commercial films. In fact, our true life, our situation and our environment should get reflected in our films.

Kodiyettam *(Courtesy: Kerala State Chalachithra Academy)*

7

Kodiyettam (The Ascent)

The Uphill Road to Growing Up

'Bildungsroman' is the German literary term for the genre that narrates the psychological and spiritual progress of an individual from immaturity to maturity and his or her recognition of his/her place as an individual in society. In other words, a 'coming of age' story. Adoor Gopalakrishnan's *Kodiyettam*, his second feature film which was released in 1977, ran for more than four months at Kottayam and elsewhere, despite its avant-garde format. *Kodiyettam,* literally meaning hoisting of the temple flag – the ascent – is a filmic bildungsroman.

Sankarankutty, its unlikely hero, is good at heart and everyone likes him for his simplicity. They know him basically as a wanderer but as the plot unfolds along the director's sympathetic and understanding delineation of character, the viewers realize that Sankaran is no caricature but a full-blown real-life character. While *Swayamvaram* portrayed the trip from illusion to reality, *Kodiyettam* focuses on the uphill journey of Sankarankutty from an irresponsible drifter to a responsible individual through a variety of experiences that help him understand the meaning of life and belonging.

A filmic plot arranges and interrelates events in narrative form so as to achieve certain artistic and emotional effects. *Kodiyettam* has two plots, the main and the subplot – such as the Gloucester story in Shakespeare's narrative *King Lear* and the Falstaff comic subplot in *Henry IV*, both serving to enlarge the perspective of the main plot with the intricate interrelation between each other. The main plot of *Kodiyettam* contours the rising graph of Sankarankutty as he ascends towards maturity in thought and deed. The subplot looks at a clandestine relationship between a socially respected, revered schoolmaster and a widow.

According to Adoor, 'My second film *Kodiyettam* is about a man who drifts. He is very much a part of society but does not really get involved. He comes to terms with himself and society on a very meaningful level only when he realises that he can love and be loved.'[40]

Sankarankutty, who is in his thirties, has lost his mother early in life. His sister, Sarojini, works as a maid in Trivandrum. She pays an occasional visit to her parental house in the village to see her brother and sends him money at regular intervals. The family's little income comes from the small palm grove adjoining the family house. Sankaran tends to loiter around the village. Adoor describes him as a 'common man', by which he means, '…a person who is not politically motivated and not even educated one. Such common people, when they are together, make up political processions and the crowd for politicians to address. That common man does not even recognize his own identity as a self or individual in the society.'

Sankaran is quite childish by nature, excited about the temple festivals, spending time fishing with the village children, drinking occasionally at the toddy shop. When he is not participating in festivals, he is summoned for political processions. He lives a carefree life without restrictions, burdens and responsibilities. The money he earns by joining a political procession is spent in the evening on booze. He does not see himself as a grown-up and does not understand the value of time. He does not know that a family means giving and receiving love, in other words, a reciprocal relationship.

The film also benefits greatly from a standout performance by Gopi in the lead role. As noted film critic and author M.K. Raghavendra says, 'Adoor's second film can perhaps boast of the best performance from any actor in Indian cinema. Gopi plays the part of Sankarankutty, an enthusiastic but wayward young man who cannot be trusted to remain true to his task or responsibilities. Adoor has always been an actor's director.'[41]

Speaking Images

Adoor's forte as film auteur lies in his masterly use of powerful images. *Kodiyettam* pulsates with the sonorous rhythms of Kerala's rural life. His use of kites is one of the best metaphors used in serious Indian cinema to suggest a fickle mind and the leisurely and idle life of Sankarankutty. Gopalakrishnan shows the kite tail stuck in the top branches of a tall tree and the village children, unable to set it free, shout for Sankaran's help. Sankaran has been ambling along the lane in leisurely fashion. He pulls the string in an effort to free the kite. But the string breaks and the kite is set afloat. The village children run after the kite with Sankaran following them. Literally and figuratively, the kite sequence is a reflection of the sort of life that Sankaran leads. Indeed, he identifies himself with the village children who seem no older than him. Rich images accompany the dialogue:

> But any kind of summarising hardly conveys Gopalakrishnan's discreet yet fruitful method. Using very little dialogue, he puts faith almost entirely on visual detail. Despite the rich ambient sound, this is very much a story told in pictures: Sankarankutty's sudden, disarming, inappropriate smile, a dog's wagging tail sweeping the dust into crescents; the churning feet of children racing through a stream; Sankarankutty's hand greedily scooping the last of the rice.[42]

Marriage can bring two persons, two souls, close together. Sankaran's sister Sarojini, aware of her brother's vagabond nature, hopes marriage will awaken a sense of responsibility in him. She approaches a matchmaker, and while her stated intention is to arrange her brother's marriage, she also hopes to set her own life in order, marry and settle down. Sankarankutty marries a girl named Santhamma, but he continues with his old ways, loitering around the village, avoiding his own house. He does not understand the implications of marriage or the responsibilities of a husband. One morning, just after their marriage, Santhamma sets about making tea for Sankaran who is still fast asleep. But a little later, when she brings him a cup, she finds that he is gone to the village tea shop to have tea with his friends.

On another occasion, just after their marriage, Sankarankutty and Santhamma, both dressed suitably, set out to visit his in-laws, he walking with unusual hesitancy. But midway, suddenly, the band of village children pulls him away to help them retrieve a ball that has fallen in a well. Santhamma, out of irritation and anger, shouts, 'Is this any time to play games?' A little boy, ignoring Santhamma's threats, asks Sankaran for help anyway. Santhama reacts angrily, 'I'm telling you … he's not going.' Sankaran confirms, 'I can't come now. I'll be back soon. Don't be cross with me.' As they walk ahead, a passing truck splashes muddy water from the potholes all over Sankaran. He grins and remarks, 'What speed!' A visibly upset Santhama frowns, 'How can we present ourselves in this sorry state?' Sankaran pacifies, 'Don't worry, it can be washed.' Yes, this is Sankarankutty…

> He is portrayed as someone who works occasionally but also depends on his sister's earnings. His is a somewhat vegetative existence. The film repeatedly alludes to the body and bodily needs, especially eating. In fact, the rites centering on the body – sex, eating, drinking – become the rites of pleasure and self-definition. There are several shots of Sankarankutty devouring food where he literally becomes a gluttonous body.[43]

'But he is not a bad character. He is available to other people – he is willing to help them out,' Adoor clarifies. At the same time, Sankaran is gullible and can easily be swayed by emotional pleas. Various incidents light up these other aspects of Sankaran's character. In one sequence, four villagers are playing cards under a tree. Sankaran, who has not visited his home for a couple of weeks, is asked where he had been. Sankaran replies that two of his friends had implored him to accompany them to the festival at the Haripad temple. When they reached the town, they stopped at a tea shop near the bus terminus but when it was time to pay, they vanished like bubbles in the air! As Sankaran did not have a single penny with him, the shopkeeper held him back and took away his shirt. Sankaran believes God will punish the cheats – and indeed, while gambling at the festival, they are caught by the police. Interestingly, Adoor uses off-screen narration by Sankaran over close-ups of the cards, signifying that the others are not listening to him with any particular attention. Only two or three shots of Sankaran's face figure in the course of the lengthy narration. When Sankaran remarks, 'There is someone watching us,' meaning 'someone' is watching from above, we see on the screen a crow perched on a branch.

Sankaran, who is about to leave for his home, learns that the elderly matchmaker is on the way to the hospital to see his grandson who has been ill and has no one to attend to him – so he volunteers to go along. The elderly man too takes advantage of the innocent Sankaran. Another time, Sankaran buys bangles at a festival for his wife as a token of his affection for her and ties them in a knot at the waist in his dhoti. Since it is late at night when the dance programmes are done, he sleeps at the temple. When he returns home, his wife first scolds, then wails loudly about her husband's irresponsible nature. Thinking he will bring a smile to her face, he hands over the gift but alas the bangles are broken into pieces! He is dejected. This too is Sankarankutty – this tender-hearted man beneath a rustic exterior…

But slowly he changes from a drifter to an individual aware of his identity as also his responsibilities. The first time Sankarankutty grows dejected is when a girl from the neighbourhood informs him that his wife has left his house after waiting for him for days on end. In a top-angle shot, Adoor shows a broken-hearted Sankaran sitting crouched on the porch of his house. The howling of a dog nearby suggests his state of mind.

Sankaran next loses his temper at the neighbourhood children who run around him in circles and annoy him. The visuals indicate that the seeds of self-knowledge are sprouting in him: he makes an attempt to take Santhamma back to his house but she refuses to go with him. Another time, we see Sankaran losing his temper – when an old mahout gets drunk and suggests that Sankaran leave his sister in his care. Pankajakshi, the lady in charge of the toddy shop, laughs out aloud when she hears the old man's proposal. But Sankaran cannot bear such insults from the old man. In fury, he attempts to stab the mahout with a glass bottle – a reaction hardly likely from the wayward avatar of Sankaran.

In one sequence, Sankaran has a passing glimpse of the familial love between teacher Sukumara Pillai, his wife and child in the courtyard of their house – but it is enough to set him brooding over the tragedy of Kamlamma, the widow with whom the teacher has a clandestine relationship. Another time, Sankaran, clean-shaven, visits Santhamma and his newly born daughter, at her parents' home. In this scene, Adoor frames Sankaran walking out of the house but looking back at Santhamma who watches him from behind the door – the cradle gently swaying between them. The three figures are kept steady in a single frame to suggest the gradual bonding between them.

As Ramesh Menon put it, '*Kodiyettam* was about a simpleton who wandered around the village flying kites with the children but who gradually became aware of his responsibilities.'[44]

Sense of Selfhood

One of the most telling sequences in the film indicating Sankaran's dawning sense of himself is when the village elders taunt him with incovenient questions about his wife leaving him. We see him in a moving bullock cart whose driver sings in pure abandon,

> Never mind this ruthless world,
> It is a creation of maya,
> Don't take it seriously.
> After all, the life you live is an illusion.
> O' wanderer, who are you?
> You who are affected
> Neither by grief nor by happiness
> Like the bullock cart that wheels along…

Being a truck driver's helper offers Sankaran an opportunity to learn about life at close quarters. Once, washing his truck in the river, he finds that a child is getting dangerously close to the water. He rushes to the child, sternly rebuking the mother, 'Careless woman! The child could have drowned!'

While the truck driver is mainly on the go, he makes it a point to visit his family at regular intervals, advises his children to study and get good grades in class. Sankaran sees that his master is a loving husband as well as a caring father. But at the same time, he has a mistress, Savitri, in a hill station. The intrinsic nature of life on a truck (movement, speed and the rules of the road) all affect Sankaran's life.

Sankarankutty, returning from a truck journey, is shocked to find a stranger digging with a spade in the compound of their house. Sarojini comes running to him and pleads, 'Don't be cross with me. It just happened.' Sankaran, a man once not at all bothered by society's censure asks her, 'But what will people think?' Sankaran's disappointment at his sister not informing him about her marriage is evident. Sarojini, instead of asking Sankaran whether he would have lunch or not, asks her husband if he wants tea, praising him for being very particular about having his meals on time. Sankaran perceives the arrival of this new person in the house as a threat.

Soon after, Adoor shows Sankaran bathing in the village pond. As he gets out of the water, Adoor closes in on Sankaran's legs as he ascends (both physically and metaphorically) the steep stairs to the temple at the top. There, as he prays, head bowed, eyes closed, Sivan Pillai, the old village drunkard, calls to him, 'Come, let's go and celebrate!' To which Sankaran points out, 'What's the point? You are already high!' The old villager answers that he can still gulp down a whole barrel! But Sankaran must now contend with the fact that his brother-in-law cannot stand the smell of alcohol. Sankaran is forced to transform himself.

On another occasion, when Sankaran returns home at night, he calls to his sister but she, instead of letting him in, tells him that his mat has been laid out for him on the verandah. He sits there, pondering over his predicament: he is an outcast in his own house and his loving sister is now clearly committed to someone else. These realities introduce him to aspects of life he was earlier quite unaware of.

Behind the Mask

The subplot of the film offers up yet more experience – the most revered person in the village, the married schoolmaster, is having an affair with the widow Kamlamma. Sankaran sometimes carries out domestic chores for Kamlamma and, in return, is provided both food and wages. Kamlamma has a son named Gopi. Sankaran is close to both of them and believes he knows her well. Once, he witnesses the schoolmaster and Kamlamma at the village temple talking to each other, then they disappear behind a pillar. On another occasion, while fishing in the brook in the company of the village boys, he notices them walking along a narrow path in the spreading paddy field. Sankaran realizes something is afoot.

Strolling by the side of the village temple, Sankaran overhears their conversation.

Schoolmaster (*in a low voice*): What should I do? Tell me.

Kamlamma (*sobbing*): I didn't ask you for anything.

Schoolmaster (*worried*): If someone sees us here together … you better go home, Kamlamma.

Kamlamma: I'm going. I won't do anything to disgrace you.

Schoolmaster: Allow me a few days, Kamlamma. Let me think it over in peace.

Kamlamma: Oh God, how will I face my child?

Schoolmaster: Now calm down. Someone is coming.

Sankaran realizes that Kamlamma is pregnant and the schoolmaster is scared of accepting the responsibility for fear of social disgrace and of his family breaking up.

Next morning, Sankaran learns from the villagers running towards the temple pond that Kamlamma has committed suicide. While the victim's body is not shown, the endless cawing of the crows underlines the tragedy. Sankaran was fond of Kamlamma and knows why she killed herself. For the first time we see him crying loudly, moved by the death of a person close to his heart. The audience too is deeply moved. Sankaran begins to feel terribly desolate.

The episode of the schoolmaster and the widow reminds us of Nathaniel Hawthorne's *The Scarlet Letter*, a story of crime and punishment set in the rigid moral environment of puritan New England. A young English lady, Hester Prynne, living in a village in Boston, is sent ahead to America by her husband. He is much older than her. He does not follow her and the conjecture is that he is lost at sea. But, while waiting for him to arrive, Hester has an affair with Reverend Arthur Dimmesdale, a young Puritan minister, resulting in the birth of an illegitimate child. Hester Prynne does not expose her lover's identity. As punishment for her sin and her secretiveness, the scarlet letter 'A' is branded on her chest to declare her 'Adulteress'. She is forced to stand on the town scaffold and face public humiliation. To avoid this, she could have committed suicide but does not since she is strong-willed and has the courage to face the consequences.

Adoor's Kamlamma, coming from a parochial Indian society, cannot endure the public humiliation that she, as a widow with a son, would have to bear for giving birth to an illegitimate child. Neither does she reveal who her lover was. Indeed, she leaves no clue as to why she killed herself. The schoolmaster, of course, retains his pure and stainless character in the eyes of society. It is left unclear whether he will come forward to bring up Kamlamma's child.

At the start of the film, Adoor shows Kathakali performers preparing for a show. The intricate stylization of make-up and costumes project the performers as larger than life, even superhuman. In the film, Sankaran peeps through the wooden partition and sees a Kathakali male performer transforming himself into a female character. The schoolmaster is considered a perfect gentleman ready to help every villager, including Sankaran, but behind the mask of gentility is concealed his cowardly character. This recalls the hypocritical Nana Phadnavis in Vijay Tendulkar's *Ghasiram Kotwal*. Of course, Shakespeare makes masterly use of masks or disguises in his dramas, whether it is Portia parading as a lawyer in *The Merchant of Venice*, or Viola as Cesario in *Twelfth Night*.

Film Like a Festival

Sankarankutty is a universal character – everyman – transcending time and space. He does not belong to any single period or represent any single section of society. He is a 'lacker' so to speak – lacking a sense of responsibility, lacking understanding and lacking maturity. *Kodiyettam* traces Sankaran's arduous journey whereby he acquires these sensibilities. Adoor uses the images of the moving bullock cart and the lumbering truck metaphorically – to signify the transition of Sankaran from immaturity to maturity, from a thoughtless to a thoughtful man, from an irresponsible person to a responsible one. Adoor says, 'This film has a very typical episodic structure. Sankaran is there in every shot of the film, and his is the overriding presence. I wanted the audience to feel nothing is fake in the film. It is as if I have just taken the camera and followed him along his journey through life.'

'Kodiyettam' – meaning flag hoisting – is a ritual performed in the temples that marks the beginning of annual festivals in Kerala. 'Kodimaram' is the flagpole in the premises of the temple used for the ceremony. The film itself resembles the structure of a typical temple festival in Kerala. Adoor begins with the ritual 'Katinavedi' (fireworks) set off at any festival's start. '*Kodiyettam* is seemingly a simple film, keeping in tune with the protagonist. But Sankarankutty's simple journey has actually a very complex structure. The milieu is a Kerala village at festival time. The internal development of the protagonist is interwoven with the development of the festival.'[45]

The ending of the film is symbolic. Santhamma is shown pushing the cradle in which her daughter sleeps. Kathakali music plays in the background. Sankaran visits her late at night. Santhamma indicates she is alone at home. 'Mother has gone to the temple festival. She can't keep away from a Kathakali performance.' Sankaran, now a graduate from the school of life, gives a pudava (sari) to Santhamma. The temple music has fallen silent, and only the sounds of the crickets can be heard. As soon as she receives the gift from him, she cries out in joy while fire crackers burst in the sky. Adoor 'happy-ends' the film with the reconcilation between Sankaran and Santhamma. Film critic Mira Binford writes, 'The last scene is a glorious conception of man's triumph and defeat.'

Kodiyettam was shot in 1975 and was released in 1977 – only in three theatres in Kerala. Yet the film with its innovative film language – and with no songs and no background score – completed 145 days at a theatre in Kottayam. It was the first film of Adoor Gopalakrishnan that Satyajit Ray saw, appreciating it as being 'mature, subtle and very human'. He inquired why Adoor did not use any background music, to which Adoor's reply was that, for him, music could never be a major factor. He preferred not to do any underlining. It was Adoor himself who, travelling through the length and breadth of central Travancore, recorded the ambient sounds on the soundtrack on a Nagra recorder.

Like *Swayamvaram*, *Kodiyettam* too was shot in the backdrop of financial hardships. The Chitralekha Cooperative had purchased a second-hand camera from Bombay, but could not afford to buy film rolls. Somehow, they managed to put together funds to complete the film. As Adoor says:

> We managed to get petty loans from many sources and completed the shooting in 1975. The film was sent for processing to the AVM Studio, Chennai. But none of us could go to Chennai for one year – because we had no money to pay for the processing! Those days I was making

a documentary on the Idukki Power Project. The then prime minister, Mrs Indira Gandhi, inaugurated the project and the state's minister for electricity wanted the completed film to be exhibited in all district headquarters of Kerala on the day of the formal inauguration. The budget allocated was far below the actual requirement and we asked for an enhancement. It was duly approved and the film got completed before the appointed time. With the budget hike, we made a marginal profit – which went into completing *Kodiyettam* and releasing it in 1977.[46]

Elippathayam *(Courtesy: Kerala State Chalachithra Academy)*

8

Elippathayam (The Rat-trap)

Through a Keyhole Darkly

Adoor Gopalakrishnan's third film *Elippathayam* – heralding a whole new language in contemporary Indian cinema – is unquestionably one of the finest works of art in the history of Indian cinema. Released in 1981, the film is set in Kerala of the1960s, at a time when feudalism and the matrilineal structure of society had faded away. It critically analyses the tragic journey of a family caught in the whirlpool of the decaying past.

Using a mixture of metaphor and lyricism, *Elippathayam* is like a poem which if read once can be understood only superficially, but affords greater enjoyment and deeper understanding if read again. Indeed, every reading opens the door to new meanings – it beguiles the general audience with its style of narration, while drawing in the cine-aesthete with its many-layered structure.

The minutiae of decaying feudalism are there right from the opening shots of the ancestral house: the viali (the lamp stand) that is considered to protect the house from evil influences, the oil lamp, the Chinese jar, the heavy ancient door, the two iron keys lying on the table, the small keyhole of the wooden door, the abandoned cot, the intricately designed wooden ceiling, and a non-functional wall clock that permanently shows twenty-eight minutes past six. The use of the keyhole images is indicative of vouyerism. Adoor himself says: 'I have used the keyhole very significantly ... as if the whole film is a peeping through the keyhole.'

One of the most distinctive scenes in the film is when the youngest sister Sridevi climbs up to the attic of their house one morning to

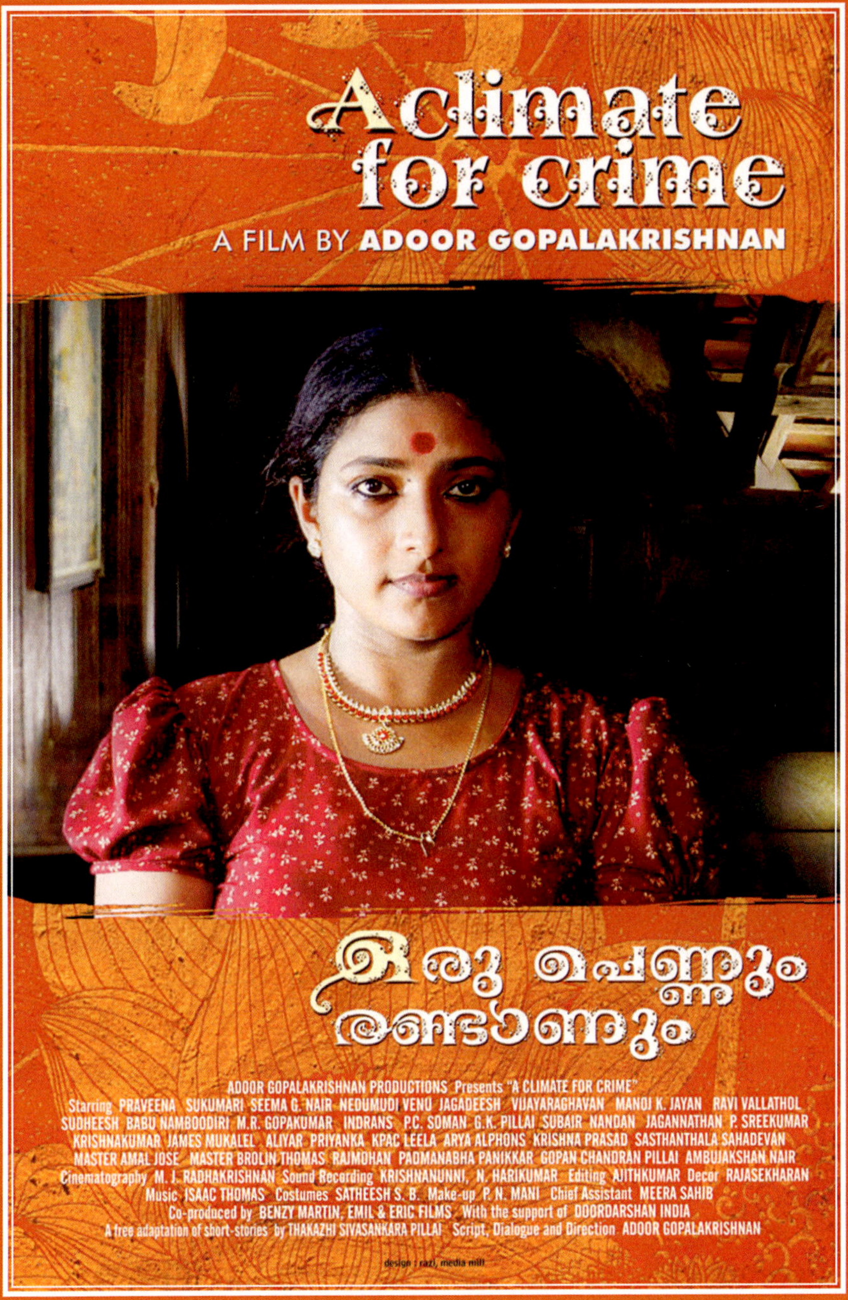

Praveena as Panki in the story *One Woman Two Men*
in *Oru Pennum Randaanum* (2008)

Mammootty as Basheer in
Mathilukal (1989)

Gopi as Sankarankutty in
Kodiettam (1977)

Ashokan as Ajayan senior in
Anantaram (1987)

P. Gangadharan Nair
as Sreedharan in
Mukhamukham (1984)

A scene from
Kathapurushan (1995)

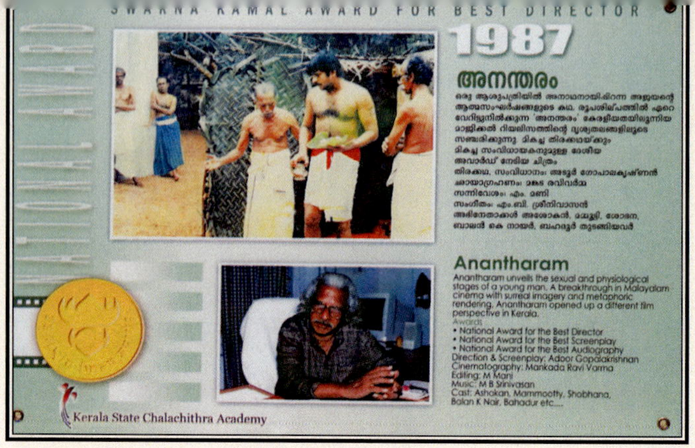

A mini poster of *Anantaram* (1987) designed by Kerala State Chalachitra Academy

A mini poster of *Mukhamukham* (1984) designed by Kerala State Chalachitra Academy

A mini poster of *Kathapurushan* (1995) designed by Kerala State Chalachitra Academy

A mini poster of *Swayamvaram* (1972) designed by Kerala State Chalachitra Academy

A mini poster of *Vidheyan* (1993) designed by Kerala State Chalachitra Academy

A mini poster of *Elippathayam* (1981) designed by Kerala State Chalachitra Academy

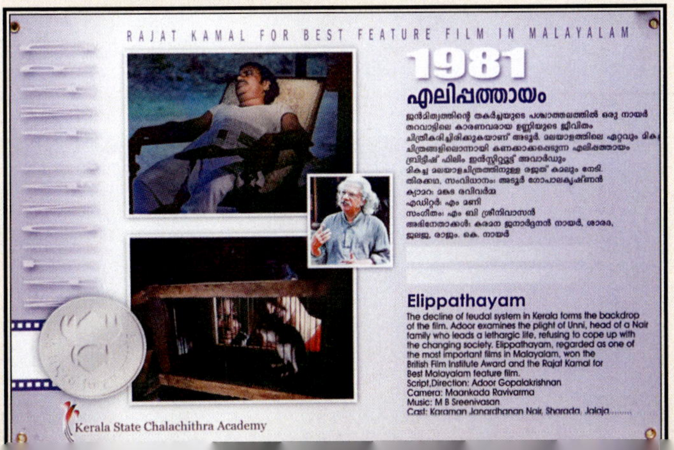

A young Adoor Gopalakrishnan

Adoor Gopalakrishnan
with his wife Sunanda

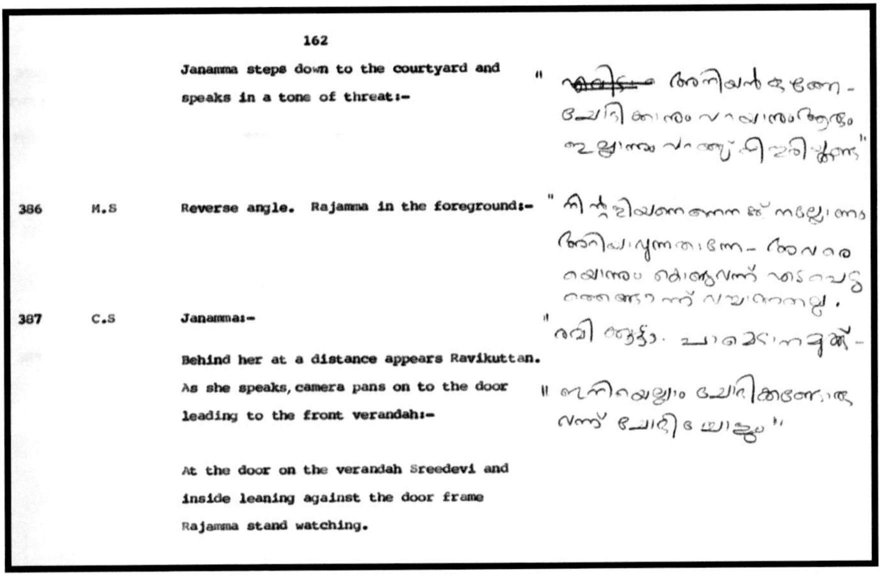

162

		Janamma steps down to the courtyard and speaks in a tone of threat:-
386	M.S	Reverse angle. Rajamma in the foreground:-
387	C.S	Janamma:-
		Behind her at a distance appears Ravikuttan. As she speaks, camera pans on to the door leading to the front verandah:-
		At the door on the verandah Sreedevi and inside leaning against the door frame Rajamma stand watching.

The shooting script of Adoor Gopalakrishnan's *Elippathayam*

Adoor with Ravi (left), producer of *Elippathayam*, and Karamama (right) the hero of *Elippathayam*

Adoor on location

Adoor explains a shot to his artist

Adoor on location, setting up a shot

Adoor signalling the artist for the final take

Adoor on set

Adoor with Devadas recording sound of a passing train

Adoor with long-time cameraman Ravi Varma

Second coming of Sreedharan in *Mukhamukham* (1984)

A scene from *Nizhalkkuthu* (2002)

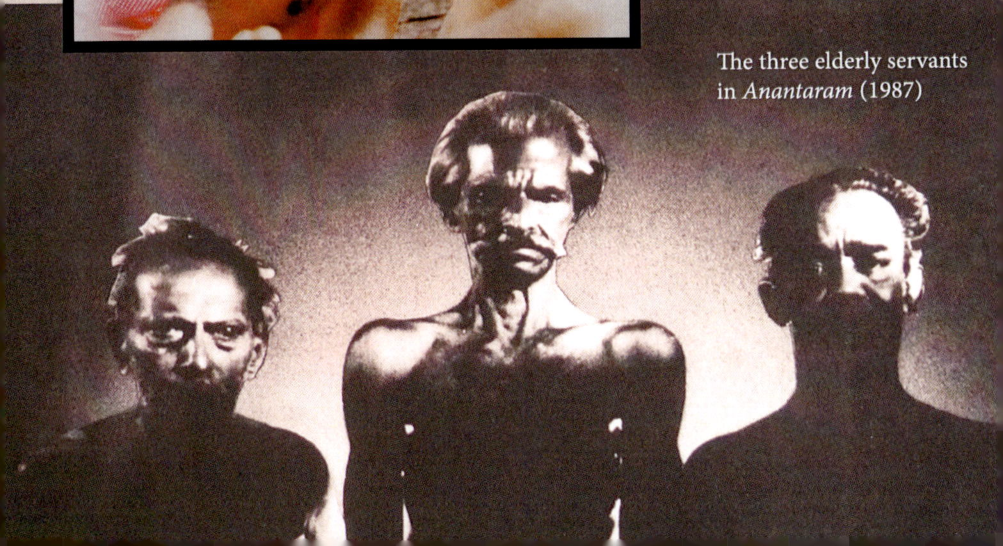

The three elderly servants in *Anantaram* (1987)

Mini Nair in *Kathapurushan* (1995)

P. Gangadharan Nair in *Mukhamukham* (1984)

Padmapriya as Kunju Pennu
and Sreejith as Pappukkutty
in *Naalu Pennungal* (2007)

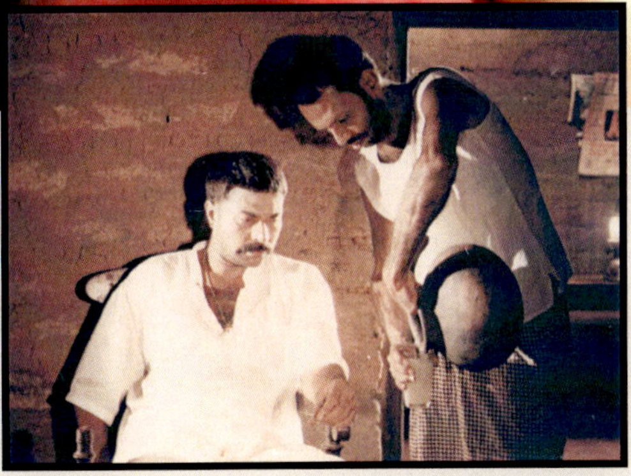

Mammootty as Bhaskara Patelar
and M.R. Gopakumar as Thommi
in *Vidheyan* (1993)

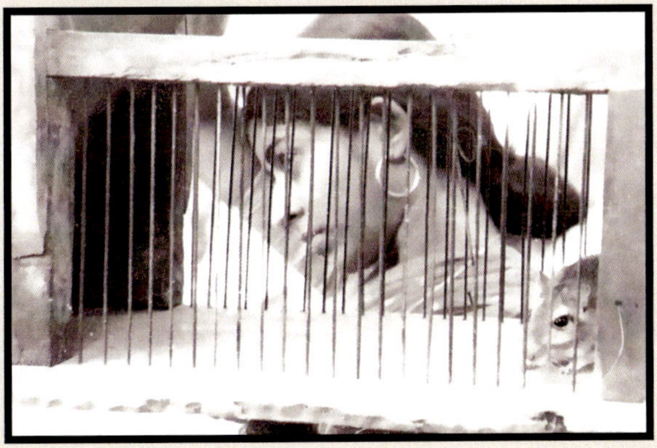

Jalaja carrying the rat-trap
in *Elippathayam* (1981)

Surendra Shah as Ravi in *A Great Day* (1964-65)

Sudharani Sharma as Mini and Appa Umarani as Chadda in *A Great Day* (1964-65)

Mani Kaul (right) as Ramesh and Surendra Desai
as delegate in *Light* (1964-65)

Sudharani Sharma as Lakshmi in *Light* (1964-65)

(Top): Madhu and Vempayam in *Swayamvaram* (1972); (Middle Left): A still from *Mathilukal* (1989); (Middle Right): A scene from *Kathapurushan* (1995); (Bottom Left): Mammootty as Bhaskara Patelar and M.R. Gopakumar as Thommi in *Vidheyan* (1993); (Bottom Right): A still from *Oru Pennum Randaanum* (2008)

fetch a rat-trap. The rat-trap, covered with spider webs, is placed on a harmonium – that traditional Indian musical instrument remindful of the rich culture of bygone days. The present family does not boast the culture cherished by their ancestors; it seems to have perished with them.

Against this context, Adoor sets two characters, namely, Mathaikutty, who works abroad, and Ravikuttan, Unni's young and spoiled nephew. Mathaikutty is shown wearing dark glasses, a collarless, colourful shirt, while Ravikuttan wears a striped shirt and long pants rather than the mundu. They are symbolic of the Western culture invading the Keralan culture zone.

The film focuses on the feudal-minded Unnikunju, who is middle-aged, egoistic, insensitive, weak-willed and lethargic. He is bogged down by lineage and a weighty past. He lives in his own world, refusing to face up to the changing world around him, not sharing his mind or feelings with others. He prefers to withdraw, like a rat, into a closed chamber. Narcissistic, he is often found preening at himself, cutting and cleaning his nails, trimming his moustache and massaging oil on his body. He is afraid of external influences, preferring to hang on to the past that envelops his ancestral house and its surroundings. This feudal and patriarchal figure rarely lifts a finger for himself, looking to his submissive sister for housekeeping. Meenakshi, a farm hand of easy virtue who lives nearby, attempts to entice him into a relationship but he is nervous and scared. An article in *Filmfare* (1–15 February 1985) commented:

> The film is essentially about the vestiges of feudalism. The crippling hold that a dead system still exercises on a family, in which a man's creed of idleness and total dependence weighs down the women and makes one of them run away. The other collapses and the man is left humiliated, helpless. Face to face with a reality he had refused to acknowledge for too long, a victim of his own paranoia.

A review in *The Business Standard* of 17 January 1982 reads:

> The film is not the naturalistic recounting of a story that has its parallels in any other parts of the world. But right from the first shot, when Unni wakes up screaming from a nightmare of a rat biting him, the elusive thought flits through one's mind time and again – is this happening or is this some phantasmagoric imaging in Unni's overheated mind?

The world around Unni is changing but he refuses to, cutting himself off from the outside world. And that world ostracizes him – casts him out. At the film's end, Unni has confined himself to a closed chamber and lost all communication with the outside world. Only his paranoia keeps him company. Once, when he opens the door a bit and peeps through, he sees the mother of a little girl rushing to pick her up when she strays into the courtyard of the abandoned house. This is one of the most poignant scenes in the film:

> Unnikunju's pathos originates from precisely this. He has nothing to give, nothing to take. His feeble attempts to cope with the new order while clinging on to the moribund values of another age, spell out a meaningless existence. In the end, his umbilical cord with society cut, nothing truly matters anymore – the shocks and trepidations of his experiences become immaterial, all that is left is the vastness of his inability to interact. He has become truly incommunicado.[47]

Adoor focuses on human attitudes and the psychology of the characters. C. Ignatius quotes him in an interview in *The Indian Express*, on 26 December 1982: 'The decay of feudalism was only the background. I was essentially trying to portray basic human attitudes which are, however, very much coloured by Kerala's life and culture.'

Sisters' Share

In her perceptive preface to the book *The Rat Trap*, Shampa Banerjee says:

> Unni is the last male descendant of an erstwhile rich land-owning family. The house he lives in is nestled amidst orchards of tapioca, coconut, banana and cashewnut, its ancient rafters bearing evidence of a craftsmanship of bygone days. It is a beautiful old house, physically encompassing the two worlds of the traditional family unit, the inner world of the woman and the outer world of the man. Through the years the house and its sprawling courtyards have witnessed unbroken cycles of birth and death in a prosperous and growing family.[48]

As already mentioned, in a matrilineal system, a married woman can stay in her parental house with her husband and her children and will be looked after by the head of the family, that is, a maternal uncle or a brother. Daughters can claim their share of the property. Our protagonist

Unni is always in fear of the family property getting divided and does not support the marriage of his sisters because it will eat into his income. Unnikunju has three sisters – Janamma, his elder sister, is married, has children and stays with her husband. Sometimes, she visits Unni to claim her share but he refuses. Once, her son Ravikuttan arrives at his maternal uncle's house and demands, 'My mother sent me … she wants her share of the crop.' Ravikuttan adds that his father is angry as Unni did not share the crop with them in the earlier harvest as well. Unni is surprised and retorts, 'What do you mean? Tell him I am not parting with any crop … Tell him that if he cannot look after his wife and children, he should send them back here.'

In the ancestral house, Unni lives with two of his unmarried younger sisters – Rajamma and Sridevi. Rajamma, the devoted sister, functions like an unpaid slave, taking care of Unni round the clock. She irons his shirts, brings him his slippers and umbrella when he is going out, boils water and cooks for him, forgetting her 'self' in the process. She suppresses her desires and dreams, never mentioning them. Janamma and her son Ravikuttan, on his occasional visit, too treat Rajamma like a drudge.

When there is an opportunity for Rajamma to marry and discover a new world outside the rat-trap, Unni rejects the marriage proposal. He remonstrates to Kesomman, the distant relative of theirs who has brought the proposal from a widower, 'Couldn't you find anyone other than a widower for my sister? Let's not discuss it further.' Rajamma continues to be very loyal to her brother and never speaks against him.

The youngest sister of the house is Sridevi, a college student lost in her own romantic world. In her room, she tries on ornaments and costumes or reads romantic books, or composes love notes like 'My dearest darling, a life without you is unimaginable…' She says to Rajamma, 'A new teacher has joined our staff. You can't imagine how handsome he is. We discussed him a lot in class. Some swore they had seen him in a film. But how could that be? Will any film actor take a teaching job here?' Study for her is an excuse to avoid her share of household work. She longs to fly out of the confining cage-like house – it is she who carries away the trapped rats to the village pond.

Escape Routes

Adoor uses certain images symbolically to manifest the different and contrasting natures of Rajamma and Sridevi. Rajamma's suppressed feelings are confined within, while Sridevi's feelings are overtly expressed. In one scene, Adoor frames the roof of the house and the well in a top-angle shot. Adoor juxtaposes images of unwashed vessels and utensils in the backyard of the house, with the sound – not the image – of an aeroplane flying overhead. Sridevi is instantly excited and enthusiastic when she hears the sound of the plane. She looks up and calls out to her sister Rajamma, 'Sister, sister, hurry up, there is a plane! Hurry up – it will soon be gone!' Rajamma emerges and searches the sky with her eyes, 'Where *is* the plane?' Sridevi dismisses her question, saying, 'Too late – it's gone. It won't wait for you.' Exposed to the glaring sun, Rajamma covers her eyes and huddles down. Sridevi asks, 'What's the matter, sister?' Rajamma tells her, 'I felt I was going blind. But it is better now.' The piercing sound of the aeroplane haunts Rajamma. She too desires to fly away like Sridevi, but she cannot as she feels duty-bound to look after her brother, as a result of which her suppressed feelings manifest themselves as severe pain. For Sridevi, the sound of the plane is a metaphor for freedom and liberty. She knows that she will, one day, soar away into the open sky.

One day, a visibly upset Rajamma, with tears in her eyes, rushes to Unni and informs him that Sridevi is missing. But Unni shows no concern, he simply advises Rajamma to search for her sister. Rajamma gives vent to her anguish for the first time: 'You're not making any effort to search for her! Or are you relieved she's gone?'

There are other occasions too when we witness the outburst of her repressed feelings. She cries out when she is by herself, 'God have mercy on me! Take me out of this hellhole!' But she doesn't share her feelings with others, preferring to keep them bottled up inside. Another poignant scene also incorporates the plane sound: here, Rajamma is once again near the well in the backyard of the house. The top-angle shot brings the roof into the frame. While washing the vessels, Rajamma suddenly hears the faint sound of a plane. She sweeps the sky with her eyes for a glimpse of it but does not see anything. As the sound of the plane rises, she grows desperate ... suddenly she feels a stabbing pain in her stomach and bends over. She does not see the plane; the symbol of freedom is denied to her. However, she finds an escape of sorts when she is taken seriously ill. She lies unconscious in bed attended by no one – till Meenakshi who visits the house discovers her. Her call for help is answered by caring neighbours who carry the groaning Rajamma in a makeshift stretcher … maybe to recovery, maybe to the ultimate freedom of death. The route they take, we note, is the one the trapped rats are carried along to the pond for drowning.

Feeding off Others

In Kerala, coconut saplings are regarded as very precious because life here revolves around the coconut tree and its bountiful nuts. It is the responsibility of the head of the family to protect them. In one scene, Unni reclines on a traditional wooden chair in the verandah, reading a newspaper. Suddenly, a cow enters the courtyard and starts devouring the coconut saplings. Instead of shooing away the cow, the slothful Unni – true heir to the feudal legacy – calls out to Rajamma to do it. In the feudal system, landlords feed off the labour of others. Another time, when thieves try to steal coconuts in the dead of the night, Unni doesn't have the courage to confront them.

In another scene set in the courtyard of the house, the aged farm manager, while separating chaff from the coconuts, tells Rajamma, 'Isn't the master up yet? The noise will wake him.' Rajamma's answer reveals the habits of this landlord. She says, 'He gets up late no matter what happens.' Unni always wakes late morning, uncaring of what is going on around. About these scenes, Adoor says:

> I wanted to explore the question of why some people do not respond to things around us in a natural way. Unni, the protagonist, stops responding to events and people around. But my question is: What does it mean to live in society if we do not act or react? When you do so, you become human – a part of society. Once you cut bonds with human beings and society, your very existence is in question.

Unni's attitude to people around him is unsympathetic and heartless. Mathaikutty, the farm manager's son, visits Unni and his family. The young man, wearing dark sunglasses and fashionably dressed, is in high spirits because of his new and fancy look. He has brought a small bottle of perfume as a gift for Sridevi. Both Rajamma and Sreedevi appreciate his gesture. When Unni walks in, he ignores Mathaikutty's presence at first, and later asks sarcastically, 'I hear that all those who come home and flaunt their riches are actually doing hard manual labour out there. Is that true?' He continues insultingly, 'Why're you looking so dark? Are you always working in the sun?'

John W. Hood writes this of Unni:

> The man's deliberate burying of his head in the sand when coconut thieves are reported to him is, in fact, a sign of social paralysis. In the maelstrom of changing times, a once influential element of society has now become an anachronism, atrophied, as enfeebled as a rat in a trap. In bringing together a number of inconsequential domestic crises, Gopalakrishnan has developed them into a metaphor for the decline of the once predominant social class.[49]

The non-functional old wall clock, used as a recurring motif in the film, clearly says time has ceased to move within the compound of this ancestral house. You can even say the unmoving clock represents Unni himself who is forever static in thought and deed. Unni remains unaffected by Sridevi's departure from the cage-like house – but as soon as the seriously ill Rajamma is carried away, he breaks down. He has lost his unpaid maid – the only person in the world with whom he has some connection. Without Rajamma, he is in utter dread of facing life. In the huge ancestral house Unni is pathetically alone. Maithili Rao writes: 'We watch Unni with a paralysed will, mesmerised by the rat's deperate struggle to escape, with detached understanding and impotent anger. With clinical precision, Adoor captures every wince and twinge of Unni's psychological and moral paralysis, the inability to act and face the grim reality of the crumbling feudal order.'[50]

At the film's end, Unni is trapped in the closed chamber of his house. In the absence of Rajamma – Unni's only hope of survival – he is overcome by paranoia and isolates himself from the outside world. In the dead of night, the villagers break open the door of his chamber, chase and catch him and throw him into the cold waters of the village pond. They wait for him to drown but he emerges with folded hands, cowering from the cold, wet and trembling.

Poetic justice has been meted out: Unni, the feudal lord who always refused to bathe in cold water, now stands before all, drenched and shivering from the cold, a helpless, trapped creature. But water is also a symbol of purification, a means to wash away sins, so throwing Unni into the water could imply a positive end – he has been given a chance to reform himself and maybe live a new life.

Writing in *The Times of India*, 10 May 1988, S. Prasannarajan has this to say:

> *Elippathayam*, as the film-maker himself says, begins with a rat chase and ends with the chase of the protagonist. There is a clear equation between the rats and the humans inhabiting the house. There is a development in the chase, the rats are killed in the movie in a very heart-touching manner – drowning them in the village pond – whereas the man who had insisted all his life to have water heated to a particular degree for his bath is himself thrown into the chilled waters of a pond at midnight.

Tony Rayns, celebrated British writer and film critic, writes: 'Gopalakrishnan has constructed the film like a cinematic rondo making every composition and camera movement count.'

Finally, the ancestral house is emptied of the people living there. But the house continues to stand, continuing to symbolize the decay and death of the feudal system.

Most Original and Imaginative

Since 1958, the British Film Institute (BFI) has been annually awarding the Sutherland Trophy – today a very prestigious award in world cinema – to the maker of the most original and imaginative film screened at the London Film Festival (earlier it was the National Film Theatre). Noted film-makers to receive the award include Yasujiro Ozu, Bernardo Bertolucci, R.W. Fassbinder, Jean-Luc Godard and Michelangelo Antonioni. Satyajit Ray's *Apur Sansar* was the first Indian film to win the award, in 1959. More than two decades later, in 1982, the BFI award went to Adoor's *Elippathayam* for 'the most original and imaginative film of the year'.

Elippathayam is Adoor's first colour film. When he was making

Swayamvaram, there was no colour film available. In those days, only big Indian producers could guarantee export of the film and recovery of the cost of imported raw stock. Small films, of course, could not provide the same guarantees. Says Adoor:

> While making *Swayamvaram*, I did not think of colour, I just made it in black and white. But when it came to *Kodiyettam*, I thought it would be good to see in colour the colourful festivals featured in the film. But it was not possible, so I had to make do with black and white stock. There was a four-year gap between *Kodiyettam* and *Elippathayam*. That year, another political party, led by Morarji Desai, came to power. Everything was liberalized. Everyone started making films in colour. Even if I had wanted to make a black-and-white film, it was not possible because the entire industry, big and small, had gone for colour! Without colour, your films would not get distributed in the theatres. The exhibitors wanted colour to attract audiences. It was a strange situation and there was no escape from it. So I too decided to use colour – and to use it meaningfully.

Mukhamukham *(Courtesy: Kerala State Chalachithra Academy)*

9

Mukhamukham (Face-to-Face)

The Myth Lives On

The Buddha uses the elephant parable to draw attention to sectarian disagreements. According to this tale, a king had an elephant brought into the palace and a group of blind men invited to touch the animal and describe their experience. One touched the head and said that the elephant was like a pot, others said it was like a winnowing pan (ear), a pillar (leg) a pestle (tail), a brush (tail tip) and so on. Of course, they were neither right nor wrong but could not come to a conclusion about the elephant's appearance since each knew the animal only from his particular perspective. The actual truth, however, could be gained only from the totality of the animal – not its separate parts.

Adoor Gopalakrishnan's fourth film, *Mukhamukham*, too deals with questions of perspective. Its layers of narrative make it interpretable from diverse points of view. One of the film posters features the protagonist's face segmented into two parts – one side of the poster shows him as a young man, while the other shows his worn-out face. Superficially, some may say the film deals with the theme of age. But it is far more than that. For some, *Mukhamukham* is an anti-communist or a political film. But while it is true that the communist movement forms the backdrop of the film, it has other thematic concerns as well, so one cannot conclude flatly that *Mukhamukham* is about communism. For yet others, *Mukhamukham* is a film not only about individual identity but also the physical self wherein that resides, the man of flesh and blood who is subjected to change and degradation. Together, the multiple narratives of

Mukhamukham offer what one may call a bouquet of varied fragrances. Says author and film critic Shampa Banerjee, 'Gopalakrishnan's fierce, controversial critique of political hero worship is an intricate pattern of sound and image where every detail contributes to the total artistic structure.'

The film, released in 1984, mirrors the socio-political picture of Kerala in the 1950s and '60s with the communist movement as its background. When the film was released, Adoor had to face vigorous attacks from a section of the media and political circles that condemned *Mukhamukham* for its scathing attack on the leadership of the Communist Party of India in Kerala. Hard-core communists in Trivandrum condemned Adoor for distortion of historical facts. Party members were all the more irate because the film was released just before the elections and would send a wrong message to the people. P. Govinda Pillai, a popular leader of the CPM (Communist Party of India-Marxist), a former chief editor of well-known Malayalam newspaper *Deshabhimani*, and a celebrated literary critic, commented:

> The film is full of major historical inaccuracies. When a Party leader goes underground, he maintains his links with the party. In fact, it is the Party that decides he should go underground and provides him with shelter and safety. This film shows Sreedharan out of touch with his Party. No one knows his whereabouts when he goes underground. This is simply not the way it happens … the erection of a memorial without verifying the death of the leader, honouring a man who is recognisably degenerate. History does not support any of these contentions. None of the communist leaders who have memorials in their name ever touched liquor.[51]

Adoor urged people to see the film in totality rather than from disconnected viewpoints. He answered the critics and the Marxists in *The Illustrated Weekly of India*, 3 March 1985:

> I have not distorted history. The central character of my film is a relatively unknown leader spreading the message of communism in a small town. I know of several such leaders who used to drink but I will not name them. It is irrelevant to the story whether the man kept in touch with the movement or not when he was underground. The Communists have missed the point completely.

Adoor tells me, '*Mukhamukham* uses the "*Internationale*" as the theme music and red as the dominant hue but it is not about the communist movement. The central character of the film happens to be a communist but he is not a reflection of the communist movement.'

The Making of a Hero

Sreedharan, a trade union leader of a tile factory, is a staunch follower of communist principles and ideology – and importantly, a messenger or carrier of these principles to others. Indeed, when Sreedharan is first introduced as a communist party worker, his face is shown reflected in the portrait of Lenin.

Structurally, *Mukhamukham* has two parts – the first ending in 1955, the second starting in 1965. The first part covers the process of the building up of Sreedharan's image as a charismatic leader while in the second, the myth of Sreedharan as a heroic figure is shattered among party workers and the people. Once a certain image is cemented in the minds of people, they would like to adhere to it. But when Sreedharan returns home after a gap of ten years, his second avatar is in total contrast to his former self. He has lost his zeal for life. He is addicted to drinking. People are immensely disappointed to see him reduced to this pathetic and pitiable state – battered by what Shakespeare calls 'the ceaseless passage of the destroyer Time!' Says film critic John W. Hood, '*Mukhamukham* presents the dissonant juxtaposition of the actuality of Sreedharan at a given time along with the popular memory of the same man from earlier times using the general interpretation of him as an icon of the proletariat as a means of reflecting the broader realities of social and party political frailty.'[52]

Industrialization Comes to Kollam

The film opens languidly with visuals of a small boat moving slowly along the river, carrying clay to a tile factory on the shore, the splashing sound of the oars merging with the chirping of birds. Pictures of humans toiling away are set against the background of a picturesque nature. Workers load clay in a wooden box, transport unbaked tiles to and fro, a grinding wheel buzzes. Inside the tile factory, the camera moves around busily to capture the movements of machines and men, driving home the point that industrialization is very much under way in the small towns of Kerala. Adoor said in an interview with Iqbal Masud in *The Indian Express* (9 December 1984): 'The idea was to convey the arrival of the industrial revolution – its rhythm in music, its hues in the image of the red-hot kiln and the neat cutting of the rectangles of clay, its impact in the cries of the workers for reinstatement.'

In this small town, the owner's agenda to mechanize production leads to conflict with the labourers, and, with no one in a mood to compromise, thereon to a prolonged strike. The workers look to Sreedharan, popular trade union leader and worker of the Communist Party of India, to voice their protest against the management. Sreedharan, an austere-looking man with a beard and a squint in one eye, is an ardent follower of communism and of Lenin's ideals. He feels the protest against the capitalist owner should continue until the retrenched workers are reinstated and given permanent jobs and legitimate wages. The workers put up a temporary shelter in front of the tile factory and the senior leaders of the trade union sit there.

Some of the workers hold up posters with the slogans, 'We shall struggle until we are victorious!', 'Long Live Comrade Sreedharan', 'Comrade Sreedharan on hunger strike!' The posters reveal the magnetic hold Sreedharan has on his followers. He is friend of the deprived, foe of the capitalists…

Sreedharan puts up a portrait of Lenin on the wall of the union office and asks Sudhakaran, a young boy of fourteen, if he knows whose portrait it is. But before the boy can reply, Sreedharan supplies the answer: that Lenin is a great leader and liberator of the proletariat. A little after, the leaders of the union organize a meeting under a tree festooned with red-coloured lanterns. Sreedharan is welcomed with a garland of red yarn and huge applause. He launches on a heart-touching and fiery speech with every worker listening to him in rapt attention. He urges them to unite and be strong so as to achieve their legitimate rights.

As he speaks, a police van suddenly screeches to a halt near the festooned trees and the police descend upon the group with batons. People run helter-skelter and scatter in different directions. Utter confusion prevails, everything turns topsy-turvy. Sreedharan is taken away to the police station.

The next day, at the tea shop, the trade union members are sitting deep in thought when the tea shop owner says to them, 'So many people have tried to form a trade union here. But there is no hope, sir. Either the proprietor will buy them off, or they'll get beaten up by police. After all, it is the rich who control the police, and the people in power.' The following day, the gate of the tile factory, which is close to the tea shop, is pasted over with posters like 'End Police Brutality!', 'Shun the Stooges of the Management', and 'Protest Meeting against Police Brutality'.

The police beat up Sreedharan very badly but when asked about it he only smiles meaningfully. In another scene, Sreedharan is attacked by unidentified assailants. He lies on the road in the dark of night, groaning in pain, asking for water. An old man, who has been sleeping on the verandah of his house, is suddenly awakened by the noise. The assailants run away under cover of darkness. The old man, with the help of his widowed daughter Savithri, takes the injured Sreedharan to their house.

Days pass as he convalesces, thanks to the attention and care given by Savithri. One night, while Savithri is attending to Sreedharan's wounds on the back and chest, the inevitable happens. Adoor masterfully portrays this passionate scene: we have a close view of the steaming cloth, she lifts and shakes it, smiles shyly at him, he stares back … and as she presses it down on his shoulder, he suddenly grabs her hand. The steel bowl with water rocks and rattles and water splatters to the floor…

The next evening, Sreedharan apologizes to her for his conduct. He tells her that in a moment of 'weakness' he lost control of himself. Savithri smiles, putting her hand on his shoulder. She leans her face against him very softly and says, 'Oh, it doesn't matter.' Then – with the old man's silent consent – they start to live as man and wife. (Later, they have a son whom Savithri names Sreeni. But by that time Sreedharan has disappeared.)

Sreedharan's spirit is indefatigable: he is not cowed down by the assailants' attack. When Sugathan, a worker in the factory, warns that there are some turncoats among the union members, Sreedharan replies that rather than oppose them as turncoats, the real victory would be to bring them into one's own fold. He continues to hold fast to his faith that they have to join hands with the movement – if not today, then tomorrow. Living by his philosophy and ideals, Sreedharan is a true leader of his people.

A henchman of the factory owner approaches Sreedharan with a proposal to meet the boss by himself. Sreedharan taunts the henchman: Will the owner offer him Scotch along with the post of supervisor? Is he expected to betray the movement in exchange for a bunch of notes?

In the very next scene, the police are shown searching the union office and vandalizing it. Adoor draws a graphic and vivid picture of the raid. In this small town in Kerala, the crowd, silent spectators in the distance, watch the police break, throw, crush everything in the office. The portrait of Lenin lies on the floor with its glass broken and the flag of the Communist Party of India crumpled on the ground. In a close shot, a hand of a policeman picks up a book with a red cover that reads 'October Revolution' and then shuts it angrily. The red ink from a broken bottle resembles blood as it splashes on the wall and on the broken glass of Lenin's portrait. The policemen emerge from the union office and attack the gathering mob with their sticks. The people run away, screaming. The sub-inspector screams after them, 'What the hell are you doing here? Revolutionaries, are you? We'll finish the lot of you!'

Events take another turn when it comes to light that the factory owner has been murdered by unknown assailants. Again, Adoor shoots the sequence in detail: the waylaid car, the huge police van, the dead body of the factory owner clad in white and lying face unseen in the gutter, the police sub-inspector walking back and forth between the road block and the line of policemen, his boots making a crunching sound, the newspaper headlines in large type, 'Business Magnate Killed', 'Gory Murder', 'Vasudevan Pillai Murdered!'. The prime suspects – the trade union leaders Sreedharan, Mathukutty and Damodaran – go underground, and thus ends the first part of the film.

Mystery of the Missing Communist

Then, for almost ten years, there is no news about Sreedharan. In those ten years everything has changed in Kerala: socially, politically and economically. Those who went underground have returned to resume their work for the party and have helped it come to power. Some by now are established as big guns in the party. The young idolizer, Sudhakaran, is now a staunch party rebel. The long absence of Sreedharan leads many to believe that he is dead; and indeed the Communist Party of India has named the party office after him. It seems only right that a leader such as Sreedharan continue to have a large number of faithful followers. But then he returns …

One night, when Savithri and her son are lying on a mat on the floor in the dim light of the oil lamp, she suddenly hears a voice which seems to be Sreedharan's. It is! Savithri feels she is dreaming. She cannot believe her eyes and repeatedly asks him where he had been all those years. But he is a tired and broken man. Even when she points to their son, Sreeni, Sreedharan does not react. He says he wants to sleep. The viewers are not given any sort of clue where he had been during those ten years and, as a result, the viewers' curiosity is aroused, coupled with confusion:

> Critics have equated sleep with lethargy or decay and have missed its importance in the film. Sleep is mysterious and it transforms the sleeper and locates him within another 'reality', but what seems even more pertinent is that the most pathetic of wretches regains his dignity when asleep. If Sreedharan had returned to his former milieu as a physical or mental wreck he would still remain a subject of the world and his misery might have left him an object of compassion. His former allies cannot justly regard him dangerous because, even if all activity is inherently political, Sreedharan demonstrates his innocuousness by remaining triumphantly inactive. Sreedharan simply exists but it is this existence that becomes abhorrent to them.[53]

Writes Shampa Banerjee:

> …Out of the darkness of ten lost years, a face returns to light: Sreedharan has come home. But is this the same man – idealist, theoretician, path-finder, dynamic leader of the working class – this worn-out old face, fossilised in sleep? Sreedharan has come as a memory redefined, a reality from the past distorted by a ruthlessly changing present. He has come as a brief illusion, a mirror to the political confusion of the times, a warning of a crisis that his comrades have chosen to ignore.[54]

Mukhamukham has a complex structure, dealing with varied issues such as youth, revolt, aging, recollection and dreams; and the answer to the question, 'What was wrong with the protagonist?' lies within these layers. Where has Sreedharan been and what was he doing all those years? That remains a mystery. Does he still possess the same magnetic personality?

Is he still a master of words? No, not at all. The revolutionary is just a shadow of his former personality. His voice is muted.

The film makes extended use of irony to showcase human relationship and psychology. When the news of Sreedharan's arrival spreads, every member of the party and others who have heard of his reputation, come to see this heroic man. They are filled with hope that this second coming of Sreedharan will change the fate of the people and reunite the split groups of the Communist Party of India. In a lengthy shot, Adoor frames Sreedharan, sitting on the verandah of his home, surrounded by his admirers and well-wishers to whom he is a father figure. They wait eagerly for a word from him, but there is none forthcoming. Indeed, he would prefer to go to sleep. The people are utterly disillusioned with him, frustrated; they wish to question him, scoff at him. When he is not sleeping, he likes to drink. He steals money from his wife to do so. His comrade, Mathukutty, who is no longer a labour leader, is well off and leads a life of leisure. He takes Sreedharan to his house and there they guzzle foreign liquor.

Where Have All the Heroes Gone?

Confused between present and past images of Sreedharan, the people long for the hero of the myth rather than that of a fallen leader:

> The return of this Sreedharan generates anxiety and panic among the people who desperately try to match the man of the image – the myth they had forged – with the reality before them. Since the party split, leaving them divided and disillusioned, they have failed to unite and act decisively as a group with a new political agenda. Instead, they have pinned all their hopes on the second coming of Sreedharan. They have invested in his image, in an intangible dream that is ten years old.[55]

As Gautaman Bhaskaran says in his book on the mastero, '*Mukhamukham* constantly taunts us through hope and disappointment, through light and darkness. Some moments seem clear, some obscure. And then, we are led into a state of confusion … that however clears a little later.'[56]

Adoor elaborates:

> People of the village cannot imagine that he is a human being after all, like everyone else who could falter and fall, age and degenerate,

> become sick and weary, withdrawn and cynical … he returns to a situation after ten years that is a lot changed too. The party is divided, his own young disciple has turned an ultra-revolutionary. The party members of the past, who are now established and influential figures in society, have become corrupt and power-hungry. In a situation like that he cannot align himself with any particular faction. The present is not something he had fought for.

In the final analysis, *Mukhamukham* is a critique on the middle-class mentality. A class which is inclined to let someone else do the work on their behalf. They want change but do nothing to bring about that change. They glory in the myth of Sreedharan as a man who fought against the capitalists – but are easily disillusioned when the passive and pathetic Sreedharan doesn't live up to his image. For instance, the constable informs Savithri's father that his son-in-law Sreedharan has a police record with many complaints registered against him. On another occasion, Savithri finds him burning letters. Do these letters hold the answers to the riddles of his hidden past? His relationship with Savithri and their son reveals yet another aspect of the man.

There is one way, however, to keep the original image intact: Sreedharan is murdered. The two split groups of the Communist Party of India march together in a funeral procession, carrying with them the portrait of Sreedharan. This is their charismatic leader Sreedharan – not the fallen and broken leader who came back to their midst. Like a phoenix, Sreedharan once again rises from the ashes to gain his place in society as a supreme leader who can show them the way.

Anantaram *(Courtesy: Kerala State Chalachithra Academy)*

10

Anantaram (Monologue)

A Story about Storytelling

Adoor Gopalakrishnan's *Anantaram*, his fifth feature, is probably the most complexly structured of his works. The film reveals the subjective thoughts, emotions, desires, cognition, and passing sensations of a character who may be named Ajayan (the protagonist of the film) or could be any other human being for that matter. Adoor, journeying into the depth and complexity of human consciousness, captures the ebb and flow of Ajayan's psyche through powerful visuals, and a narrative with nuances and overtness both. The film is inspired by a real-life story about an adopted child who is brought up by a doctor.

Adoor writes in the article 'Image, Imagination and Creativity', '*Anantaram* can be translated as "... And then ..." or "Whereupon", a term frequently used by the narrator in traditional storytelling. The central character of the film is no artist or writer. But this film is about storytelling, in fact, the very process of storytelling.'

In the film, Adoor employs a kind of interior monologue (a first-person narrative), providing us with the flow of perceptions, thoughts and feelings of the protagonist and which remain unvocalized in dialogue. Through this novel technical device, Adoor enables the viewers to visit the inner mind of his character. Ajayan seems an ordinary enough personality, but later reveals schizophrenic tendencies. He selects specific incidents from his life to present his self to audience – incidents which point to repressions lurking below the level of his conscious mind and hidden from the outside world.

> In the process, the protagonist of *Anantaram* goes on to reveal the layers of his scarred psyche in his constant endeavour to discover himself. Through the portrayal of the existential dilemma of this sensitive young man, Adoor has sculpted to near perfection a new cinematic form ... this sort of narrative exploration has never been seen on the Indian screen so far...[57]

Adoor began his travels into the recesses of the human psyche with *Elippathayam* in which the protagonist Unni, assailed by worries, fears and doubts, traps himself, like a rat in a cage, inside a closed room. *Mukhamukham*'s main character Sreedharan journeys from being a strong leader to a broken one. The theme of disturbed mental balance is carried even further in *Anantaram*.

Ajayan tells his story twice through a voice-over: in the first part of the film, his birth, parentage, obvious intelligence, exceptional talent, erratic behaviour are presented in chronological order. In the second part, however, the narration hints that he is unable to distinguish between fact and fiction, reality and dream, memory and actuality. Speaking to S. Prasannarajan, Adoor said: '*Anantaram* examines creative expressions as a process of perception, selection and arrangement of experiences. In other words, it is a film about storytelling.'

Suranjan Ganguly writes in *A Door to Adoor*:

> *Anantaram* is, conceptually and formally, perhaps Gopalkrishnan's most ambitious film about the outsider in which he seeks to describe the inner world of a schizophrenic who can't separate fact from fiction. The film is structured as a pair of parallel narratives that are authored by the protagonist Ajayan, a college student in his early twenties. He tells us the story of his life through a voice-over, singling out specific events which he believes can throw light on the formation of his self. This film, then, is a monologue, not only because of the words we hear but also because of the images we see which originate in the mind of the narrator.

Says the Adoor retrospective brochure *Adoor Gopalakrishnan: Poet Laureate of Indian Cinema*:

> An audacious experiment spiked with gentle humour, *Monologue* mimics the process of artistic creation by operating on three levels:

> experience, memory and the crafting of memory and experience into art. The protagonist, a precocious orphan named Ajayan, tells the story of his withdrawal from society twice – once in a straightforward, if selective, fashion, and once by interweaving fantasy and reality until even he cannot distinguish between the two.

The film opens with the cry of a child in a hospital ward, as a voice says, over the visual of the child, 'They call me Ajayan. I'm also known as Ajaya Kumar. Neither my mother nor father gave me this name. I have not known my mother or my father. Perhaps the woman who gave birth to me paid a price by my birth. That woman unburdened her shame in the labour room of this hospital and escaped into anonymity.' In other words, his birth itself is a disgrace.

The voice continues, 'I surely was not the first baby to be abandoned in this hospital. But I don't know why I was not placed in an orphanage or given in adoption. When doctor uncle retired, he took me away with him.' The narrator himself does not know why he is brought up by the doctor instead of being sent to an orphanage. This raises a suspicion not only in the mind of the viewers, but also in the narrator's mind. In one scene, when the doctor is examining a patient in the hospital, he suddenly hears a child bawling – which seems to pain the doctor as much as if he hears his own son crying. In another scene, when a nurse gives the child Ajayan a strong thump on his back, the doctor rushes to embrace the child and ticks off the nurse, 'Why did you hurt him?', then turns to the child, 'From now, your uncle will see no one hurts you.'

Ajayan tells us that he was extremely brilliant at studies, in sports and in classical vocal music – a child prodigy in the true sense of the term. But he laments that he was a lonely child, 'I don't know the reason. Even in my own age group, there was no one I could call a true friend. I'd nothing to say to them nor had they anything to offer me. Actually, my only friend was Balu, doctor uncle's son, then a medical student, who stayed with us over his vacation.'

Balu, the doctor's son, and his foster-brother Ajayan share some good times together. For a short period, Ajayan has intense feelings for Lata, an older girl of the village, but threats from two older boys put an end to that infatuation. About his mother, Ajayan is unequivocally bitter: 'That woman who gave birth to me, if ever we meet, I'll strangle her.'

As he grows up, Ajayan faces what he feels is rejection by the family. While Ajayan is studying in the university, his doctor uncle dies, but he is not informed. Ajayan is upset, 'The news of doctor uncle's death was intentionally conveyed late to me. Who was he to me anyway? My uncle? My foster-father? Or my real father? Why did they do this? Deny me even a last glimpse of him?'

His sense of isolation and rejection are intensified after this incident, and his sense of belonging either to the family or to the society around totally frayed. Ajayan feels a gnawing sense of loss. But Balu tells him, 'In one way, father was lucky. He was not bedridden even for a day. He died of cardiac arrest. It was over in minutes. I wrote you a telegram but my uncle stopped me from sending it. Ajayan, were you here to take part in the last rites, it would have posed many problems and questions.'

Forbidden Attraction

In the first part of the story, as narrated by Ajayan, a problem surfaces when Balu marries Suma. Ajayan finds himself attracted to his sister-in-law but cannot approach her. Sexual repression leads to further personality disorder. In one of the scenes, Adoor takes an extreme close-up of Ajayan's eyes hinting at the turmoil below. In another scene, on his way back to the university, Ajayan is unsettled by the recurring image of his sister-in-law. He begins to veer between imagination and reality, and a masterly visualization by the director captures the essence of this conflict. Ajayan is sitting at his table in his hostel room and the words 'Sleep and Dream' are scrawled on the facing wall. Ajayan is writing a letter. Then we see Suma weeping and tearing a letter, with Ajayan's voice-over saying, 'My dear brother, forgive me! I don't wish to hide anything from you. What use will it be to do so? I don't know how to say it. I can't forget the look of her. I cannot forget her eyes! However much I resist, her presence haunts my mind! The more I struggle, the more she stays with me. However much I fight against it, my love for her grows stronger! This letter could have been written to her, ignoring the respect due to a brother's wife. But would that do any good? You're the one who should know about this. I burn all over with this forbidden passion! I want you to be cruel to me! Why did you shower your love on me? Why make me feel so guilty? No, I can't forgive you. I hate you! I hate you!'

Adoor cuts the scene back to Ajayan writing the letter. He now declares that he does not have courage to write such a letter – making it clear to viewers just how confused his mind is. Writes S. Prasannarajan in *The Times of India*, 'Two recurring symbols in the film *Anantaram* are pen and paper. Ajayan also paints. In his study are books like Albert Camus's *Outsider*, Gabriel Garcia Marquez's *One Hundred Years of Solitude*.'

The first part of this narration is cut short when Ajayan's roommate knocks at the door of his room. When the door is not opened, Ajayan's hostel mates start peeping through the glass of the door. Everyone, including the viewers, is scared that something terrible has happened. Suddenly, the narrator's voice continues, 'I think there is a lot more to be said.'

Road to Schizophrenia

In the second half of the film, Adoor goes over Ajayan's childhood to probe the root causes of his sense of alienation which leads to schizophrenia. His talent, his sharp wit, intelligence and exceptional brilliance do not find a mention in this part. In an interview with Jyoti Punwani and Ajith Pillai, published in *The Sunday Observer*, 20 September 1987 when *Anantaram* was released, Adoor said:

> In the first part, the narrator relates the high points of his life and tells you a cogent story. In the second, he says, maybe I haven't told you enough. The characters are the same, the way they develop is the same, but you realise that the roots of his development are not what you'd been shown earlier. In the second story, you become aware that these other things were also part of his childhood. Till then you supposed that he had been put down by society because he was so brilliant. But you're not shown how various negative experiences acted upon him. This can be perceived fully after the film ends, on reflection the story becomes complete. It's a kind of exercise for the audience, they have to think about it and work out the developments. There is no attempt to hand over the complete story to viewers on a platter.

Ajayan grew up in doctor uncle's big house. His foster-brother Balu, who was a medical student then, visited home only in the vacations, while most of the time his doctor uncle was out on tour. Under such circumstances, he was brought up by the three old retainers, the cook, the driver and the compounder. In this second half of the film, the narrator unveils the other face of his childhood, 'I grew up in isolation. In a way, I used to like being alone. My childhood still lives with me. Did Balu have a childhood? To my mind he did not. My earliest memory of him was of a mature person. He was studying in a far-off town. His mother had died when she was quite young. Doctor uncle was always on tour and seldom at home. Under the circumstances, this house was run by three elderly servants whose authority was unbridled. The cook, Raman Nair, ate almost all that he prepared. I never saw that old car driven outside. All the same, the driver Mathai spent all his time repairing the car. Very few came to the dispensary. It was routine for the compounder to sleep all afternoon, snoring loudly.'

They become the nightmares in the later stage of his life. These three old men – three male witches – give birth to confusion and fear in the fragile mind of young Ajayan, and go on to dominate his nightmares. In one scene set in the kitchen, Raman Nair is swallowing a hard-boiled egg; Ajayan enters and asks the cook where he found so many eggs. Raman Nair, pointing to a hen perched high on a raft above, says that Mathai (the driver) lays the eggs. Ajayan is confused. On another occasion, late at night the three old men are found sitting in the verandah, drinking from a bottle of arrack and an ounce glass. Asked what they are drinking, they tell him it is a medicine to alleviate their sorrows. In another scene, a terror-struck Ajayan watches a woman walking across the verandah on a rainy night. The woman suddenly disappears like a bubble in the air and the three describe her as a yakshi, an enchanted spirit. The book of Grimms's fairy tales which his foster-brother gives to Ajayan further fuels his imagination. Like a magician, Adoor plays tricks with his visuals: in one scene, Mathai is drawing water from the well on a rainy night and gets soaked through and through. But as soon as he reaches the verandah, his clothes are completely dry, with not a drop of water on him. Another time, we see Mathai in the steering seat of the car. As the frame is in mid close-up, we assume that Mathai is driving the car but when the camera is panned right, we find a tractor is towing away the car. Indeed, viewers too get confused occasionally between what is reality and what fiction. This is the setting in which a child, a lonely and isolated child, is brought up.

What has been disturbing Ajayan since his childhood is an elusive image in his mind of a loving and caring woman. Having been deprived of a woman's love and affection, he pines for it. But in real life, love and care are distant stars for him. When he shows his affection for a senior schoolgirl, he is threatened by two older boys; there is the ghostly yakshi who visits the big house; and finally, there is his hatred for his mother for abandoning him in the labour room – all these produce misogynistic tendencies. In the second part of the film, Ajayan describes an imaginary relationship with Nalini, a university student, but viewers are left wondering if she is no other than his sister-in-law Suma. His meeting with her at the bus stop, in his hostel room, walking on the beach, seem to be real enough – though perhaps not so. The appearance of Nalini in his life might be a figment of Ajayan's imagination. As Adoor said to Jyoti Punwani and Ajith Pillai:

> Nalini could be real or imaginary or both. The realm of the imaginary merges into the real. This interplay of real and imaginary is such that just as the director and the audience seem to settle down into thinking all this is imaginary, something so concrete occurs that it all becomes real. But just when you have started to think 'all this must be true' – it starts seeming imaginary.

One night, Ajayan rushes to Balu's room, alleging that Suma is unfaithful. When Balu advises Ajayan to take his medicine, we realize that he is mentally disturbed. Adoor keeps Suma in the frame as the narrator says, 'I am not sure if I have told you the complete story. There may still be some things I have forgotten to relate.'

The realization that Ajayan is suffering from a mental ailment creates a kind of sympathy in the minds of the viewers. Says Adoor, in an interview with C.S. Venkiteswaran:

> No one really knows for sure what causes mental illness. Similarly, no one knows why one becomes a writer or an artist. The reasons are mysterious. Is it genetic, social, circumstantial, sheer grit, or something else? No one really knows. A madman has no method with his materials. When there is a method to madness, it becomes creation.

One More Story

According to Suranjan Ganguly, 'Ajayan's attraction for Sumangala and his justification of that passion by inventing Nalini may have roots in his childhood experiences, especially his abandonment and his sense of being an outsider at home as well as in a world that refused to acknowledge his talents. But this is only one of the many possible readings. Ajayan offers us his own interpretation and, at the end of the film, seems ready to give us another one. And then possibly another. The search for truth must necessarily go on.'[58]

The film ends with visuals of a child counting numbers as he hops up and down the steps to the pond in the big house, always looking straight at the camera. Adoor freezes the frame at this point, leaving us to wonder if there's yet another version of his childhood to come forth. As Adoor says:

> Once Ajayan finishes the narration and as the audience takes it as his whole story, he tells us it is only a part and goes on to recount a second one. Having finished it, he reveals that it is not the whole story either. His tales are of a tormented mind caught in a web of confusions, a crisis of identity and the ambivalence of relationships and belonging. The film ends where he starts his third story.

The magical elements in the film, the confusion between the real and the imaginary, remind us of Ingmar Bergman's *Wild Strawberries* (1957) about the egotistical Professor Isak Borg who, travelling by car from Stockholm to Lund, experiences nightmares, daydreams, old age and even impending death. This makes him re-evaluate his life. However, the multiple narrative technique used in *Anantaram*, for some reason, was not duly appreciated abroad. But in India the film received both state and national awards for Best Director in 1987, and cineastes particularly applauded its complex structure and open ending, its polyphonic narrative and striking visuals.

Mathilukal *(Courtesy: Kerala State Chalachithra Academy)*

11

Mathilukal (The Wall)

Journey through the Mindscape of a Writer

Mathilukal is another tour de force from Adoor Gopalakrishnan. The film, based on the well-loved autobiographical novella by the legendary writer Vaikom Muhammad Basheer, is not simply a recreation of a powerful work but is transformed by Adoor's innovative cinematic language. A very special story is reshaped into a complex and beautiful film which rejects conventional methods of narration, design and pattern. The interrelationship between the source text and the adaptation is very important as far as the thematic structure is concerned.

Mathilukal (meaning 'walls') is Adoor Gopalakrishnan's first film adaptation. In adaptation, the auteur of the film has the liberty to redesign the source text, not wholly, but according to the needs of the screenplay. It is not that there must always be a verbatim translation of the words into visuals. Satyajit Ray's first film, *Pather Panchali* (1955), was the film adaptation of the autobiographical novel *Pather Panchali* by Bibhutibhushan Bandyopadhyay. Ray said he chose it because it had certain distinctive qualities like humanism and lyricism and the truth of life lived. Ray also 'rewrote' parts of the novel, for instance, the death scene of the old aunt, Indir Thakrun. In the novel, the event takes place in its earlier section, in a village shrine in the presence of some elderly members of the family. In the film, Ray shows her dead on the wayside as Apu and Durga wander through the jungle. Another alteration is the train sequence. In the novel, Apu and Durga make a vain attempt to see the train but in the film they run through the fields and manage to catch a glimpse of the speeding train. We can see many more such variations in the film.

In *Mathilukal*, Adoor too makes changes in the source text. According to Adoor:

> When I take my story idea from elsewhere, I don't feel obliged to be fully faithful to the original work. Because once I take up a story, I assimilate it and treat it as my own. And through the different stages of film-making the material keeps growing organically. In that process I am not bothered about what the writer had written or what he had originally intended. It is my own inspiration that comes first. Also I am very particular that my work should not end up as a mere film version of the adapted literary work. I always try to lend it different dimensions and interpretations which the writer may not have even intended. The writer should not feel worried about these changes because his original work is there, intact. Anyway, the ultimate product that emerges will definitely be a tribute to the genius of the author.[59]

Basheer's novel is told in the first person narrative. The story is based on his experiences in the Trivandrum Central Prison in 1942. Social analyst Krishna Chaitanya writes of how the Muslim community in Kerala remained very conservative for a long time. Most took to small trades while a few became wealthy merchants, but education was neglected by even the rich stratum of the community. A great awakening was pioneered entirely from within the community by philanthropists who provided funds for educational and vocational institutions, and by intellectuals who provided the leadership. This awakening brought some gifted writers to the forefront of the literary scene – Vaikom Muhammad Basheer being one of them.[60]

Basheer, a humanist, a staunch freedom fighter and litterateur, is known for his unconventional writing style. His works include *Baalyakaalasakhi* (Childhood Friend), *Mathilukal*, *Entuppappakku Oranendarnnu* (My Grandpa had an Elephant), and *Pathummayude Aadu* (Fatima's Goat). 'The merit of Basheer's works is that, under the garb of presenting social problems, he unfolds the working of the human mind. The hopes and frustrations, and the joys and sorrows of humanity are presented vividly through his characters.'[61]

Basheer was actively involved in the freedom struggle. In 1930, he arrived in Calicut to take part in the Salt Satyagraha but was arrested and had to spend a period of three months in jail. This did not dampen his zeal and enthusiasm. Out of jail, Basheer organized an anti-British movement and edited a revolutionary magazine called *Ujjivanam* (Uprising). The British were frequently harassed by his activities and issued a warrant for his arrest. He fled from Kerala and returned only after seven years. In 1941, however, he was arrested and made to wait for a long time for his trial. When it took place finally, he was sentenced to two-and-a-half years' imprisonment and later sent to the Trivandrum Central Jail.

A Not-so-simple Love Story

Adoor read the story in the annual issue of a popular Malayalam weekly, *Kaumudi.* The novella portrays Basheer's relationship with Narayani, a woman prisoner from whom he is separated by high walls. This exceptional love story attracted many directors but they were not confident about making a film without physically presenting the heroine on screen. I have heard of at least half a dozen attempts that got aborted at this crucial point. One director even suggested to Basheer that they show a different woman every time Basheer talked to Narayani across the wall!

But for Adoor, it was a puzzle that served to stimulate his imagination: 'Then, twenty years later, it occurred to me that I should address the challenge head-on and took the decision to make an all-male film. *Mathilukal* was, in fact, a real challenge for me because of two reasons: firstly, creating a character without even showing her, and secondly, narrating the internal journey of the writer. It was a story told in the first person and the hero was the writer himself. It became a film on a story as well as its author!'

Khalid Mohamed in an interview published in *The Times of India* 4 March 1990, quotes Adoor:

> I liked the idea that by showing a man who is infatuated by a disembodied voice, I could create a very complex love situation. Basheer is a great writer and he narrates the story in first person. So, the 'I' element had to be gone into in detail. So, I re-read the entire literary works of Basheer. He has written nearly twenty-five moderately sized novels and several short stories. My job was to understand the

> man. And I saw he wrote only about himself, he drew only from his own experiences.

And in an interview with Prema Viswanathan published in *Time Off*, 4 March 1990, Adoor added:

> I must say, despite the fact that this is the first literary script I have handled, I was not restricted at all by it. It is precisely because I wanted to lend it a totally different dimension from its fictional form that I decided to flesh out the character of Basheer to the fullest extent possible. I spent a long time talking to him, observing him, trying to understand the different facets of his conscious and unconscious mind. I spoke to people who knew him, read through all his works. In effect, I got under the skin of the character.

And in the interview with Khalid Mohamed in *The Times of India*, mentioned earlier, Adoor said:

> I thought it would be a simple film to make, but it was forbidding once I got down to it. The jail conditions, costumes, prison conduct, modes of punishments, everything had to be researched. There's very little material in the archives. Fortunately, my chief assistant Meera found a 1928 book, *Prison Administration Regulations of Travancore*. It was a life-saver – now we know so much about prisons that we could probably run one ourselves!
>
> Reinhard Hauff (the German film-maker) is a specialist on prison conditions. He saw the film and said that he liked the idea of nothingness, of time hanging heavy instead of going into the clichés of savagery and cruelty. Hauff said he had been told by prisoners that they even spend hours just watching a fly buzzing around!
>
> In my film, I have dramatized the routine, the regimen itself takes a central place. I'd gone to three central prisons in Kerala. Even a bath becomes a celebration because it takes time. In one scene, I've shown a visibly disturbed Basheer pacing up and down the jail verandah, while the other prisoners are taking their afternoon siesta. I have suggested that there is a little abnormality in every artist's mind, they even crave for it.

After completing the film, Adoor screened it at Calicut for the writer: 'Basheer saw the film and enjoyed it a lot. When I went to his seat at the end of the show, he said to me, "Not a dull moment."'

Mathilukal opens with the following words in the frame:

> A free adaptation of Vaikom M. Basheer's autobiographical story, *The Walls*.
>
> Period 1942-43, Travancore – a small principality on the southern tip of British India. The nationwide Gandhian struggle for freedom from British rule was at its peak. In Travancore, the rulers had a soft spot for the movement led by the National Congress. With freedom within sight, their ambitious Chief Minister was already scheming to declare Travancore a sovereign state, independent of the Indian Union. Consequently, freedom-fighters in the jails of Travancore enjoyed a few privileges forbidden to others.

The opening titles are displayed against a frozen image of a police constable. The police inspector and Basheer exchange pleasantries. He tells Basheer that because of the war, every essential commodity is in short supply. Even paper needed for writing is not available. Basheer is behind bars in a police station along with petty criminals. He has been languishing in the lock-up for almost a year without trial. Already an established creative writer, he is taken care of by the elderly police inspector, an admirer of his who provides him with paper to write despite the shortage. The inspector suggests Basheer go on hunger strike which is the only way his case will go to court. Valuing his advice, Basheer proceeds to act on it.

In court, the magistrate declares that Vaikom Muhammad Basheer, son of Abdul Rahiman, is proved guilty beyond doubt under Penal Code Section 111: 'He is hereby sentenced to two years RI and a fine of Rs 1000. If the fine is not paid, the term of RI is to be extended by six more months.'

Most Popular Prisoner

Basheer is then shifted to the Central Jail. On the way there, two friendly police constables give him two bundles of beedis, a box of matches and a blade. When he is taken to his cell, the head warder seizes the forbidden goodies but later returns them to Basheer as their friendship flowers.

In the jail, Basheer meets many political prisoners and hard-core criminals who love and revere him, not because he is a freedom fighter, but because he is a creative writer. Basheer, for this reason, gets special care from all. He is provided with tea, sugar, beedis, additional helpings of egg and fish and other special foods. No one shows any resentment against such privileges. Basheer is hospitable and friendly with the other inmates and with the jail superintendent. He takes matters in his stride. He doesn't take sides. He plants red roses and waters them, tries to catch a butterfly or scolds naughty squirrels.

In real life, Basheer was handsome though balding a little. In the film he is shown doing regular exercise to keep himself physically fit. Being a follower of Mahatma Gandhi, he shares his time with other political detainees; as a political prisoner, he enjoys special privileges in the prison such as being allowed to walk around the jail. Jawaharlal Nehru, who stayed in the Dehra Dun jail for fourteen-and-a-half months, narrates his prison experiences in the essay, 'Animals in Prison'. He felt less lonely in the cell when he realized wasps, hornets, lizards and squirrels were constant companions. The cells were very small, so the prisoners were given special permission to stroll in the grounds. Nehru regarded this as a great privilege because he could enjoy the beauty of the fields, the public road and, above all, the Himalayas. Such sights relieved the monotony and loneliness of his days and helped him feel less stifled. Prisoners undergoing long terms of imprisonment grow emotionally starved and very often pets and nature fill part of that vacuum. Of course, the prisoners could let their imaginations carry them over the confining walls …

The film doesn't make prison a harsh place. If you go by the rules, it's even a 'deluxe' life, as one of the characters remarks. Once, Basheer is asked by the head warder to make tea for a prisoner who is to be hanged in an hour. 'Is he desperate?' Basheer asks. The warder replies, 'He went to the latrine five times.' Basheer's comment to the warder reflects his philosophy of life: 'There are two ways of facing death – either crying or laughing. Ask him to face it laughing. Let him smoke beedis if he is used to them.'

Then a young jailor brings the news that all political prisoners are going to be released soon. Their joy knows no bounds at the prospect of freedom. But Basheer's excitement plummets when he learns his name is missing on the release order. There must surely be some mistake?

Coping with Time and Emptiness...

Basheer is left alone and disappointed in the desolate jail. The emptiness devours him. He takes to strolling in the deserted corridor of the prison, he walks in the garden, talks to the trees, squirrels and the roses. He even hatches a plan to escape from the jail but later abandons the idea.

Basheer tells the young jailor that a strange fear, which he has never known before, has descended on him, draining him of his strength. He says to a tree, 'Dear friend, this is not the old Basheer. I'm completely changed. I'm trapped in solitary confinement. I'm here all alone.' He then turns to a squirrel that starts calling to its mate, 'Oh, you're teasing me, aren't you? I'll lock you up inside the cell and that blasted warder will keep guard.'

But how has Basheer changed from his former self? Formerly, we saw his sense of humour at play, how he shared light moments with fellow prisoners, enjoyed leisurely time with his rose plants and animal friends, and was an integral part of the prison. But loneliness changes him. He has forgotten to laugh. In one particular scene, Basheer is shown strolling up and down on the verandah of the jail. It is a lengthy shot without any cut and it reflects his lonely and disturbed self. The use of the background score in this scene intensifies Basheer's sorry state.

Of Roses and Dry Twigs

One day, Basheer is whistling as he strolls leisurely along the towering prison wall. Suddenly the voice of a woman from the other side of the wall catches his ear. The conversation between Basheer and the unseen woman is very significant as it reflects the artist's creative mind and shows how it contributes to the development of the story:

Woman's Voice: Who's that whistling there?

Basheer: It's me.

Woman: Don't you have a name?

Basheer: Basheer, I'm a humble writer, sentenced to two-and-a-half years. Now, I'm alone here, all my friends are gone. And your name?

Woman: Narayani.

Basheer: A beautiful name. Age?

Woman: Twenty-two.

Basheer: Beautiful age. It's RI for you. Isn't it?

Woman: Yes, fourteen years.

Basheer: So, it's a case of murder? How long have you been here?

Woman: One full year. What a life!

Basheer: We've entered the jail almost together.

Woman: Will you give me a rose plant?

Basheer: How did you know about the rose plant?

Woman: It's a jail after all. Everyone knows everything. There are no secrets here. Will you give me the rose? Why don't you answer?

Basheer: Narayani, I'll gift you all the rose plants of this earth.

Woman: I want just one, will you give it?

Basheer: What a question! Wouldn't I?

Woman: I'll throw a dry twig up when I come. Will you come?

Basheer: Yes!

Woman: I'll throw the dry twig up. And I'll wait for you.

The rose has always been used as an image of fantasy, imagination and love. Adoor is quoted by Iqbal Masud in an interview published in *The Indian Express* on 18 March 1990: 'The rose is not used as an obvious symbol of beauty. In the film, it stands for the unreal. It connects to the voice on the other side of the wall.'

Suddenly, the empty space is filled by the sweet voice of a woman. Life now seems to take a new and fresh turn for Basheer. He falls in love with Narayani though separated from her by the high wall. He throws rose plants across the wall for her and exchanges promises of love. Basheer is now revitalized. He waits eagerly every morning to listen to the alluring voice of Narayani and waits eagerly for her twig to be tossed up. No matter that Narayani is in jail for killing her husband, he loves her regardless.

There is also a special message conveyed by the Basheer–Narayani love affair: Basheer, a Muslim by religion, who is charged with rajadroha (treason) against the state, falls in love with Narayani, a young Hindu woman of twenty-two. This indicates Basheer's cosmopolitan outlook and his image of a society without religious friction. 'It is perhaps the most successful portrait of a Muslim writer shorn of his religious antecedents and projected as completely secular – a feat that could possibly have been accomplished only in Kerala, where the Muslim minority has been able to enter the mainstream of Indian life.'[62]

Unheard Melodies Are Sweeter

As said earlier, Narayani is never seen in person in the film. Romantic poet John Keats put it this way in his famous 'Ode on a Grecian Urn': 'Heard melodies are sweet, but those unheard are sweeter…'

Unheard or unseen objects generate a sense of mystery and feed the urge to attain the seemingly unattainable. In the case of Basheer, he knows he has to wait for the arrival of his release order – which is uncertain. Meanwhile, he has to pass long days in a deserted prison. Has he, out of frustration and loneliness, created an imaginary character named Narayani to keep him company?

The creation of Narayani's character is a sort of 'willing suspension of disbelief', a phrase coined by Samuel Taylor Coleridge: 'My endeavours (in *Lyrical Ballads*) should be directed to persons and characters supernatural, or at least romantic, so as to transfer from our inward nature a human interest and a semblance of truth sufficient to procure for these shadows of imagination that willing suspension of disbelief for the moment, which constitutes poetic faith.'

In other words, invented and incredible situations may be presented in such a way that viewers begin to believe in them as if they were real. The conversations between the separated lovers in *Mathilukal* are so vividly presented that viewers can well believe the woman is real, of flesh and blood. Like Ajayan in *Anantaram*, one is unable to distinguish between fact and fiction. Indeed, Adoor conjures up the most sensuous of scenes through conversation between the two figures who have not laid eyes on each other:

> Basheer: Are there no roses in your jail?
>
> Narayani: No, not even one.
>
> …
>
> Narayani: How is your face?

Basheer: Fair, hair cropped. I am afraid I may go bald soon.

Narayani: The eyes?

Basheer: Small, like an elephant's.

Narayani: Mine are also like an elephant's but big. The chest?

Basheer: A bit broad.

Narayani: Mine is also broad.

Basheer: My hips are narrow.

Narayani: As far as my hips…

Basheer: The colour?

Narayani: Of?

Basheer: Of your pretty face?

Narayani: Fair.

Basheer: I can get the scent of woman…

In the novella, Narayani plans with Basheer to meet him at the jail hospital a few days later. But before that, unexpectedly, his release orders arrive. Basheer protests in a loud voice, 'Who needs freedom? Outside is an even bigger jail!' The novella ends with Basheer, rose in hand, standing outside the prison gates.

In the film, when they plan to meet each other, Narayani says, 'It's Monday today. Thursday at eleven at the hospital. Black mole on the right cheek. Don't forget.' Basheer replies that he will be holding a red rose…

But the ending is different. Basheer yells out, 'Free world! What free world? Out there is a bigger jail. Who cares for this freedom?' On the other side of the wall, a dry twig is being tossed up, it rises and falls against the vast blue canvas of the sky. Basheer's eyes are focused on the rising and falling of the dry twig; as his eyes fill with tears, the visual of the twig slowly gets blurred…

Freedom Reframed

Writes Suranjan Ganguly, 'The film shows how Basheer transcends the limits set on his liberty through the power of his creativity. In the process, the freedom fighter radically reformulates his notion of freedom. True liberty, he discovers, doesn't lie in scaling the walls of the jail but in the mind. The prison cell, then, is also an existential space that serves as a setting for his meditations on identity, selfhood and escape.'[63]

In an interview published in *Indian Film Culture* (August 2010) by Bikas Mishra, Adoor said:

> The writer had always been affirmative that there was a real woman on the other side of the wall. She was serving her term there because she had murdered her husband. But in my film, I brought in the element of ambivalence. Maybe she was a real character – maybe not. She could be a figment of the writer's imagination. I wanted to bring in a new dimension.

Is Narayani a creation of Basheer's fertile imagination? Adoor told Gita Aravamudan in an interview published in *The Indian Post* (15 November 1989):

> I am exploring the mind of the creative writer. The woman who comes into his all-male world could be real or be a creation of his mind. As a writer he can create, recreate, interpret or efface things. He can build upon absolutely nothing! He is above all this and yet bound to everything. Only a writer or artist gets this freedom.

People can create such characters out of utter frustration. For instance, the childless couple in Edward Albee's *Who's Afraid of Virginia Woolf* invent a son who studies abroad and stays in a hostel. While their imaginary son dies at the end of the play, the love story of Basheer and Narayani (whether real or imaginary) ends in separation.

An aspect of the film that drew widespread acclaim is Mammootty's performance. About casting Mammootty, Adoor is quoted as saying:

> My effort was to cast someone who suits the self-image of Basheer during that period of his life. In his writings, Basheer always talks about his appearance as handsome, well built and strong. But the popular image we have of him is that of an old man. In the film, he is in his youth, so I thought Mammootty suited the role eminently. I couldn't be happy with a lesser actor in that role. It was my intention to capture the image Basheer had of himself. When he saw the film, Basheer joked to his wife, 'Mammootty is not as handsome as I was but he approximates!' The two characters Mammootty portrayed in *Mathilukal* and *Vidheyan*

> are opposites: one self-reflective and creative, the other, a ruffian, devoid of any sense of sophistication or finer feelings...

To Adoor, sound is as important as the visual in films. In fact, he always prepares a separate script just for sound. In *Mathilukal*, he outdoes himself in his creative use of sound – he fashions a sensuous heroine from just a voice! According to Resul Pookutty (the 1995 FTII graduate who won an Academy award for Best Sound Mixing in *Slumdog Millionaire*):

> Adoor and Mani Kaul are real masters when it comes to sound. So was the late Aravindan. I was awed by the way Adoor used sound in his films. My favourite film is *Elippathayam* – for all reasons. Adoor uses sound to extract drama, while for Aravindan, it was for lyrical purposes. I must add that Adoor uses music as a leitmotif while many top commercial film-makers use it just as a narrative tool.

N. Harikumar, who has been working as a sound recordist with Adoor after P. Devadas, has this to say:

> Adoor Gopalakrishnan always uses natural sounds. For example, we could match the sound of the door with another door sound. But Adoor sir will not allow that. He will prefer to record the sound of that particular door. In *Mathilukal*, there was a big jail door. Since we would not get permission later to record the sound of that jail gate, Adoor sir saw to it that ample door sound was recorded during the shooting time itself.

In 1989, *Mathilukal* carried away four National Awards: for Best Direction, Best Actor (Mammootty), Best Regional Film and Best Audiography. Satyajit Ray's reaction after watching *Mathilukal* at the International Film Festival of India at Calcutta in 1990 was short: 'Marvellous, Adoor!' Ray even candidly admitted before the assembled journalists that Adoor was his favourite Indian film-maker.

Vidheyan *(Courtesy: Kerala State Chalachithra Academy)*

12

Vidheyan (The Servile)

The Zamindar Who Wasn't

Adoor Gopalakrishnan's *Vidheyan* (released in 1993) is a magnum opus that explores the master–slave relationship in a south Karnataka setting, about a decade and a half after Independence. During British rule, the main landlord or the influential person in a village was entrusted with the task of collecting land revenue from the people. Known as Patel in Karnataka, he was addressed as 'Patelar' as a mark of respect. The Patelar enjoyed full legal power and was the centre of power in the village. He was often a source of terror for the villagers.

Following Independence in 1947, the feudal-like zamindari system prevailing in Indian society was abolished. But some of them continued to live in the style of zamindars or feudal lords long after they had been replaced by regular revenue officials. In Dakshin or south Karnataka (a border area between Kerala and Karnataka), even during the 1960s, there were Patels who dominated and exploited the villagers, particularly the submissive immigrant farmers. *Vidheyan* critically examines the psychology of power and submission.

The notion of selfhood, according to scholars, is a socially constructed phenomenon that recognizes two selves, one independent, the other dependent – which have no separate meaning and identity until one acknowledges the other's existence. Hegel (*Phenomenology of Spirit*) says: 'The two exist as opposed shapes of consciousness, one the independent consciousness whose essential nature is to be for itself, the other, the dependent consciousness whose essential nature is simply to live or to be for another. The former is the lord, the other is bondsman…'[64]

In *Vidheyan*, zamindar Bhaskara Patelar is the independent consciousness and the minions of Bhaskara Patelar in general, and Thommi in particular, are dependent on him. The existence of the Patelar gains significance only in the acknowledgement of Thommi and other underlings.

The master–slave relationship has been graphically portrayed in world literature. In Daniel Defoe's hugely popular adventure novel *Robinson Crusoe*, its hero describes the greeting he gets from Friday the 'savage', '…he kneel'd down again, kiss'd the Ground, and laid his Head upon the Ground, and taking me by the Foot, set my Foot upon his Head; this it seems was in token of swearing to be my Slave forever.'

Another master–slave relationship (in Shakespeare's *The Tempest*) portrays Lord Prospero's despotic treatment of two servants, Ariel and Caliban. Says Ariel, 'I prithee/ Remember I have done thee worthy service/ Told thee no lies, made thee no mistakings, served/ Without grudge or grumblings: thou didst promise/ To bate me a full year.' Reminding Ariel of how he rescued him from the horrid witch, Prospero threatens, 'Any more complaints … and I will confine you in an oak tree for twelve winters!'

The opening titles of Adoor Gopalakrishnan's *Vidheyan* appear against a visual of an armless chair with a gun leaning against the wall. The chair itself symbolizes the power and domination of the zamindari autocracy – but its lack of arms suggests its inherent decay. And, of course, the gun reminds one of the brutality and violence of the one-time autocrats.

Slaves in the Making

The Christian couple Thommi and his wife Omana, among other immigrants, come from conditions of abject poverty in Wayanad (a hill district of Kerala) to Dakshina Karnataka in search of employment and better opportunities. In the pre-Independence period, land masses were mapped on the basis of what was cultivable land for paddy, and the surrounding areas for wild growth to provide green manure for the rice fields. Most of the areas around the paddy fields were kept vacant. They were not meant for cultivation as this part of the land was not as fertile as the rest. This resulted in large stretches of unsurveyed land lying vacant on which the settlers encroached. Priya Menon says in her dissertation, 'Liminal Resistance: Local subjection in *My Story*, *Vidheyan* and *The God of Small Things*':

> *Vidheyan* is set in Dakshina Kannada at the dawn of Indian independence where an ex-feudal Bhaskara, belonging to the British-enforced Patel system of administration, continues to reign supreme by terrorising the local population that consists mainly of immigrant settlers from Kerala. Adoor differentiates the indigenous Dakshina Kannada population from the settler-group by assigning Malayalam to be spoken by the settlers as opposed to the Konkani-Tulu used by local Kannadigas. (Bhaskara Patelar, who behaves as if he is still lord of the village, is fluent in both Kannada and Malayalam.)

The film opens with Thommi sitting idly at a tea shop, staring vacantly ahead. The whimsical and tyrannical Bhaskara Patelar sits in the armless chair in the toddy shop across the road, surrounded by his henchmen. He has a big moustache and is also big of build and barely fits into the chair. The crouched figure at the tea shop across the road catches his eye. Calling Thommi a 'son of a bitch', Bhaskara proceeds to harangue him about where he lives, how much land he has encroached, how old his wife is and whether she is good-looking or not. He kicks Thommi and spits betel juice in his face. The opening sequence at once introduces us to the inhuman brutality of Bhaskara Patelar and the vulnerability of the landless immigrant labour.

When Thommi returns home angry and helpless, further humiliation awaits. Patelar opens the door from inside his hut while Omana's sobbing can be heard. Patelar leaves with his attendants and crosses the stream nearby.

The next morning, Thommi vows to his wife Omana in an outburst of hate and helplessness that he will cut the Patel to pieces. A little later, when one of the henchmen summons Thommi, he replies in a fit of rage, 'Who is he to summon me?' Fully aware of the consequences, the henchman warns Thommi, 'Don't you want to live here?' Thommi presents himself to the Patelar and, to his amazement, he is gifted a dhoti for himself and a sari for his wife. The Patelar says to Thommi, 'I fixed for you to work here as a bartender from today.'

Goodbye, Rebellion!

The evil intentions of Bhaskara Patelar are clear: Thommi will be slave to the Patelar while Omana will be his sex toy. Thommi, out of fear, raises no objection and remains mute while his wife Omana is regularly raped by Patel. Thommi's desire for rebellion and vengeance is dampened by his friends who advise him to be practical. Thommi suggests to Omana, 'Shall we go away from here?' She replies, 'Where to? We didn't make it in Wayanad so we decided to try here. Where'll we go now?'

Saroja, wife of Bhaskara – she is the voice of his conscience – is a soft-hearted woman who advises her husband against indulging in inhuman acts. She is all sympathy for Thommi and Omana. For his part, the Patelar, not liking his wife's interference, hatches a plot to do away with her. But when Bhaskara attempts to shoot her, a misdirected bullet hits Thommi instead, wounding him severely. Meanwhile, the relationship between Bhaskara and Omana becomes an open affair and even Thommi accepts it. Thommi tells his wife: 'Omana, now your body smells only of Patel sir's scent. I like this smell. But you are mine alone. One day I'll buy this scent for you.'

M.R. Gopakumar, who played the role of Thommi, says: 'Adoor sir is a perfectionist, he aims to reveal the inner character with every scene. For that particular scene in which I tell Omana that I like the smell of Patel sir's scent on her body, Adoor sir took almost ten takes – normally there are three or four. I did not dare ask him why, but he is the kind of film-maker who will take and retake till he is completely satisfied with the character's performance.'

Talking of performances, Mammootty received the National Award for his brilliant performance in *Vidheyan*, following his award-winning turn in *Mathilukal*. His collaboration with Adoor – particularly in *Anantaram* as an elder brother of Ashokan – is a perfect example of Adoor's skill in moulding and designing characters according to his vision. Writing in *The Hindu*, Shobha Warrier quotes him:

> I noticed Mammootty in K.G. George's films. In fact, I noticed him right in his first film *Mela* ... I am always looking for actors who can portray my characters. Ashokan was the main character in *Anantaram*, but I needed another actor as his elder brother. Now, this elder brother

> was better than him in looks, profession and in real life. So my search was not for just an actor, but one who was attractive and imposing – physically and personality-wise. Mammootty was the man who came to mind when I thought of the character. Usually, a star prefers to act in films that consolidates his position as a star and not to jeopardise it. Mammootty is not like that. Take his role in *Vidheyan.* Were he concerned about his stardom, he would not have acted in it – there were negative shades to the character. In fact, we made him look unattractive and ugly, to suit the thoroughly unlikeable character. But he had no qualms about enacting it. That is why I call Mammootty a courageous actor – he is willing to go beyond the trappings of a star.

Thommi becomes Bhaskara's chief accomplice. A defiant Caliban says to Prospero (*The Tempest,* Act I), 'You taught me language, and my profit on't/ Is I know how to curse. The red plague rid you/ For learning me your language!' But Thommi protests not at all, his initial urge to cut the Patelar to pieces having become subservient to the demands of survival.

In an interview to K. Santhosh (*The Hindu*, 2 July 1993), Adoor said, 'Thommi's fidelity to Patelar is unshakeable.Yet deep down in his heart the natural human urge to revolt remains alive. In the end, when Patelar tragically dies, Thommi is at once aggrieved and relieved.'

Thommi introduces a wealthy merchant Yusuf Picha to Bhaskara: 'He needs help to find his brother who is missing.' But in a cruel and inhuman act that baffles Thommi, Bhaskara savagely beats up Yusuf, leaving the trader to die on the roadside. 'What wrong has he done?' Thommi cries out loudly, holding on tightly to Yusuf Picha who lies immobilized on the ground.

Bhaskara, who has little respect for women, again reveals his dark side when he teases Kuttappa Rai's son and his young bride in the open street. These events unite Yusuf Picha and Kuttappa Rai in a common aim to eliminate Bhaskara Patelar once and for all. The two meet Thommi to convince him that a tyrant like Bhaskara should be killed. Yusuf says to Thommi, 'Don't be scared. We must kill the Patel.'

In fact, Thommi is not concerned about the killing as much as the prospect of losing his provider. He asks them, 'Then who will be there for me?' So they make Thommi an alluring offer, 'We'll give you 100 rupees and make you a peon at the panchayat office.'

However, the night they finally fire at the Patelar, they miss their target and the Patelar escapes with minor wounds.

Meanwhile, Bhaskara has not abandoned his plan to kill his wife. He finally succeeds, then tries to pass it off as suicide. But others, particularly Saroja's brothers, refuse to accept this. Bhaskara picks up Thommi from his house in the dead of the night to accompany him to his nephew's town house where he believes he will get shelter. But to his utter shock, his nephew turns him away on the grounds that Bhaskara is a fugitive.

Bhaskara and Thommi have no alternative but to find shelter in the dense forest. In an interview with C.S.Venkiteswaran, Adoor said:

> From the moment they enter the forest, they turn into two ordinary human beings. All social connections and disparities severed, we find them eating from the same food packet. Loyal Thommi is contemptuous of the nephew who does not even allow Patelar inside the house. It is only then that Patelar realises the deep trouble he is in, and the fact that he is a fugitive from the law. All relationships end there.

The two, erstwhile master and slave, remain hiding in the forest. As they are trying to cook something, suddenly they hear the sound of gunshots. Thommi runs away and hides behind a huge rock. He sees Bhaskara raise his gun in surrender to Saroja's brothers. They shoot the Patelar down. Thommi slowly approaches his master, looks at him and cries out, 'Master, it cannot be!' Then he takes the gun from the dead man's hand, lifts it high with both hands and flings it into the water.

He is emotionally confused whether to rejoice at the death of his tyrant master or grieve because his master was also his provider. Thommi runs rapidly home to his wife, crying out loudly that his master is dead. According to Adoor,

> For someone who knows Thommi, his final run may not be one of liberation. He is running out of relief. But there is also an element of sadness in it: his cry of joy resembles a wail. He realises in an elemental way about the Patelar's misuse of power – which is evident in the act of throwing away the gun into the river.[65]

M.R. Gopakumar says the character of Thommi changed his image as an actor: 'Initially, Adoor sir had looked for another actor to play the role, but fortunately, it came to me. In the novel, the character of Thommi is a kind of caricature. But my role in the film gave me everything – a new recognition, and a new energy. I have played so many characters but Thommi is the best I have ever acted in my life – the kind of character one gets to play once in a lifetime. After seeing *Vidheyan,* Hollywood director Spielberg wanted to cast me in *Lost World* – the second part of *Jurassic Park.* But alas I could not go because of a visa problem.

Gopakumar narrates another behind-the-scenes story of the shooting of one of the last grim scenes of the film – which ended on a comic note. 'Mammootty was ready for the take with blood all over his face and costume. The shoot was happening near a waterfall when it started to rain, sparking off the possibility of a flash flood. So we had to pack up for the day in a hurry. Mammootty and I were the first to emerge from the dense forest on to the road, make-up and all in place. There we were, the blood-painted Mammootty and I, standing on the highway, no doubt looking forlorn. Besides, we were scratched by thorns and bushes on our journey up. A number of vehicles passing by stopped to inquire what the matter was. There were curious students too who wished to know more. Fortunately, before a crowd gathered, the rest of the unit arrived and we were able to make our exit.'

From Novella to Screen

Adoor's *Vidheyan* is a cinematic adaptation of the novella *Bhaskara Patelar and My Life* by Paul Zacharia, a renowned Malayalam writer. It had been published in 1986 in the *Mathrubhumi Weekly.* On visits to his farm in Dakshina Karnataka, Paul Zacharia was inspired by the stories he heard from the local people of the atrocities committed by an authoritarian Patelar. These real-life stories sparked off a fictional work, in which Zacharia added many fictional elements such as the killing of the Patelar's wife. At the same time, he incorporated real elements such as casting dynamite into the river to kill fish. Zacharia narrates the story in the first person, in the voice of Thommi. It begins with Patelar calling him from the other side of the road:

> I saw Bhaskara Patelar for the first time one evening in Udina Bazaar. Squatting on the edge of a shop verandah, I was thinking about my sorrows. The sound my frayed mundu made as it gave way little by little at the back kept pace with my thoughts. Suddenly I heard someone call from the other side of the road…

And at film's end he says:

> I covered Patelar with grass and twigs. Then I took his gun, walked along the bank of the river, climbed on a rock and threw the gun into the rainbows that fluttered in the waterfall beneath me. I felt a kind of relief. And also, a kind of courage. Crossing the river I ran to Ichilampadi, to tell Omana that Patelar was dead.

In an interview with K. Santhosh (*The Hindu*, 2 July 1993), Adoor Gopalakrishnan mentions the revisions he made in the original story:

> I have altered the total tone of the story and the characters. The two women – Sarojakka, Patelar's wife, and Omana – assume importance in the film whereas they play little part in the novelette. Patelar kills his wife for her property in Zacharia's story. I have changed that. I use only one murder – Patelar killing his conscience. That is the turning point of the story. On the whole, it shows how unchecked power creates problems.

One of the most poignant – and poetic – scenes in the film is the temple pond scene when Bhaskara orders Thommi to throw the dynamite sticks in the pond to kill the holy fish. Thommi, against his will, throws the sticks into the pond one by one, but they do not explode – could it be Divine Will? In the novella, the last stick of dynamite thrown in the pond explodes, but that is only after the two of them have left its bank. In the film, the dynamite does not explode at all.

Adoor says he used the plot of the story to explore the subterranean landscape of the human mind. Here, terror – the oppressive form of power – joins hands with servility in a pathological alliance of interdependence. Each of them, oppressor and oppressed, is the source of sustenance of the other. *Vidheyan* is a study of the psychology and structure of power – and also an attempt to examine what lies buried beneath an obsessive servility.

Author and film critic Mark Schilling called the film 'a striking examination of the dynamics of power in a society still shaking off the last vestiges of feudalism'. For film critic Derek Malcolm, *Vidheyan* was the best Indian film he had seen in the Indian Panorama till then, a significant work of India's major director after Satyajit Ray. *Vidheyan,* I believe, will continue to live on in Indian cinema space as a masterpiece on the master–slave relationship that transcends time and place.

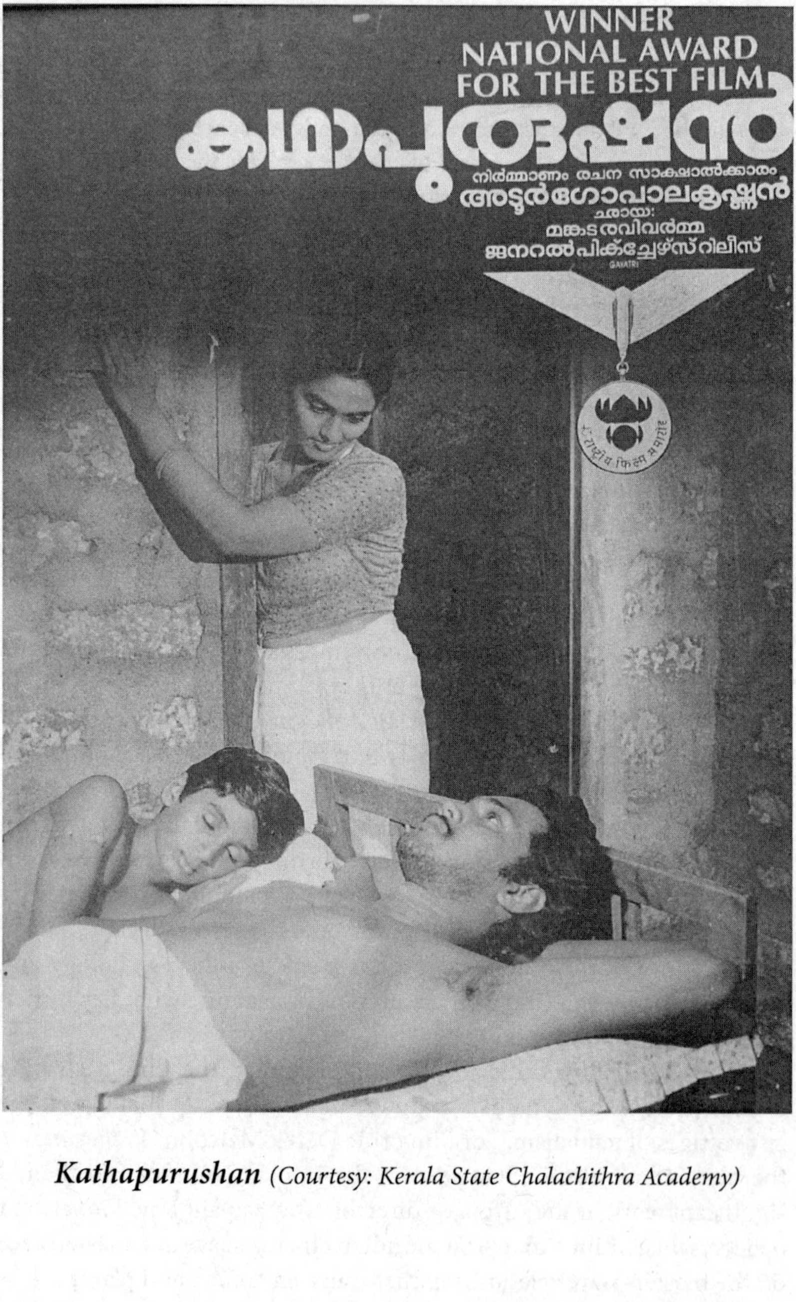

Kathapurushan *(Courtesy: Kerala State Chalachithra Academy)*

13

Kathapurushan (Man of the Story)

Turbulent Times

In the course of the twentieth century, the people of Kerala witnessed several historical events, both national and regional: the national movement culminating in Independence in 1947, the assassination of Mahatma Gandhi in 1948, the Communist Party of India coming to power through the general elections in 1957, the split in the Communist Party of India in 1964, land reform bills, the rise of the Naxalite movement in the late 1970s, the declaration of Emergency in 1975, the rise of communal politics, all of which left a deep impact on the nation – and Kerala.

Translating those epoch-making happenings into celluloid is no easy task. *Kathapurushan* (released in 1995) eschews a conventional narrative style and documents the social and historical events of the state and country through the personal experiences of the protagonist, Kunjunni – which technique brings a new dynamic to the narrative.

In an interview with Deepa Gahlot published in *The Times of India*, 18 Februrary 1996, Adoor said:

> The film is factually and historically true – I am talking of happenings I know intimately. You cannot understand the life and culture of Kerala without knowing the changes of the last quarter-century … I have seen the sunset of the feudal system, the coming of independence, the democratic process. All this has brought about a sea-change in attitudes and lifestyles, in the relationship between man and his land.
>
> There have been remarkable changes – not all necessarily for the

> better. Kerala was the first state to introduce land reforms, the first state in the whole world to have a communist government voted into power. The Naxalites were an ultra-faction of the Marxists that resorted to armed revolution. You know the stories of terror and violence then there was a period of cooling off and settling down after the outburst…

Placing the film in his own time and surroundings allows the director to incorporate his own life's experiences, the socio-political changes occurring in his time. But, as Adoor clarifies, he is not making a historical film. The 1940s were the period of his childhood and *Kathapurushan* deals with parts of that period and the decades that follow. Adoor draws on the past only to vivify the present. As he tells Vinu Abraham, there should be a time gap between present reality and past happenings so as to better comprehend the varied dimensions of past events.

Kathapurushan was shot at Adoor Gopalakrishnan's ancestral house, Medayil in Pallickal, indicating how autobiographical the film is. Like Kunjunni, Adoor was deprived of paternal love as a child. Adoor's parents had been living separately for some years, but unlike the film, Adoor's father never got married again while Kunjunni's father acquires another family.

The Eternal Storyteller

Kathapurushan opens with a close shot of a squint-eyed old man who is narrating to viewers a story of long long ago. Adoor says, 'The eternal storyteller tells the universal and timeless tale of a demon and a prince. The story he relates at an abstract level is actually about the establishment demanding submission from the individual. But it is the individual rebellion that makes life worth living.'

The old man's story is set in a fearsome and terrible forest which is home to elephants, bears, tigers, leopards and bison – where nobody ventures alone. It is so dense that it is dark even during the day. Once, a prince, defeated in battle and on the run, reaches this dense forest with his faithful wife and their son. A man-eating demon rules over the forest. All of a sudden, the earth begins to quake with his footfalls, and the air with his roaring. The prince draws his sword, readies to attack. But the demon makes the prince an offer: You give me your son and I will spare you and your wife. As for a son you can always have another one. The prince ponders for a while, then says: True, we can have another son – but you will continue to be here! What happens to all the other young boys traversing the forest? The prince, not waiting for a reply, flourishes his sword in his hand and rushes at the demon.

Suddenly, Adoor cuts to a closed door. An old lady opening the door says, 'It's tough. It's a breech delivery.' A few moments later, a second lady opens the door partly to announce, 'She has delivered a boy but it does not cry.' Eventually, to everyone's relief the child, thumped on its back, cries out.

The family astrologer foretells the future of the newborn baby: The feet of the child has come out first, making the delivery painful and dangerous. According to the planetary positions, as the delivery has not caused any injury to the child or the mother, either he or his mother could be handicapped in the future. (Kunjunni starts limping when he is released from prison and thus the prediction comes true.) Moreover, the child is not fated to enjoy paternal love and care.

John W. Hood writes in his book, *The Essential Mystery:*

> History eventually brings Kunjunni, his wife and son into confrontation with a modern version of the cannibalistic demon in the forest. But the world as a forest, dominated by the predatory beast, has probably always existed, even in the seemingly tranquil world of tradition in which landowning families such as Kunjunni's could find particular fulfilment. While the servants at home kept their place, there was a happy relationship between them and their masters as seen in Kunjunni's maternal grandmother's attitude to Veluchar and to Meenakshi's mother and father … But with rapid and momentous historical change this tranquility is dispelled.[66]

As he grows, it is found the child stammers as he tries to speak. In preschool, Kunjunni is more interested in watching the goat outside the classroom than in reciting the difficult consonants. The village schoolteacher, flying into a rage at Kunjunni's inability to pronounce the words properly, is harsh with the child, no matter that he belongs to a landowning family.

Adoor says, 'The protagonist's stammering is a kind of metaphor. Kunjunni is a normal enough child but the oppressive school system makes him reclusive. And while he stammers at the start of the film you see that he does not do so by the end. He is utterly taken aback when his book is proscribed by the government but he takes pleasure in the ban. As a writer with artistic sensibility and a social conscience, he is glad to disturb the status quo. The system does not want a different – and humiliating – voice to drown its own.'

Kunjunni, as the only son in the family, is brought up with utmost love and care by his mother, maternal grandmother and the estate manager named Veluchar (who fills the void left by Kunjunni's biological father). He is Kunjunni's constant companion. Meenakshi, the daughter of their maidservant Janamma and the elephant-keeper Pachupillai, does not reveal her feelings of love for Kunjunni.

Kunjunni grows up and goes to university for higher studies where he is attracted, like other youth of the time, to the ideology of communism. Kunjunni's maternal uncle, Vasu, had been sent to England to study but had joined the national struggle under Mahatma Gandhi and lost contact with his family. One day, he returns home. He has by now abandoned Gandhism for Marxism, and become an active member of the underground wing of the Communist Party of India.

One of the most touching scenes in Adoor's film is when Veluchar informs the grandmother that Gandhi has been shot to death at a prayer meeting the previous evening. Kunjunni is deeply affected by the news. Veluchar, the grandmother, Meenakshi and Kunjunni mournfully watch the procession of Congressmen lamenting Gandhi's death. Kunjunni weeps without restraint and his grandmother tries to pacify him, 'Don't cry my child. We're helpless.'

As time passes by, Kunjunni's mother gradually grows feeble despite medical treatment. Kunjunni is called from the university with the news that his mother is on the brink of death. The grandmother also sends for Kunjunni's father who has been long separated from his wife.

One of the villagers who had assembled for the funeral asks, 'Where's her husband?' Another villager comments that Kunjunni had managed to arrive before her death though he was located far away. But Kunjunni's father arrives only after his mother is gone.

First Elected Communist Government

In 1957 a communist government came to power in Kerala – the first in the world to do so through a democratic election. Its first historic step was to legislate the Land Reform Bill which sought to disinherit the feudal lords and provide agricultural lands to the tillers. Kunjunni's grandmother cannot afford any longer to keep the maidservant Janamma – for long a trusted member of the family – and her three daughters and is forced to send them away. Kunjunni is heartbroken too at this parting but he remains a mute spectator. He feels that communism is the answer to all the evils of society and he joins hands with the ultras to provide intellectual leadership to the movement.

The Naxalite group launches a series of attacks on police stations. Newspaper headlines repeatedly read: 'Policeman Killed', 'Communists Invade Police Station', 'Constable Murdered', 'Extremists on a Rampage'…

Kunjunni has been running a printing press in town that publishes inflammatory literature. He becomes the prime suspect behind such attacks and is arrested. In the police station, Veluchar pleads with the inspector, 'He wouldn't kill even an ant. He's charged of murder. God will not forgive you.'

Eventually, the court declares Kunjunni innocent. He is a lonely man, poor in companionship but rich in experience. He sets out limping (a souvenir of police atrocities) in search of Meenakshi to find that she has remained unmarried and learnt tailoring to support her family. When Kunjunni expresses his desire to marry her, her father says, 'My daughter is not for a stuttering criminal. If he still insists, tell him to pay ten thousand rupees and take her away. He cannot have her for free.' Kunjunni, who knows the father's character well, says he will pay up. Meenakshi, disgusted with her father's attitude, retorts, 'So, you would sell your daughter for a drink!' Kunjunni marries her and takes her to his ancestral home.

One day, all of a sudden, Kunjunni's uncle Vasu visits them, this time completely transformed. He is clad in saffron clothes, has become an ascetic and is in pursuit of spiritual salvation. He wants his share of property to be handed over to his wife, three daughters and son as he has failed to provide anything for them. Kunjunni sells the ancestral house, properties and other belongings to an eager buyer – whose father was once a servant there. He shifts to a small house in a remote area, so that they can concentrate on farming and writing.

Kunjunni has almost stopped thinking of his father whom he had met only once. Suddenly a man appears at Kunjunni's house, introducing himself as a schoolteacher. He says Kunjunni's father happens to be his father too! There was no formal wedding and his parents had just decided to live together. His two younger sisters were married and settled. They were all fairly well off. Only after growing up had they learnt they had a half-brother. Kunjunni might find it hard to forgive his father but he had been bedridden for the past six years and of late, had been talking about Kunjunni. He would like to see him before his final departure from this world. This information evokes mixed feelings in Kunjunni but he agrees to visit his father. When he returns home that night, he tells his wife, 'It was all over by the time I reached there.'

Kunjunni completes writing his novel, titled *The Hard Consonants*, which is published with the help of a friend. One morning, Kunjunni's son reads out a newspaper item about the book being banned. Kunjunni reads the news for himself: the state government has issued an ordinance restraining the publishers from selling copies of the book. The book has already become a best-seller and has been receiving much critical attention. Kunjunni exults at his triumph, 'How ugly is the face of truth! So must we act without affecting anybody? Without disturbing anything?' Kunjunni anticipates his arrest. Significantly, in this scene where he lambasts the power of the state, he does not stammer at all. All three – father, mother, son – realize that the unachieved has been achieved at last. Then they laugh and sing aloud in pure abandon. And their song is composed entirely of consonants.

Once again, the scene cuts to the old man narrating the story of a prince, his wife and their son. He continues from where he left off: The demon says, 'Wait, wait, you don't think about the consequences. You're rash. You are a foolish prince. I'll give you one more chance. If you dote so much on your son, I'll spare him. All right? Instead give up your wife for me. It's a long time since I had a pretty lady for my meal. And don't grieve over her. You can take another beauty for your wife.' Once again, the prince rushes forth in anger, 'You wicked demon!' The demon reasons, 'Hold on. In this combat, victory will anyway be mine. So you decide whom I should choose for my meal.' The prince brandishes his sword and leaps forward. 'What makes you so sure you'll always be victorious?' The film ends with the prince challenging the demon to mortal combat…

Film critic Saibal Chatterjee writes (*Outlook*, 31 January 1996):

> *Kathapurushan* is a powerful yet touching testament to the invincibility of the human spirit, a document that explicates Adoor's humanist credo: no matter how destructive the ravages of time and the depredations of oppressive political systems are, the free will of the individual is bound to assert itself in ways that are as impressive as they are surprising ... He is Kunjunni, a character afflicted with a stammer but endowed with inner strength that helps him turn every experience of life, both triumphs and defeats, into an intellectual propellant. Every flash point becomes a new beginning – his love for the maid's daughter, the deaths of his mother and grandmother, his disillusionment with party politics, his involvement in the Naxalite movement, his arrest and subsequent torture by the police ... the rich texture of *Kathapurushan* and the elliptical editing is near perfect, no shot is held a split-second longer than it should be, the outdoor sequences are visually lush ... *Kathapurushan* is a cinematic creation of the highest order...

Nizhalkkuthu *(Courtesy: Kerala State Chalachithra Academy)*

14

Nizhalkkuthu (Shadow Kill)

Even Hangmen Are Human

George Orwell's essay of August 1931, titled 'A Hanging', is set in Burma where Orwell served with the British Imperial Police from 1922 to 1927. It describes the execution of a condemned man without mentioning his name or the crime he has committed. Orwell minutely observes and describes how the prisoner was taken from his prison cell to the gallows and how unbearable and inhuman an act it was. When the hangman tightened the noose on the prisoner's neck, he cried out a sort of prayer, 'Ram! Ram! Ram!' Orwell recalls how later all of them, native and European alike, quite amicably had a drink together and a good laugh at an anecdote told by one of the group … while just a hundred yards away lay the dead man …

In the same way, in *Nizhalkkuthu*, Adoor Gopalakrishnan is critical of capital punishment but instead of interpreting the mental state of the prisoner just before the noose is fixed on his neck, Adoor analyses the psychology of the hangman and the fact that he is a man with all-too-human feelings and failings. Adoor breaks the stereotyped notion of a hangman, painting for us a picture of a normal human being leading a normal family life like others in society.

While working on *Mathilukal* in 1989, Adoor was drawn to the idea of making a film on crime and capital punishment. Some years later, he came across a short news item in a local paper about a hangman who happened to be the last professional hangman of the erstwhile Travancore state. He found the story of the hangman's life stirring, and after seven years of research and study of this theme, Gopalakrishnan made *Nizhalkkuthu*. Vinu Abraham wrote in *The Week*:

> Though set in the 1940s, *Nizhalkkuthu* is not a period film, says Adoor. While researching the film, he learnt that executioners were made to live on the periphery of the state's border so that social contact and interaction with the mainstream was kept to the minimum. The executioners of Travancore lived in a village in Kanyakumari district in the southernmost part of the princely state. It was after a year-long search that Adoor zoomed in on Pottakulam village. Countless trips to the area resulted in the discovery of the old house that resembled the original and suited the central character …
>
> Even as his writing was in progress, an assistant told him that *Dhruvam*, a Malayalam film released then, dealt with the story of an executioner. 'I immediately dropped the idea and began work on my next film (*Vidheyan*).' But later when his wife saw the film on TV and told him that it had no bearing on the hangman's story, Adoor went back to work on the script.[67]

The title 'Nizhalkkuthu' refers to an episode in that ancient epic, the Mahabharata. Son of the blind king Dhritarashtra and the blindfolded queen Gandhari, Duryodhan, eldest and most powerful of the Kaurava siblings, wants to kill his five Pandava cousins so as to become sole ruler of the kingdom. He orders tribal sorcerer Malayan to use black magic (known as shadow killing) to eliminate the Pandavas. Malayan, initially reluctant to obey, ultimately agrees to perform *nizhalkkuthu*. The shadows of the Pandavas are created through black magic and then killed. As their shadows fall, so do the flesh-and-blood Pandavas. Malayan returns home and describes the killing to his wife who is so infuriated that she kills their own son so the father may feel the same pain as Kunti, mother of the Pandavas. Malayan's wife rushes to see Kunti who has meanwhile sought Lord Krishna's help to bring her sons back to life. Which Krishna does. He promises that Malayan's son too will regain life. A parallel can be drawn between the story of Malayan's wife killing her innocent son to punish her husband and the killing of innocent victims through capital punishment as shown in the film.

Nizhalkkuthu is set in the early 1940s against the backdrop of the struggle for independence in the princely state of Travancore. Kaliyappan, son of Chinnappan of Nagercoil (located on the border between Tamil Nadu and Kerala), is the last living hangman of the Travancore dynasty. He lives on the outskirts of the village with his wife, son Muthu, and youngest daughter Mallika. His eldest daughter Madhavi is married to Vasu and they have a daughter. Kaliyappan's son Muthu is a staunch follower of Gandhi. He turns vegetarian and joins the freedom struggle. The people of his village are surprised that at public meetings Muthu speaks against capital punishment, thus deprecating his own father's profession.

Killer-Healer

Nizhalkkuthu opens with a background note, letters in white flashing on a black screen: 'In the early 1940s before India became independent, death by hanging was a common punishment in the princely state of Travancore, South India. The State had its own professional executioner, traditionally the head of a designated family. Placed in a border village, he was kept away from mainstream society. The Maharaja granted him many privileges and monetary benefits with every hanging. The rope for the hanging was made by the inmates of the central jail. After use, it was kept with the hangman in his prayer room. The rope, when ritually burnt, was used as holy ash to heal the sick.'

Kaliyappan is haunted by a feeling of guilt that the last man he hanged was innocent and so seeks relief in drink. Film critic Maithili Rao describes the scene (*Cinema in India*, January–March 2003):

> We first meet Kaliyappan at that ubiquitous Kerala institution – the wayside thatched liquor den where men congregate singly or in a group to down the faintly milky brew poured readily into thick glass tumblers by the ever-obliging owner/attendant who also doubles up as gossip-cum-wizened philosopher. Kaliyappan is placating his unquiet conscience, mumbling his thoughts aloud. He is convinced that the last man he hanged was innocent. But there is no way that he can atone for his guilt except to regard himself as not only the instrument of the state but also a tool carrying out the will of Kali, the wrathful dispenser of divine retribution. The camera trains its unrelenting gaze at this old man of uncertain gait and mournful eyes staring out of a stubbed, stoic face. He prostrates before the kumkum-daubed picture of Kali,

> muttering fervent prayers that invoke her compassion and celebrate her unsparing justice.

Kaliyappan is a devout worshipper of Kali, the mother goddess. He who puts an end to so many lives by tightening the noose – supreme irony! – also heals people by treating them with the holy ash from burning the hangman's rope. Both Kaliyappan and the people who leave a few coins in payment firmly believe in the miraculous power of the holy ash. One rainy night, when Kaliyappan returns home from the arrack shop, he finds a worried mother with her sick child awaiting this healing touch. He treats the child by applying the ashes from the burnt rope on its scalp.

Kaliyappan is the antithesis of the conventional image of an executioner being insensitive and loathsome. Instead, he is humble and meek and a family man – a loving husband and father. Adoor says in an interview with K.B. Venu published in *Cinema in India*, April–June 2002:

> *Nizhalkkuthu* is about how empathy evolves in us at different layers and levels. I have an executioner as the protagonist in this film. Society maintains some set notions about both the executioner and the condemned who he hangs to death. We do not consider them as individuals in their specific social and cultural milieu and understand them objectively. The protagonist of this movie should alter your conventional notions of an executioner as the envoy of death. After all like all of us, he too does his job and earns his bread. He too has his family and children.
>
> *Nizhalkkuthu* is also about the process of brutalisation that goes on in our society. Whether you want it or not, you become part of the system. It is only when you identify yourself with other fellow-beings that the process of empathy begins. Then you start responding as a fellow creature … Cinema should be a social document. It can be fiction, not fictitious. It becomes relevant as it attempts to do social, psychological and philosophic probing.

Opposing Elements

In some outstanding cinematic sequences, Adoor juxtaposes scenes of utter contrast, for instance, in the latter part of the film, when the jailor narrates a heartbreaking story, the tragic denouement is preceded by descriptions of the natural beauty of the village.

In an earlier scene, a class teacher who is explaining a poem to the students expounds on the certainty of death. At the same time, Kaliyappan's youngest daughter Mallika attains puberty – a sign of fertility and life. Fertility is set against Death, two opposing elements making up the natural life cycle. Maithili Rao describes the scene (*Cinema in India*, January–March 2003):

> Adoor frames Kaliyappan's family within the dismal greys of a spartan house against the lush green countryside; the camera often cuts to the swaying palms rustling against the tiled roof of the house, subtly underlining the isolation of this Tamil-speaking family from the Malayali ethos. The hangmen were deliberately settled by the State in border areas and the judicial task of taking life was confined to the 'outsider'. Interaction with the locals is limited to holy ash-distribution.
>
> The one person in the family who mingles with others – Mallika, the young daughter – is withdrawn from school when she reaches puberty. There is a deliberate build up of the primal contrast – death versus fertility – in the sequence set in school. The teacher expounds the philosophy of death's inevitability as he explains an obviously classic text while the camera tracks the heavy blood trickling down an ankle. The dark skin under the enveloping *lehanga*, the silver anklet, the deep red of the blood and the startled, almost frightened face of the nubile girl – all enact an ancient ritual …

Mallika's puberty ceremony and celebrations are elaborated in bright detail while the preparations for the hanging are in stark and sombre contrast.

One day, the maharaja's messenger delivers a royal order to Kaliyappan, summoning him to perform an execution. The messenger reads out the order: 'It is hereby ordered by His Highness, the Maharaja of Travancore, that as the court of law has proved, beyond doubt, that one of his subjects has committed the heinous act of premeditated murder, the sentence of death by hanging to be executed on Friday, 7 September 1941. So it is hereby ordained that the hangman, Kaliyappan, son of Chinnappan, residing at East Street, Nagercoil, should proceed to cleanse himself with penance and prayers and be fit to carry out the execution.'

Kaliyappan, already physically and mentally torn, tells the official that he is very old and sick and would not be able to stand the strain. He pleads to the official to look for another person. The official reminds Kaliyappan that His Highness looks after him, gives him food and clothing, and grants him a house and tax-free farm land. So it ill behoves him not to carry out His Highness's order.

Kaliyappan resigns himself to carry out the hanging and embarks on the rituals of self-cleansing. But as the day of execution approaches, the villagers, who gather in his courtyard, realize that Kaliyappan's magical powers to heal are increasing. As for Kaliyappan, he feels that his prime duty is to help the sick with the rope ashes, rather than carry out another hanging. But he finds that the supply of healing rope is coming to an end. The only way to obtain more is to conduct another hanging...

After completing the rituals at home, Kaliyappan is taken to the capital with police escort for the next morning's execution. It is ironical that his son Muthu accompanies him on this bullock-cart journey – Muthu who is a follower of Gandhi. But the young man silently accompanies his father, not raising any objection, nor citing Gandhian principles.

Who is the Criminal? Who the Hanged?

On the eve of the execution, the hangman, according to tradition, has to remain awake the whole night. To keep him awake, usually the warders offer alcohol. But they discover to their chagrin that excessive drinking is instead putting Kaliyappan to sleep.

To keep him awake, the warder narrates a poignant story about a romance between a thirteen-year-old girl and an orphaned flautist, set in a serene and beautiful village. One day, that serenity is suddenly shattered. The flautist and the girl go to a dilapidated house in the middle of the jungle to be together. The boy leaves her for a short while and asks her to wait for him and to continue practising on the flute. But her brother-in-law, who has been following her, seizes her, rapes and kills her. But there is some evidence pointing to the flautist as killer. In spite of knowing the real culprit, the father and the girl's family hide the truth, since a family member is involved.

In his inebriated state, Kaliyappan imagines that the victim in this horrendous story is his daughter Mallika and the culprit is his own son-in-law. He asks what happened to the flautist. The warder grins and says that he is the very boy Kaliyappan will hang at dawn! These words echo like a thunderclap in his ears and Kaliyappan collapses.

The jail superintendent has no alternative but to hand over the responsibility of the hanging to Kaliyappan's son, Muthu. Muthu, the Gandhian, dressed in black and wearing the required headgear, his face and figure heavy with sorrow, walks out to carry out his first execution. Ilaiaraja's music carries the scene to great heights of misery. Adoor said to film critic Lalit Mohan Joshi:

> In the narration of the story, I wanted to use all the five elements of Nature in their raw and untamed manifestations: the Earth in the shape of the primeval mountains and virginal valleys with tall trees and lush vegetation; the Air in the form of the insistent wind that blows through the plains and fields and lends the palmyra trees personality and expression; the Water that cleanses and sustains life and lashes down in torrents swelling streams and soaking the farms; the Fire that lights up the dark and enlightens the mind and soul, and that also burns and reduces everything into ashes; and the Sky, the overwhelming expanse of which makes all human drama and trials look trivial and inconsequential.[68]

In many scenes, the director uses the palmyra tree as one of the characters in the film – a mute and silent witness that observes both the bright and dark side of events. In one instance, Kaliyappan and his wife observe how the son-in-law leaving the house looks upon his sister-in-law Mallika with a sensuous gaze. The camera is close to Kaliyappan's face. His expression of puzzlement and suspicion is unforgettable. Then Adoor cuts to the tall palmyra tree which stands just behind their house. On another occasion, the single tree witnesses the messenger of the Travancore maharaja conveying the order for execution. To make the palmyra tree more human, Adoor focuses on the sound of the tree.

Nizhalkkuthu's sound recordist N. Harikumar says, 'After shooting, we went to collect ambient sound. The ambient sound differs in the early morning, in the afternoon and in the evening. As I have said to you, Adoor is very particular about recording the morning sounds in the morning, evening sounds in the evening. The palmyra tree produces a peculiar sound or noise. We were recording sound then in the analogue format which had some limitations and could not reproduce that peculiar sound clearly. I was tense because Adoor, who is very particular about his soundtrack, was insistent on using only that sound. One of the sound engineers of the film, Dominique Vieillard from France, had with him a good recorder and microphone which was able to record the sound. However, the location was very windy which complicated matters. And of course, it had to be the same palmyra tree and at the same location, in a remote corner of Kanyakumari. But if you listen closely, you can hear a sound of the palmyra tree when it is in the frame.'

S. Sivaraman, GM (Technical Operations) in Chennai's Prasad Lab, testifies to Adoor's meticulousness. 'Adoor is a perfectionist and does not compromise – he wants to get the best results from the technicians of the lab. He will reject and reject until the prints arrive at the right look and colour. He knows exactly what he wants and is very particular about the results – that's why his films are well appreciated all over the world, and that's why all the technicians are eager to do their best for him.'

Celebrated film critic Chidananda Dasgupta wrote on *Nizhalkkuthu*:

> With *Nizhalkkuthu*, Adoor reaches new heights, bringing together various strands developed in earlier films. For the first time in his work there is a lyrical passage of deliberately emphasised, declared, visual charm in the love scenes, in the faces and body of the characters and also in landscapes. A remarkable story, written by Adoor himself, leaves us thinking more than ever before. The many strands of the story, especially the story within story, make the film rich in ambiguities. What makes it even more interesting is a curious detachment in recounting the love story; it is as though we have seen it all before and will do again. That it is obviously a variation of the Radha-Krishna legend is only a small part of the feeling it arouses in us ...[69]

Das Gupta goes on to remark that the hangman is altogether the opposite of any image that the word might conjure up. All facile assumptions are challenged. The picture that emerges, instead, is of a man caught up in a mesh of his time and circumstances – which seeks to rid us of the very habit of making ready assumptions. The audience is forced to think of the universal meaning hinted at, of numerous ordinary people who must often act as hangmen of sorts, handing out punishments, deserved or undeserved, to people for whom redemption comes too late.

In the earlier part of the film, Adoor introduces two villagers (one from an upper class, the other his assistant from the lower rungs of society) discussing how a big man escaped punishment and an innocent boy was made scapegoat and condemned to death.

On another occasion, the two are debating the sin of killing an innocent man. A number of questions arise. Who is accountable to God for the death of the innocent? The assistant feels that the maharaja must answer to God as he is the one who pronounces the death sentence. But the master points out that the maharaja is not technically responsible as he issues a pardon for the man to be hanged which is intentionally delivered only after the hanging is done. This is so that the maharaja may escape the karmic consequences of this sin.

Then who is responsible? Is it the hangman? But ironically, the hangman always offers prayers to Goddess Kali before the execution, pleading that he is just a medium in her hands. His prayer, 'You are the sin as well as the sinner', signifies that he passes the blame to Goddess Kali herself.

'How does one death help another life?' is the question that is tearing Kaliyappan apart. He is just a puppet in the hands of the system – a puppet that cannot raise his voice against the Travancore maharaja. Kaliyappan cannot determine the course of life because he is chained to forces he cannot escape from. Played by Oduvil Unnikrishnan, his emotional and psychological conflict hits you full force.

As the drama builds in the film, the camera seems to inch closer and closer. Adoor's long-time cameraman, seventy-five-year-old Ravi Varma, though unwell, was persuaded to join the *Nizhalkkuthu* crew while Sunny Joseph was chosen as standby for safety. Mankada Ravi Varma had been the cinematographer on all of Adoor's films right from *Swayamvaram*. He recalls how they shot for one of Adoor's best works, *Elippathayam*, in a village where the power situation was miserable. 'As we had no money to hire a generator, we had drawn electric power from the mains of the house we were shooting in. But the supply was erratic. There were days when we used to sit idle for hours waiting for the supply to come on. Somebody from the unit would go to the electricity board office on a bicycle to speed them up! We had to bear with many difficulties. But we were so passionate about films that we were willing to sacrifice everything.'[70]

It all turned out worthwhile for Ravi Varma, who found the experience intellectually enriching. The film went on to win the state's best cinematography award for Varma and Joseph. It was the script that convinced him to say yes to the film-maker. As usual, Adoor first sent the script of *Nizhalkkuthu* to Ravi Varma and followed it up with a call the very next day to know his reaction. Says Varma, 'It was quite different from anything he had written earlier. Unlike his earlier films, it had a very strong story element. It had more depth too. The story was half sentimental and half intellectual, which again was something new as far as Adoor's films are concerned. I told him I liked the script very much. It is always better to have a second opinion about your script because you cannot be objective about what you write. And even better to have the opinion of somebody who knows you and who has been working with you.'

For Sunny Joseph, '*Nizhalkkuthu* was an inspirational experience. I learned many things from the shoot, especially how to mould actors into characters. I have been fortunate to receive the affection and attention of two of the great creators of Malayalam cinema – Adoor sir and Ravi Varma sir.'

Naalu Pennungal *(Courtesy: Kerala State Chalachithra Academy)*

15

Naalu Pennungal (Four Women)

Awareness Rising

The process of modernization in Kerala society in the early decades of the twentieth century can be seen as the product of the anti-colonial, anti-feudal struggle that paved the way for profound changes in class relations and societal norms; the reform movements that sought to cleanse the society of evils like untouchability and social segregation on the basis of caste, polygamy and female servitude; the struggle against feudal mores which led to a thorough restructuring of the family, not only among the oppressed classes but also among the privileged strata.

The effects of this radical process were most visible in the cultural realm. Artistic works imbued with reformist zeal appeared in large numbers. The spirit of enlightenment characteristic of the times led to a wholesale critique of the decadent feudal culture (which had reduced women into sex objects, the mere playthings of caste-Hindu overlords) and conferred a certain measure of dignity upon women ... they began to emerge on the social scene as actants with the rudiments of individuality...[71]

The repressed voices of women inspired creative writers in Malayalam to raise their own: the 1950s was an epoch-making era as litterateurs like Thakazhi Sivasankara Pillai, P. C. Kuttikrishnan (Uroob), P. Kesava Pillai (P. Kesavadev), Sankaran Kutty Pottekkatt, et al. turned the light on to feminine identity in their works.

Adoor Gopalakrishnan, always a voracious reader, had even as a schoolboy read Thakazhi, Basheer, Kesavadev, and admired them all.

Though he was not enamoured of doing films for television (which get shown a few times and are then forgotten), when Doordarshan proposed to Adoor that he should make a film on stories by the celebrated Thakazhi Sivasankara Pillai and, what's more, agreed to give him theatrical rights, he was more than agreeable. In preparation, Adoor read almost four hundred of Thakazhi's stories but this time with the perspective of whether they would suit the medium of cinema. *Naalu Pennungal* was the first film in the assignment and was followed by *Oru Pennum Randaanum* in 2008.

The film, set in the verdant Kuttanad area in Kerala, follows the travails, in the face of social constraints, of four village women from the 1940s to the 1960s. As Adoor said to John Mary, in an interview published in *Outlook*, women have always had a strong presence in his films, whether it is Sita in *Swayamvaram*, Santhamma in *Kodiyettam*, Rajamma in *Elippathayam*, the grandmother in *Kathapurushan* or the unseen woman prisoner in *Mathilukal*. In another interview, he added that in many of his films the weaker and indecisive ones were the male characters. In *Naalu Pennungal*, Adoor raises a characteristic ironic voice against male chauvinism. Film critic C. Gouridasan Nair agrees part of the way:

> Adoor's films are (largely) centred on men caught in a world of crumbling structures and ideologies. Women are there mostly to reflect the existential dilemmas of his male protagonists, without any inner life of their own. But Adoor's *Naalu Pennungal* (Four Women) focuses on women, four of them, each trapped in stations and situations in life that call for a tremendous amount of endurance and resistance.

This is Adoor's third film to be adapted from a written work, after *Mathilukal* and *Vidheyan*. The four women are drawn from four independent short stories by Thakazhi Sivasankara Pillai, one of the most prolific of Malayali writers and recipient of the Jnanpith Award. All the four stories depict the plight of women in mid-twentieth-century central Kerala, the limited space and time in which most of Thakazhi's stories dwell upon. In the course of the four stories – *The Prostitute*, *The Virgin*, *The Housewife* and *The Spinster* – we witness the rising level of self-awareness in the women.

Film critic Paresh C. Palicha writes in his article, 'Adoor's *Naalu Pennungal*: A Unique Experience' (5 November 2007):

> The thin line between promiscuity and morality, fidelity and desires, and also the clash between wishes and deprivation is what the auteur par excellence tries to explore in *Naalu Pennungal* ... The four stories are set in an era when social upheaval and turmoil seemed to be settling down. But people are still shocked when individual women make drastic choices. The brilliance of these stories shines through as they happen on the cusp of a change.

The four women in the film belong to four different strata of society. The first is a street prostitute, the second a farm worker, the third is a lower-middle-class housewife and the fourth is from the ranks of the middle class. The social milieu thus changes from story to story – as the dress indicates. For example, the kaili is usually worn by the working class, the *roukka* is a traditional sort of slack blouse worn by women of the upper class and finally, there is the modern sari and blouse worn by characters in the fourth story. The opening title of the film is placed against the flowing water of a river during the daytime, while the closing title is set at the time of twilight.

There is a passage of about twenty-five years from the first film to the last. The characters in the stories do not have any direct link with one another but each casts reflections on the others. It is for the audience to discern how the stories add up to a whole picture.

In *The Prostitute*, the heroine and her avowed husband, a head-load worker, are not aware of their rights, and unquestioningly accept the punishment for prostitution dealt out by the court. In *The Virgin*, Kumari is representative of all those girls who are blamed for the break-up of a marriage though really the bridegroom is at fault. *The Housewife* leads a fairly contented life with her husband, until a visiting classmate disturbs the placid waters. *The Spinster* depicts how the elder sister is bypassed by a suitor and the younger one selected. This too is a common occurrence in many Indian families.

'*Naalu Pennungal* deals with women's problems. (But) it is a timeless creation that would always be valid. It goes beyond the time in which it is set,' says Bina Paul Venugopal, the artistic director of the International

Film Festival of Kerala. The film had a successful run in Kerala and was the most popular of Adoor's films on the international festival circuit.

Tribute to a Favourite Writer

Naalu Pennungal afforded Adoor an opportunity to work on short stories (and short fiction films) for the first time. Here was an author he had grown up reading, and here was the chance to pay him a tribute. Short stories often deal with a single idea, but Adoor likes to layer his films not only with multiple levels of narration but also details of the period, its people and relationships, so that the story comes alive on screen._

The Prostitute draws a picture of Kunju Pennu, a street prostitute who knows her mother's name was Bhargavi but doesn't know who her father is. She regularly tucks a jasmine into her hair after her bath every evening to attract customers. An honest hard-working orphan, Papu Kutty, who lives in the same town, offers to marry her and wishes to live with her despite knowing her profession. He says to her friend, 'I'll care for her with all my heart. And she'll be a good support to an orphan like me.'

Kunju Pennu and Papu Kutty sleep on the pavement as they are homeless. Bonded by love, they decide to live as husband and wife and do not feel the need of a formal marriage. Kunju Pennu says to Papu Kutty, 'Look here, I'm the wife and you are my husband, right?' To which he replies, 'That's already decided between us.' And so Kunju Pennu gives up her profession as a prostitute and begins to work as a labourer, carrying gravel on her head for laying roads. A surprised supervisor asks her what made her take up hard manual labour, to which she replies that she needs to earn a decent living. Disbelieving, he taunts her, 'Poor thing, you look exhausted. Why tire yourself? I could send you the money you need!' She retorts, 'Please don't say such things. I'm living with my man.'

Kunju Pennu now begins to dream of leading a life of respect and dignity. She will leave her past behind, she will work hard to earn her livelihood. Her friend advises, 'It's time you left the pavement. You should find a roof to sleep under with your man, set up a home with him.'

But the town people cannot believe what they are seeing. One of the drunken town rowdies misbehaves with her, 'What! You've the nerve? Since when have you started playing the virgin?' The result is a furious brawl between the rowdy and Papu Kutty. The rowdy decides to have his revenge.

One night, when Kunju Pennu and Papu Kutty are sleeping peacefully, they are woken up and arrested by the police. In court, the official reads out the charge, 'On the night of 30 June 1946, at 11.30 p.m., you two were found in a compromising position on the pavement adjacent to the shop of the wholesale dealer Damodaran Pillai and were taken into custody by the police and produced before the court.' Kunju Pennu resolutely states that it is not illicit sex as they are husband and wife. Even the judge insults them: 'No home, no hometown, no parents and they claim to be husband and wife!' He rules that they remain under custody for fourteen days.

In the next court session, the rowdy Joseph testifies as a witness, 'This woman, Kunju Pennu, is a street prostitute. And Papu Kutty is a ruffian who arrived here recently.' Since the helpless couple cannot legally prove they are a married couple, they are sentenced to fourteen days in jail for the crime of prostitution. Gautaman Bhaskaran says in *Adoor Gopalakrishnan: A Life in Cinema*, 'As Kunju Pennu and Papu Kutty are taken away, we realise how cruel the system can be, how unrelentingly insensitive.' Critic Palicha writes:

> The story predictably has an ironical ending where the couple is separated and punished for aspiring to build their future together without any official sanction. But the sweet gist of the story lies in the depiction of the intimate relationship between the couple, where they discuss their wages or dream of having a roof over their heads.

Daughter Returned

The second film, *The Virgin*, talks about a young woman Kumari who runs her home with her meagre earnings. Her ailing father and her mother depend on her. Her father boasts to a neighbour, 'To be honest, today it is she who runs this house. She took over when I fell ill and started to work as a very young girl. Mother and daughter look after me, she buys all my medicines. She is unlike other girls of her age. She won't waste a paisa – she even manages to save from her meagre earnings.'

Kumari is of marriageable age, yet the proposals of marriage don't work out. Many believe that the fault lies in her stars. Then there is a proposal from the adjacent village: the boy is Narayanan who runs a small shop at the boat jetty. He is the only son of his mother, who is all praise for him, '... won't spend a paisa, doesn't drink, no friends at all. Won't smoke even a beedi. I've raised him that strictly. The one habit he cannot get away from is watching every film on the first day of its release ...'

In no time at all, the marriage is arranged. However, on the very day he takes Kumari home, he says to his mother, 'Mother, I'm leaving for the shop. I expect good business. It's a festive day at the church.' Thereafter too Narayanan shows no inclination for physical contact with his wife. Once, Kumari takes the initiative to attract his attention in bed but he declines, complaining about the sultry weather. This strange behaviour of her husband is not explained. Eventually, Narayanan takes Kumari to her parental house and, after partaking of a hearty meal, leaves never to return.

Rumours spread over her husband leaving her thus. The illiterate village women gossip, 'It's difficult to find a man of such good character. The girl has no morals. He came to know about it.' Another woman comments, 'Her looks are so misleading.' Even Kumari's mother is confused. 'Why is he not taking you back? It's been a month since he left you here...' Kumari, who knows first-hand that her husband is disinterested in sexual relations, cannot reveal to society why they are not truly husband and wife. The ending suggests an image of a woman on the rise. When Kumari's father is speaking to the village boy about her divorce, Kumari who overhears their conversation, suddenly comes out of the house to clarify, 'There has been no marriage. Then why quarrel over a divorce?' Firmly stating to her father that 'We are not man and wife,' she goes in. In the next frame, Adoor shows her father, her mother and the village boy looking at her with astounded faces.

Resisting Temptation

The housewife of the third story is Chinnu Amma, who leads a happy and contented life with her husband, Raman Pillai, in spite of being childless. The third person in this triangular tale is Nara Pillai, a father of eight, whose mother lives in the same village as Chinnu Amma.

Nara Pillai is known as a person of good character who dutifully visits his old mother every now and again. According to one of the village ladies, if a meal is offered he joins in, no matter who offers it. 'Last time, he shared simple rice gruel with us and said that it was the best he had tasted in a long time. He helps the needy. He is very kind.'

One day, Nara Pillai, who is an old classmate of Chinnu Amma's, drops in at her home and, in the course of their conversation, learns that she is childless. He insists that the problem is with her husband. Pillai, aware of how a woman longs for a child of her own, narrates a story of a rich landlord in Rajapalayam who owns a huge expanse of land but does not have any children. He prayed to the gods at all the major temples but in vain. However, he had a handsome horse-cart driver and one day, the landlord's wife asked the driver to have an oil bath, apply perfume and come to her room. She followed him in and locked the door. This is one of the most sensual sequences in Adoor's cinema.

Nara Pillai's sweet talk sparks a psychological conflict in Chinnu Amma. She tells her husband, 'He's so affectionate. After all these years he still visits relatives and friends.' Chinnu Amma's mind vacillates between having a clandestine relationship with Nara Pillai and remaining faithful to her husband. But she soon regains control over herself and refuses his proposal. 'No, my friend. No, you better go, return to your town. Go and look after your wife and children.'

In the last scene, Adoor pans the camera from the window of the house to a room where two elderly women are shown sitting and listening to Chinnu Amma with rapt attention. Chinnu Amma herself, also aged now, is outside the frame but we can feel the strength of character in her voice. 'Maybe I could have had a child to look after me in my old age. But, then, how can one be sure? Today at least I have my honour and virtue intact.'

Learning to Live on Her Own

The Spinster tells the tale of Kamakshi, a girl belonging to a middle-class family comprising her widowed mother, an elder brother and two sisters. The film opens with repeated knocking at a door and a male voice whispering, 'Kamakshi, open the door,' and a woman's reply, 'No, please go away.' The male voice insists, 'But you asked me to come, Kamakshi …'

The narrative then goes back to the events that led to this night. To begin with, there is a marriage proposal for Kamakshi – but the groom chooses her younger sister, the more attractive and youthful Subhadra.

Once, when Kamakshi is returning from the village pond, a young man whistles at her. An elderly villager passing by, protests, 'Do you know her? She may not be married yet but she is not the kind of woman you think. Go your way!'

Her worried mother asks the matchmaker, 'Can't you find a good proposal for her? She's over thirty now. We want someone from a decent family and of good character. The younger one is also growing up … I can die in peace only when Kamakshi settles down.' But that is not to be. Kamakshi's elder brother, after a long wait, gets married and, in due course, her youngest sister Sarojam too. Suddenly, the mother dies and Kamakshi is left all alone in the house.

Kamakshi has no alternative but to shift to the home of her sister Subhadra. Everything goes well in the beginning. Subhadra's husband expresses regret to Kamakshi for rejecting her, 'What I did to you is unpardonable.'

Some village women mistake her for the wife. And her sister starts imagining Kamakshi is having an affair with her husband. Kamakshi overhears her sister saying to her husband, 'I hear such malicious rumours. They say you're keeping us two sisters as your wives … mother has gifted her the house and enough to live on. Let her go there and leave us in peace.' Kamakshi, in a fit of rage and embarrassment, returns to her ancestral home, refusing to live either with her brother or her sisters. She tells her younger sister Subhadra who has come along with her, 'Have you not heard the saying, "Like the pillar holds the house, one should hold oneself." I've now become the pillar of this house.'

Then the narrative returns to the beginning of the film. A man knocks at the door but this time, the camera focuses on Kamakshi who says, 'Please go away. I'm not the kind of person you think. It was a mistake. Please pardon me. My mind wavered a little – but it will not do so again. It should not be impossible for a woman to live her life without a man …' The fourth story ends at this point where, flouting social norm, Kamakshi decides to live on her own.

Nandita Das, who plays Kamakshi, talks about her experience:

> Kamakshi represents the vulnerability to societal pressures that women often have to put up with. While it is a kind of period film, the theme is still relevant to our contemporary society. Even now the identity of a woman is largely dependent on her marital status. But through all the ages women have rebelled and negotiated their circumstances to

> find their own inner strength. Kamakshi, for me, also represents that strength.

Why did Adoor choose Nandita Das for the role? He says, 'When I wrote the script, I thought Nandita Das would be most suitable for that role. Also, she looks very much like a Malayali, you cannot tell that she is an outsider. It's probably because of her Oriya roots.'

Since Adoor usually does not take non-Malayali actors as he is very particular about the spoken word, Nandita Das recalls that she was pleasantly surprised when he called her to play the role. Though she had known Adoor for long, she had never had the opportunity to work with him. 'When he told me the story, I found it both compelling and relevant … He is one of the very few eminent film-makers who have really stuck to their commitment to good cinema. So it was an honour to have been asked to work with him.'

In *The Prostitute*, the challenging role of Kunju Pennu, a street prostitute of the pre-Independence era, went to another non-Malayali, Padmapriya Janakiraman, who debuted in a Telugu film in 2003. When I ask how she prepared herself for this role, she says, 'Well, other than mentally getting ready to work with Adoor sir, since there is not much material available in real life or on the net about street prostitutes of that era, I really didn't know what to prepare for. Sometimes it is probably best that way … Imagine you are blind and your partner leads you everywhere, it builds some sort of a very special bond. It is not easy to let go and allow yourself to be led, but it was what I did with Adoor sir.'

Did she face any difficult situations in playing the part? Besides working without a language prompt, she says laughing, 'One of the scenes began with me spitting and, you know, women from the area spit in a certain way. We were shooting outdoors and had an audience which was expert in spitting in that particular way on a daily basis. I was obviously not getting it. So we reshot many times. I don't know what the audience was thinking, but it seemed to me a bit funny. Anyway, my shamelessness and Adoor's resilience made sure we got the spit right for the camera and I have since then become an expert in spitting that way – not in public though!'

One of the finest scenes in *The Spinster*, aesthetically speaking, is when Kamakshi returns to her ancestral house in a slow-moving boat. The rippling sound of the rivulet is used as an image to interpret the psychological state of Kamakshi. In another set-up, Kamakshi is positioned in the doorway of a dark house, and against the backdrop of the bright daylight, Adoor frames her shadow to imply the trials and tribulations she will face.

While focusing on gender identity, *The Spinster* weaves in the disenchantment of the people of Kerala with the new government of 1957 set up under the leadership of E.M.S. Namboodiripad. After the scene involving the man knocking at Kamakshi's door, Adoor cuts to a conversation of elderly persons who criticize the leaders of the newly formed government: 'All would be well, we were told, once the British were driven out. But where are we now? Look at our leaders. Leading street processions and governing the state are poles apart! You need to have the maturity, credibility, discipline – and foresight. We need to plan for tomorrow for our future generations. What use are the promises they made so far, were they at all practical?'

Adoor Gopalakrishnan's *Naalu Pennungal* premiered in the master's section of the 2007 Toronto International Film Festival, sharing the screen with film-makers like Eric Rohmer, Claude Chabrol and Ken Loach, and was screened thereafter in more than fifty international film festivals round the world. At the 2008 Brussels Film Festival, it was one of the international films selected to compete for the prestigious L'Age d'Or prize for original and path-breaking cinema. In India, *Naalu Pennungal* won Adoor Gopalakrishnan his fifth National Award for Best Director.

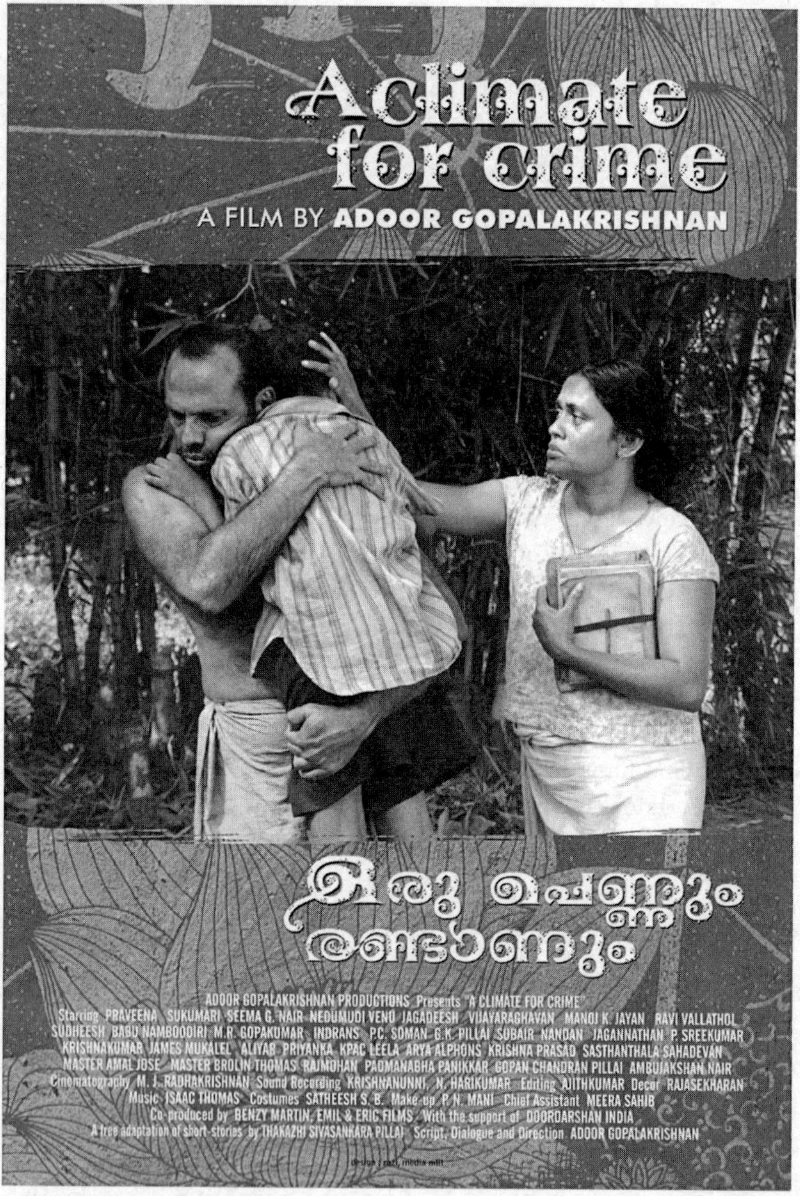

(Courtesy: Kerala State Chalachithra Academy)

16

Oru Pennum Randaanum (A Climate for Crime)

In the Season of Shortages

Oru Pennum Randaanum (again based on stories written by that doyen of Malayalam literature, Thakazhi Sivasankara Pillai) examines crimes, small and big, and raises philosophical queries about the basis of crime and what crime is constituted of. The film is original in approach and has a slow meditative pace and mystic appeal. The strains of philosophical thought and mystic beauty lying beneath the surface of the stories of social issues provide the film a distinctive place in the array of quality cinema in India.

The success of the film with audiences may be attributed to the fact that viewers have accepted and appreciated the larger issues layered behind the façade of the simple stories, thanks to Adoor's style of presenting the stories through metaphor and allusion. Add to this Adoor's keen sense of humour and dramatic acumen which are always draws.

Oru Pennum Randaanum is more reflective than passionate, and maintains a detachment in the mode of expression which is generally considered a distinctive quality of his film-making. C.S. Venkiteswaran writes in his article 'The Work of a Master' (*The Hindu*, 5 June 2009):

> *Oru Pennum Randaanum* is a rumination upon the gaping chasm between law and justice, one that sucks human lives and destinies into its vortex ... the film captures their seismic rumblings through the lives of people in this faraway place, which turns out to be a microcosm of

> the larger picture: that of history churning people's lives, and pressing upon its horizon ... Significantly, the detached format of the film shuns temptations of condemnation, sloganeering or explication. It does not resort to 'explaining' away human lives through any social or psychological reasons, nor does it treat its characters as pieces in a jigsaw puzzle. They are all there, all too real creatures of nature and culture, living out their destinies in all its unpredictability and quirkiness...

The film (released 2008) covers the period of the1940s in the princely state of Travancore. The Second World War had a terrible impact on British India, with a growing dearth of basic goods and mounting unemployment, scarcity of day-to-day requirements like food, clothing, kerosene and petrol. Unemployment escalated while hoarding of grains became routine. Set against this backdrop, the four stories in this film relate to crimes committed by the deprived as well as the comparatively privileged landed gentry. Adoor says:

> The four chapters of the film tell stories independent of each other. What connects them is the recurring theme of crime. Starting from simple, parable-like tales about ordinary people, the narrative slowly takes on complex issues of love, loyalty and morality. It culminates in the contemporary legend of Panki, the irresistible village beauty whose loves and relationships are not circumscribed by marriage. Unlike in my earlier films, here I have used dialogue predominantly to comment, endorse or simply report on the course of the plot in a narrative form akin to that of the epics where reportage plays a major role in making the experience larger than life.
>
> When someone narrates a story whether from the past or present, he inserts his own adjectives and emotions to describe the events and the characters so as to captivate or impress his audience. No storytelling can be fully objective: the subjective element gathers new dimensions each time a story is told and retold. The story of the Mahabharata is about the rivalry between cousins. One set is virtuous and the other, valiant but villainous. The fight becomes one of virtue versus vice. The elemental storyline is embellished and details keep piling up into sub-stories and incidents and several characters get appended along the way. The real and the appendages become inseparable. In this way, simple stories take on epic proportions in narration.

The four chapters of the film *The Thief*, *The Police*, *Two Men and a Woman*, and *One Woman, Two Men* reflect the socio-political state of Kerala just before Independence. In the first story, *The Thief*, a son ardently longs to reform his father who is by temperament and need a thief; in the second, two corrupt policemen plot to frame an innocent rickshaw puller in a case of burglary. *Two Men and a Woman* is about a university student who is mentally tormented after impregnating a servant girl, while in *One Woman, Two Men*, two men fight over a woman who is unwilling to indicate whom she prefers.

The official website of the International Film Festival of Rotterdam has high praise for *Oru Pennum Randaanum*, for the superb depiction of each story that captures the echoes of a past time and place, yet is universal. It noted: 'Although this never-ending search for a better life, human dignity and love is seriously rendered, it still radiates the romantic idea of human endurance, hope, guilt and a sense of justice. That makes this rather calm and lyrical film, which is obviously deeply culturally rooted, universal.'

Through the Eyes of a Schoolboy

The background to *The Thief* is the era of shortages of basic requirements in British India as a result of the Second World War. This story about crime and punishment is narrated through the eyes of a schoolboy.

Kunjunni (brilliantly played by young Amal Jose), known as 'son of a thief' in school, is constantly embarrassed to find his father, Neelantan, getting involved in theft. Neelantan argues that he has no other choice because thieving helps him sustain his family. Once, Kunjunni gets involved in a brawl over the profession of his father with his classmate Kurien.

Neelantan approaches Kurien's father, Mathai, and warns him not to pass on the prejudices of parents to children. This stricture from a thief offends Mathai who in retaliation reports to the police that Neelantan should be locked up. This is done. Kunjunni persuades his mother to talk to his father about giving up stealing.

Two years go by. It is an unforgettable emotional moment when Kunjunni comes home from school one afternoon and finds a full meal and new clothes laid out for him! At once he realizes that his father has been released from jail and is back to his old ways. Kunjunni says to his mother, 'Where have you got new clothes for me? Has father come? You are lying, mother. Father must have come.' But Kunjunni's mother hugs and caresses him, saying she will tell his father not to steal any more.

One of the various narratives woven into the film/films is the story Kunjunni relates from his school book to his father about two friends, Malyan (fat and strong) and Madhavan (thin and intelligent). Strolling through a dense forest, they vow to remain united whatever dangers the forest poses. But when they see a large bear approaching, Malyan rapidly climbs a tree while Madhavan does not know how to. Instead, he lies down on the ground, and holds his breath. When the bear nears, it smells his ears, then presuming the boy is dead, slowly ambles away. When Malyan clambers down he is curious to know what the bear whispered into his friend's ears. Madhavan replies, 'It advised me not to believe a fake friend!' Implying to Neelantan that he should give up his unlawful activities and stay loyal to his family. But Neelantan has his own philosophy to justify his actions, 'I cannot get a job, how then do I feed myself and my family?'

M.R. Gopakumar, who played the role of Neelantan, says, 'I worked very hard to get the character perfect. The scene in which I am in the lock-up and my wife and son are crying and praying to the policeman to release me is one of the most touching scenes in the film. In Malayalam films, scripts are given to the actors before the shots. But Adoor sir prefers to read the script and explain the situation, the mood and tone of the scene. Also in his films, unlike the usual ones, there is no prompting, however long the duration of the shot. Before the shot we are told in detail about our performance. The way he reads it out I always listen to him with rapt attention.'

Policing the Police

The second story, *The Police*, again set in Kerala of the 1940s, zooms in on the corruption prevalent among the police force. An upright police inspector is posted at a local police station to probe an 'unsolved' case of a theft in a merchant's shop. Complaints have been received against the head constable Kuttan Pillai and his assistant constable Mathu (played by veteran actors Nedumudi Venu and Jagannathan respectively) that they have shared the loot in cahoots with the culprit.

Sternly, the police inspector gives the two scheming policemen a week's time to solve the case, failing which they have to face dire consequences. As they have taken their shares of the booty, they hesitate to arrest the culprit. In a state of extreme confusion they go to a toddy shop to mull over developments.

In course of their debate, Mathu notices a rickshaw puller from Ernakulam opening an envelope of money from the folds of his dhoti and takes advantage of this golden opportunity. The honest richshaw puller is accused of burglary and threatened with severe consequences if he does not confess to the crime. Moreover, he will lose all his savings if he tries to defend himself. Mathu convinces the rickshaw puller to admit to the crime for which he would be jailed for a maximum term of ten days. But this so-called 'criminal' is devastated when the judge sentences him to six months' imprisonment. He has no choice but to accept his fate. This is the so-called justice of the legal system! Police brutality, their manipulations and the legal machinery are plainly satirized in this story.

A Different Kind of Test

Two Men and a Woman is another satire, this time about members of the inhibited middle class who take advantage of the poor. University student Krishnankutty is infatuated with a servant girl working at the lodge where he stays. He seduces her but when he finds she is pregnant, he is terribly scared that his family will be socially disgraced. Being completely dependent on them, he is aware that once his errant act is revealed to his family, particularly his uncle, they would stop paying for his tuition. Besides, according to the matrilineal system, he is under obligation to marry the daughter of the head of the joint family. He falters between his responsibility to his family and the girl he has impregnated. The choice seems to be between suicide and abortion.

He seeks help from his lawyer friend and together they undertake a tortuous journey to a quack who performs abortions. But here, Adoor gives a dramatic twist to the story…

The film is intricately designed. Witness the scene of the journey across the river, set in a slow boat on a still night. The main characters, Krishnankutty and Unni, his advocate friend, are pensive and silent while the boatman (who is their classmate) holds forth philosophically on the quirks of destiny which made him a boatman rather than an educated young man like them. He got married when he was just twenty-one years old and soon fathered three children. Krishnankutty and Unni listen to the boatman, saying nothing, exchanging looks. But the boatman's philosophic venting is an eye-opener for the guilt-ridden Krishnankutty. It could be the reason why the irresolute young man finally decides to marry her and defy his family, in spite of discovering that the girl is in fact not pregnant.

A May–December Wedding

The fourth story, *One Woman, Two Men*, centres around Pankiamma, a woman of elegance and beauty, who captures the imagination of the village men. The elderly Rama Kurup gives up everything, including his wife and children, to tie the knot with her. A marriage between an old husband and a young wife is inevitably fraught with problems. He is possessive and shoos away the curious people who loiter outside his house. He is suspicious of his wife's behaviour and rightly so as it turns out when one night he finds Panki's lover, Kittu Kurup, in their room. Rama stabs Kittu. Kittu survives. Rama is arrested for attempted murder but released on bail. These scenes are not picturized by Adoor but the information is conveyed through an elderly woman Bhagirathi narrating this drama to her bedridden husband, and adding a fresh dimension to the film.

However, as the case proceeds in the court of law, supporters of the two sides clash in the street, killing people in the process. The court rules that both Rama Kurup and Kittu Kurup be imprisoned for three years each for provoking murder and mayhem. Panki, urged by each man to side with him as witness, is impartial. In prison, the men patch up their enmity and decide to face Panki together on their release.

In one delectably shot scene, Kittu Kurup describes the incident to the police from his hospital bed. The camera first focuses on the saline bottle on the stand by the bed, then slowly tilts down to catch the face of Kittu Kurup. As he goes on describing the confrontation, the camera pans at a snail's pace to the right of the frame to bring into focus the other characters standing there: the policeman, the doctor, the nurse and family members. Both tale and listeners are revealed in this gradual way.

The ending of the story is riveting as the one-time rivals now turned friends arrive to confront Panki at her home – but, as they soon find out, the joke is on them! Panki now has a third man in her life!

Redrawing the Short Story

The proposition to make films based on the popular short stories of Thakazhi Sivasankara Pillai was made by Doordarshan, India's national channel, to Adoor who was asked to choose any of the literary works of the veteran writer. *Naalu Pennungal* and *Oru Pennum Randaanum* were the result. Both films share the same geographical and temporal setting, and a four-story structure based on four independent short stories in each case.

As regards the adaptation, Adoor said to Gautaman Bhaskaran:

> … Making these two movies based on short stories was quite challenging because a good short story is invariably about one idea that is etched economically in words. When you attempt to make a film based on it, suddenly it turns out to offer several possibilities at the same time. So, one needs to take the liberty of redrawing its contours anew keeping the basic idea for inspiration, but proceeding on your own without fear or doubts about transgressing the terrain of the writer.
>
> I like and respect Thakazhi's work. But I think it also becomes mine when it is crafted into a movie … it is a free adaptation, not a literal one.

Adoor does not give us purely upright or utterly corrupt characters in his works – his true-to-life characters are painted in shades of grey. He shapes, reconstructs and moulds the characters from his chosen perspective. The characters are all played by perfectly selected, highly talented actors: M.R. Gopakumar as Neelantan, Praveena as the fickle Pankiamma, veterans Nedumudi Venu and Jagannathan who play the policemen, Krishnakumar as the rickshaw puller, Master Amal Jose as the naive son of a thief – with Adoor as the perfect artisan to mould these lifelike and universal characters. Journalist Saraswathy Nagarajan (*The Hindu*, 7 August 2009) quotes Adoor in the article 'Crime in the Time of Scarcity': 'Unlike a play, there is no emotional continuity in a film as far as an actor is concerned. It is only the director who knows the film in its totality and so only he can etch out the characters. I cast good actors who can give me what I have visualized in my characters.'

N. Harikumar again records Adoor's zeal for capturing authentic location sound: 'Adoor sir is very particular because every sound adds to the viewers' aesthetic pleasure – whether it is the sound of footsteps, breaking glasses, the cawing of the crow, the chirping of birds, the rippling sound of the river, the clanging sound of the door, the bleating of a calf, or an owl's hoot. He himself returned to the location for another four or five days to collect all the sounds which could not be recorded at the time of shooting.'

Oru Pennum Randaanum bagged numerous Kerala State Film Awards, for Best Feature, Best Director, Best Script, Best Sound, and Second Best Actor to Praveena. The film also travelled to international film festivals in New Jersey, Dubai, Goa, Houston and Rotterdam, gathering accolades all the way.

Conversation with a Maestro

Parthajit Baruah: Do you think it necessary to have any formal training to be a film-maker?

Adoor Gopalakrishnan: It is not essential but it is easier when you familiarize yourself with the equipment and the language of cinema. If you stay an outsider, you are limited to that extent. It is always desirable to learn the basics because you can build on that knowledge. On the other hand, there are many film-makers who have never been to film schools – like Satyajit Ray or Werner Herzog.

PB: Have you been interested in film-making since your childhood?

AG: I had never thought of becoming a film-maker before I went to film school because basically I was a theatre person. I was writing plays, producing them and acting in them throughout my student days. But after one year of study at the Film Institute at Pune, I weaned myself away from the influence of theatre and got involved in cinema. It was all a lucky accident.

PB: Ritwik Ghatak was the vice principal when you were a student there … you have always said you were fortunate to have him as a teacher.

AG: Ritwik Ghatak was a man of letters, a great teacher, an intellectual and above all a great film-maker. As students, we looked up to him with great reverence and learnt many valuable lessons from him.

PB: As a student, you made a comedy, *A Great Day*, but during the forty years of your cinematic journey, you have never tried to make a single comedy.

AG: I have come to realize that you can't impose comedy from the outside. Then it looks laboured and artificial. It has to grow from within a situation. A certain sense of fun is always welcome but the situation and characters should lend themselves to it. I think there is subtle humour in most of my films. The only exception perhaps is *Mukhamukham* – it was too serious a theme for humour.

PB: Two leading film-makers from Kerala, Aravindan and John Abraham, were your contemporaries. How did you relate with them?

AG: Both Aravindan and John Abraham were my friends. I played a major role in coaxing Aravindan to make his first film. He was a good friend till some of his clannish friends contrived to keep us apart. But what was unpardonable was that they did not let him have the doubts an artiste is entitled to and has to struggle with to reinvent himself in his pursuit of cinema. He owes it to his 'friends' that he did not develop the potential he had. John Abraham was my junior at the film institute by two years. He was talented and was a favourite of Ritwik Ghatak. But film-making demands too much of you. One gets enervated and frustrated in the Indian situation as the organized industry is very hostile to anything that is original and innovative. John was very promising and showed flashes of brilliance – but unfortunately he lacked the innate strength and discipline to withstand the pressures associated with film-making. In his case, alcoholism offered him an escape from the realities enveloping cinema.

PB: Why is cinema important to you?

AG: Cinema is the greatest art form the human mind has given shape to. It lends meaning to my life – it is what I live for. I am always under the magic spell of cinema and it is truly wonderful how through it I can share my experience of reality with the viewers.

PB: Do you set out to preach to people through your films?

AG: No, not at all. There is no preaching. I just want to share my experience with the larger audience. Viewers should get the same sort of aesthetic experience from cinema as from other art forms like painting, music and dance.

PB: What are your views on entertainment as provided by our cinema?

AG: For me, the ultimate aim of every art is to entertain its viewers and perceivers. Audiences seek entertainment from cinema as from any other art form. Unfortunately, in our country entertainment is quite often understood in a very superficial way – films must entertain you not with vulgarity, but intellectually and emotionally.

PB: It is quite difficult to obtain funds for serious cinema in India. Did you have difficulty in finding finances right from *Swayamvaram*?

AG: Right from the start of my career I have had funding problems. It continues to be so even after I have made eleven films. The only respite was when Mr Ravi of General Pictures produced four of my films.

PB: Your films are watched by audiences all over the world. Do you watch your own films?

AG: Yes, my films have been travelling all over the world. But I do not like to watch my own films. However, during international film festivals, it is the practice to introduce your film and follow it up with a face-to-face conversation with the audience after the screening.

PB: What time do you prefer for writing your film script? Do you write during your journeys?

AG: I do not write while travelling. Otherwise, I write whenever I feel like it – usually at night, till 1 a.m. or so. Then you are not disturbed by phone calls. I make up for some of the lost sleep by napping in the afternoon.

PB: Films like *Mathilukal, Vidheyan, Naalu Pennungal,* and *Oru Pennum Randaanum* are adapted from literary works. What aspects of those stories touched you to give them a film form?

AG: You may have read a particular story some time in the past just for the pleasure of reading – but it continues to haunt you. You mull over some of the ideas but are not totally satisfied yet to start work on it. Then you revisit the story that left an impression on you and re-examine whether it would lend itself to a cinematic recreation. And whether the original has enough energy or potential to be reinterpreted and recreated. In case of the stories I have adapted, this was the process I went through.

PB: Which films do you prefer making? Films based on your own original stories or adapted stories?

AG: I am at ease with both. I have never felt obliged to be 'faithful' to the original text. I come to own it even as I adapt a story by a writer. My effort is always to go beyond the original inspiration whether it is sourced from within or without. Every time I have adapted a story, I have gone beyond the text and lent it an interpretation of my own. It doesn't simply stop at the story. This does not necessarily mean a negation of the original text. In fact it is in praise of it.

PB: You have always worked with a crew of 'regulars', whether on the camera, sound or music…

AG: Ravi Varma, who is now no more, has been my longest associate. Interestingly, I happen to be the director with whom he has worked most too! In other cases, his association did not go beyond one film. I got to know of Ravi Varma through his brother (my junior at the film institute) who told me that his elder brother was keen to work with film-makers dedicated to serious cinema. He was already working for the BBC and making documentaries.

When I completed writing the script of *Swayamvaram*, I forwarded it to him in Madras. Promptly came his reply: he was very pleased with the script and he foresaw it opening a new direction for Malayalam cinema. He was all too eager to work the camera for this project.

My films have been few and far between. But Ravi Varma worked for all the documentaries and feature films I made ever since. He had the rare quality of refusing to make compromises. As a person, he lived a very simple life but had deep convictions about cinema and culture. He was very well read and had excellent taste in literature and arts. I found in him, although he was very senior to me in age, an ideal companion to discuss one's thoughts and doubts and approach for advice (not necessarily about film-making).

Little energy was wasted in convincing him about the structure, composition, angle or movement in a shot as he would have already read my basic script as well as the shooting script in advance. In fact, he was the only other person in our unit who knew exactly what I was doing.

When I went to Chennai to brief him about the production of *Nizhalkkuthu* in 2002, he had become weak and sickly what with his advanced age and frugal food habits. He advised me to opt for another cameraman. This was not acceptable to me and after a lot of persuasion he agreed to come. When he arrived on the location for the shoot, happily, he was his old self full of enthusiasm and vitality. He surprised all of us including his associate, ace cameraman Sunny Joseph. I had requested him to help in case Ravi Varma got too tired to carry on.

The cinematography of this film was exceptional – but regrettably it happened to be the last film we worked together on.

Another long-time associate of mine was M.B. Srinivasan, the music composer. He had an uncanny sense of cinema and again our association started with *Swayamvaram*. He saw the rough cut and was very enthusiastic about its freshness of approach. From thereon he became a constant companion and associate. He belonged to the leftist movement, having worked with the Indian People's Theatre Association. He was always prepared to listen to you and was very understanding and cooperative. He had the advantage of a thorough knowledge of both Western and Indian music, and his mind was always open to new ideas. Together we carried out many experiments with the music track: increasing and decreasing the speed of the recorded music to create special effects which no other music composer had dared till then. MBS, as we would call him, was a wonderful human being whom I lost with his untimely death a couple of years after we worked together on *Anantaram*.

Another long-time associate was my editor, M. Mani, who edited my films from *Swayamvaram* to *Kathapurushan*. Then the whole system of editing underwent a change. The new technology required editors to be technology-savvy and many of the old-timers had to quit the scene. My dear editor and gentle friend had no option but to leave the profession.

Yet another close associate was Sivan, whom I have known since college days. With me, he adapted to doing the work of an art director at which he proved very efficient. He would make props and special properties required for the film at the shortest notice and I always depended on his resourcefulness. He could not join us in the production of *Nizhalkkuthu* for personal reasons and his place was taken by Marthandam Rajasekharan who has worked with me for the last three films.

How can I not mention P. Devadas, who was my institute mate and constant companion in the beginning of my career even preceding *Swayamvaram*. For a short period he did freelance work with other film-makers but eventually joined the Chitranjali Studio as the chief sound recordist. I did most of my post-production work with him, until he succumbed to a heart attack. There followed Krishnanunni and Harikumar and I have had perfect rapport with both of them.

And, of course, there is my chief assistant Meera Sahib, my loyal and dependable friend and colleague. Popularly known as Meera, he is often taken for a lady by those outside our unit and by viewers who see Meera's name regularly on the credit list of my films! He was a senior bureaucrat in the state service, retiring as head of the Bureau of Economics and Statistics. Starting from the *Kodiyettam* shoot, he has worked with me from the script stage to the very completion of every film that I have made, including the documentaries I made in between.

PB: How do you spend your day when you do not have appointments?

AG: When I am not working, I enjoy reading books and journals.

PB: As a father and as a husband do you think you have been able to give quality time to your family?

AG: Yes, I am basically a family man. I spend most of my time at home. I go out only on work.

PB: Do you worry about routine domestic problems when you are not busy in creative work?

AG: As you know, I take a long time to make my films. There are always long intervals between them. I am very much involved in everything. Like every other middle-class householder I do everything myself – like paying the electricity bill and so on. I lead a simple life, but I am not aloof or cut off.

PB: You make films with a gap of five to seven years between them. What is the reason?

AG: I work and rework on my films. As I research every subject of my films, it takes time. It is like a long period of meditation.

PB: Besides your published plays, you have written four books on cinema. Which readers are these books aimed at?

AG: The four cinema books are for those who have a desire to know about cinema history, its aesthetics, or simply its technical side.

PB: You are a film-maker, writer and playwright. You have achieved a lot. Do you think there are certain things still unfulfilled?

AG: As long as I am capable of making films, I will keep on making them. From time to time, I have been asked about my dream project. But I have no such thing. Every film is a dream till it becomes reality!

Notes

1. Chidananda Dasgupta, *Seeing Is Believing*, Penguin Books India, 2008, p. 248.
2. A. Sreedhara Menon, *A Survey of Kerala History*, DC Books, 2008, p. 14.
3. Ibid., p. 20.
4. Ibid.
5. Avinash C. Pandeya, *The Art of Kathakali*, Munshiram Manoharlal Publishers Pvt. Ltd, 1999, p. 41.
6. Balakrishnan, *Kathakali*, Wisdom Tree, 2004, p. 12.
7. Madhumita Das, thesis titled 'Changing Family System Among a Matrilineal Group in India'.
8. Ibid.
9. K. Ramachandran Nair, *The History of Trade Union Movement in Kerala*, published by the Kerala Institute of Labour and Employment in association with Manak Publications Pvt. Ltd, 2006, p.19.
10. Ibid.
11. Ibid., p. 20.
12. A. Sreedhara Menon, *A Survey of Kerala History*, DC Books, 2008, p. 301.
13. C.S. Venkiteswaran, article titled 'South Asian Cinema: Some Notes on Communist Ideas in Malayalam Cinema: Hope, Disenchantment and Nostalgia', published by South Asian Cinema Foundation, London, p. 158.
14. Janaky Sreedharan, article entitled 'Marriage and Family in Malayalam Cinema', in *Women in Malayalam Cinema*, Orient Blackswan Pvt. Ltd, 2010, p. 69.
15. Ibid.
16. Amaresh Datta, *The Encyclopaedia of Indian Literature*, Volume 1, p. 753.
17. Shyam Benegal, *A Door to Adoor*, South Asian Cinema Foundation, first edition, 2006.
18. Ratheesh Radhakrishnan, article titled 'Soft Porn and the Anxieties of the Family', in *Women in Malayalam Cinema*, Orient Blackswan Pvt. Ltd, 2010, p. 194.

19. Erik Barnouw and S. Krishnaswamy, *South Indian Film*, Oxford University Press, second edition, p. 14.
20. Meena T. Pillai, *Women in Malayalam Cinema*, article titled 'Becoming Women: Unwrapping Femininity in Malayalam Cinema', Orient Blackswan Pvt. Ltd, 2010.
21. Inderpal Grewal and Caren Kaplan, *Scattered Hegemonies: Postmodernity and Transnational Feminist Practices*, University of Minnesota Press, 1994, p. 84.
22. Shohini Chaudhuri, *Feminist Film Theorists*, Routledge Publication, 2006, special Indian edition, p. 35.
23. Patricia Waugh, *Literary Theory and Criticism*, Oxford University Press, 2006, p. 321.
24. Darius Cooper, *The Cinema of Satyajit Ray: Between Tradition and Modernity*, Cambridge University Press, 2007.
25. Richard von Busack, 'RvB's After Images: *Ankur* (1974) by Shyam Benegal', posted on 7 September 2007.
26. Gautaman Bhaskaran, *Adoor Gopalakrishnan: A Life in Cinema*, Penguin Books India, 2010, p. 117.
27. Ross Murfins and Supriya M. Ray, *The Bedford Glossary*, Macmillan Press Ltd, p. 357.
28. Gautaman Bhaskaran, *Adoor Gopalakrishnan: A Life in Cinema*, Penguin Books India, 2009.
29. Jonathan Rosenbaum, 'Ritwik Ghatak: Reinventing the Cinema', published in *Rouge*, 2006.
30. Gustavo Costantini, professor of sound design and editing at the University of Buenos Aires, 'Leitmotif Revisited', Filmsound.org.
31. Andrew Dix, *Beginning Film Studies*, Viva Books, first Indian edition, 2010, p. 33.
32. Chidananda Dasgupta, *Seeing is Believing*, Penguin Books India, 2008, p. 243.
33. Gautaman Bhaskaran, *Adoor Gopalakrishnan: A Life in Cinema*, Penguin Books India, 2010, pp. 40-41.
34. Adoor Gopalakrishnan, 'Return to the Roots', *The Indian Express*, 19 September 1999.
35. Interview with C. Ignatius in *The Indian Express*, 26 December 1982.
36. Iqbal Masud, 'Requiem for Lefty', *The Indian Express*, 9 December, 1984.
37. C.T. Venkiteswaran, '*Swayamvaram*: Classic Prophecies', in *A Door to Adoor*, South Asian Cinema Foundation, first edition, 2006.
38. *Filmfare*, 1–15 April 1978.

39. Interview with M.D. Riti, *Filmfare*, 16–31 March 1984.
40. Ibid.
41. *The Asian Age*, 26 December 1997.
42. Georgia Brown, *Voice*, 23 April 1994.
43. Suranjan Ganguly, *A Door to Adoor*, South Asian Cinema Foundation, first edition, 2006, p. 12.
44. *India Today*, 31 October 1990, pp. 173-74.
45. Prasanna Ramaswamy, 'Face to Face', *The Hindu*, 25 November 1990, p. 19.
46. To K.B. Venu, in *Cinema in India*, April–June 2002.
47. K.G. Kumar, 'Celluloid magic', *The Indian Magazine*, August 1984.
48. Shampa Banerjee, 'In the shadow world of Unni', *The Rat Trap*, Seagull Books, Calcutta 1985.
49. John W. Hood, *The Essential Mystery*, Orient Blackswan, revised edition, 2009, p. 168.
50. Maithili Rao, 'The Apolitical Humanist Projects the Sky on a Dew Drop', *A Door to Adoor*, South Asian Cinema Foundation, first edition, 2006.
51. Venu Menon, *The Illustrated Weekly of India*, 3 March 1985.
52. John W. Hood, *The Essential Mystery*, Orient Blackswan, revised edition, 2009, p. 169.
53. M.K. Raghavendra, *50 Indian Film Classics*, HarperCollins *Publishers* India, 2009, p. 236.
54. Shampa Banerjee, *Face to Face*, Seagull Books, 1985.
55. Suranjan Ganguly, 'Narratives of Dislocation', in *A Door to Adoor*, South Asian Cinema Foundation, first edition, 2006, p. 17.
56. Gautaman Bhaskaran, *Adoor Gopalakrishnan: A Life in Cinema*, Penguin Books India, 2010.
57. S. Prasannarajan, 'Adoor trip into the recesses of the human psyche', *The Times of India*, 10 May1988.
58. *A Door to Adoor*, South Asian Cinema Foundation, first edition, 2006, p. 22.
59. In an interview to K.B. Venu in *Cinema in India*, April–June 2002.
60. Krishna Chaitanya, *A History of Malayalam Literature*, Orient Longman Ltd, first published, 1971, reprinted 1995.
61. A. Sreedhara Menon, *A Survey of Kerala History*, DC Books, 2008.
62. Prema Viswanathan, 'A disquieting denouement', *Time Off*, 4 March 1990.
63. 'Narratives of Dislocation', *A Door to Adoor*, South Asian Cinema Foundation, first edition, 2006, p. 22.
64. As Hegel says in 'Master-Slave dialectic', *The Norton Anthology: Theory and criticism*, W.W. Norton & Company, New York, London, 2001, p. 633.

65. Interview to C. S. Venkiteswaran.
66. John W. Hood, *The Essential Mystery*, Orient Blackswan, revised edition, 2009, p. 185.
67. 'Hangman's Hymn', *The Week*, 6 January 2002, p. 64.
68. '*Nizhalkkuthu*: The Epic Conflict', *A Door to Adoor*, South Asian Cinema Foundation, first edition, 2006.
69. Chidananda Dasgupta, *Seeing Is Believing*, Penguin Books India, 2008.
70. Courtesy Shobha Warrier.
71. Extracted from T.K. Ramachandran, 'Notes on the Making of Feminine Identity in Contemporary Kerala', *Social Scientist*, January–March 1995.

Student Films at FTII

(1964–65)

LIGHT

(Dialogue exercise)

Black and white; Hindi; 10 minutes

Credits: Script and Direction: Adoor Gopalakrishnan; Cinematography: Suresh Nair; Sound Recording: P. Devadas; Editing: M. C. Bhuyan

Cast: Mani Kaul (Ramesh), Sudharani Sharma (Lakshmi), Suma (Baby), Subhash Ghai (Doctor), Govardhan Asrani (Assistant Surgeon), Pratima Naik (Nurse), Surendra Desai (Delegate 1), G.K. Sharma (Delegate 2), Vinay Malhotra (Delegate 3)

Adoor Gopalakrishnan's dialogue exercise *Light* was based on a Malayalam one-act play written by the well-known playwright, T.N. Gopinathan Nair. The film narrates the struggles of a poor family: Ramesh, an employee in the electricity department, his wife Lakshmi and their only daughter Baby. The film opens with Ramesh reassuring his wife that Baby will be fine if she takes her medicine. The employees of the electricity office are on strike for better work conditions and Ramesh, who earns little, is in no position to afford a frock for his daughter, which she asks for. When Baby goes out of the room to play, Lakshmi says to Ramesh, 'Pity. She has only one frock – that too is in rags. She has been pestering me for a new frock for several days … We don't have the right to call ourselves parents.'

One of the workers, returning from a meeting with the bosses, informs Ramesh that they are looking into the matter but cannot do anything immediately as there are many important jobs pending. Ramesh, in extreme fury and frustration along with his colleague, and other workers hatch a plan to cut power supply from the control room in the peak hour to teach their bosses a lesson.

In the meantime, with Baby's condition deteriorating at home, Lakshmi shifts Baby from the house to the hospital. Baby's condition is declared critical and she has to be operated upon.

Ramesh, totally unaware of these developments, cuts the power supply from the control room. In the dark, the doctors have to stop the operation midway … even as Ramesh shakes hands with the other workers saying that their mission has been successful.

Incidentally, the editor of the film, M.C. Bhuyan, is my uncle. He graduated from the same batch as Adoor. Sudharani Sharma, who later joined Hindi cinema, was the young mother in the film as well as the heroine of Adoor's diploma film. Asrani went on to become a leading comedian in Bombay cinema. Two of the then acting course students who featured in the exercise, Mani Kaul (he later switched disciplines) and Subhash Ghai, went on to notable careers as directors.

A GREAT DAY

(Diploma film)

35mm; Black and white; Hindi; 12 minutes

Credits: Script and Direction: Adoor Gopalakrishnan; Cinematography: Indu Kalpa Hazarika; Sound Recording: Anantha Padmanabhan; Editing: W.Y. Mohiley; Producer: Jagat Murari, principal, Film Institute of India

Cast: Surendra Shah (Ravi), Sudharani Sharma (Mini), Appi Umrani (Chadda), Surendra (Milkman), Rashid (Boy)

Adoor stepped into the world of cinema, technically speaking, on the day he made his short comedy film, *A Great Day.* The hero of the film is a lethargic young man named Ravi who stays in a hostel. The untidy condition of his room suggests the nature of the occupant. Posters of film actresses are hung on the wall. A dilapidated transistor radio sounds only when it is thumped upon. There is a clock on the table and bits of paper on the floor. A bicycle leans against the wall. Unpolished shoes. Uncleaned utensils. A toad sits on a bowl…

A Great Day opens with Ravi snoring. He is covered head to toe with a bed sheet. At 9.15 a.m. there is a sudden knocking at the door: 'Sir, milkman.' Ravi has a rope attached to his wooden door in such a way that he can open it by simply pulling the rope. The milkman, seeing him still in bed, says, 'Sir, are you feeling ill?'

'Today is Sunday. I'll sleep throughout the day,' Ravi replies.

The milkman places the milk bottle on the ground near the door and closes it behind him. After a while, a young boy of six or seven knocks urgently. He has a letter in his hand. When the boy gets no response, he pushes open the door and steps inside. The milk bottle falls. Ravi wakes up. The frightened young boy runs away. Ravi gives chase.

Ravi reads the letter: 'My father has come here and we're coming to your room. Only after meeting you will he agree to my marriage with you. Clean yourself up and the house. I'm saying this because I know your habits … We'll be there at 9.30 a.m. Yours, Mini.'

By the time he has finished reading the letter it is almost 9.20 a.m. The rest of the sequence is pure comedy as the would-be father-in-law arrives in a luxurious car to catch Ravi, clad in lungi and banian, chasing the toad out of the room with a broom. He mistakes him for the servant. 'Hey, come here. Is your master at home?' A shocked Ravi stares at the old man. Getting no response, the old man snarls, 'Are you dumb?' Mini, who is sitting beside her father, introduces Ravi as the boy they have come to meet.

Inside, the father is shocked to see the untidy condition of the room but his mood changes dramatically as the camera pans slowly along the photographs of the smiling heroines. He is obviously enjoying the sight. The camera pauses at a photo of one of the heroines baring her beautiful teeth, then moves on to an extreme close-up shot of Ravi's teeth. Ravi is disappointed to see his would-be father-in-law leave the house without wasting a moment. He lies despondent on the bed …

But all's well that ends well. An elated Mini rushes in to inform him that her dentist father has agreed to their marriage as he approves of Ravi's teeth!

Filmography

1972

SWAYAMVARAM (ONE'S OWN CHOICE)

Black and white; Malayalam; 125 minutes

Credits: Story, Screenplay and Direction: Adoor Gopalakrishnan; Co-Scenarist: K.P. Kumaran; Producer: Chitralekha Film Cooperative; Cinematography: Mankada Ravi Varma; Music: M.B. Srinivasan; Sound: P. Devadas; Art Direction: Dathan and Sivasakthan Nair; Editing: A. Ramesan

Cast: Madhu (Viswanathan), T. Sarada (Sita), Lalitha (Kalyani), P. K. Venukuttan Nair (Smuggler Vasu), Thikkurissi Sukumaran Nair (Tutorial College principal), Karamana Janardhanan Nair (his manager)

Prizes: National Awards for Best Film, Best Direction, Best Actress (T. Sarada) and Best Cinematography

Festivals: New York, Washington, Moscow, London, Paris, Nantes, La Rochelle, Pesaro, Helsinki, Ljubljana, Munich, Fribourg, Colombo

1977

KODIYETTAM (THE ASCENT)

Black and white; Malayalam; 128 minutes

Credits: Story, Screenplay and Direction: Adoor Gopalakrishnan; Producer: Chitralekha Film Cooperative; Chief Assistant: Meera Sahib;

Cinematography: Mankada Ravi Varma; Sound: Adoor Gopalakrishnan (Effects), Ramachandran; Art Direction: Sivan; Editing: M. Mani

Cast: Gopi (Sankarankutty), Vilasani (Sarojini), Lalitha (Santhamma), Adoor Bhavani (Santhamma's mother), Thikkurissi Sukumaran Nair (schoolmaster), Aziz (truck driver), Radhamani (truckdriver's mistress)

Prizes: National Awards for Best Regional Film and Best Actor (Gopi); Kerala State Awards for Best Film, Best Direction, Best Screenplay, Best Actor (Gopi) and Best Art Direction

Festivals: New York, Washington, London, Paris, La Rochelle, Nantes, Helsinki, Berlin, Munich, Pesaro, Ljubljana, Fribourg, Adelaide, Tunis among others

1981

ELIPPATHAYAM (The Rat-trap)

Colour; Malayalam; 121 minutes

Credits: Story, Screenplay and Direction: Adoor Gopalakrishnan; Producer: Ravi, General Pictures; Chief Assistant: Meera Sahib; Cinematography: Mankada Ravi Varma; Music: M.B. Srinivasan; Sound: P. Devadas; Art Direction: Sivan; Editing: M. Mani

Cast: Karamana Janardhanan Nair (Unni), T. Sarada (Rajamma), Jalaja (Sridevi), Rajam K. Nair (Janamma)

Prizes: National Awards for Best Regional Film and Best Audiography; Kerala State Awards for Best Film, Best Cinematography and Best Audiography; British Film Institute Award for the most original and imaginative film of 1982

Festivals: Cannes, Paris, La Rochelle, Nantes, Pesaro, Munich, Ljubljana, London, Washington DC, Chicago, Seattle, Houston, New York, Hawaii, Alexandria, Sao Paulo, Sydney, Melbourne

1984

MUKHAMUKHAM (Face-to-Face)

Colour; Malayalam; 107 minutes

Credits: Story, Screenplay and Direction: Adoor Gopalakrishnan; Chief Assistant: Meera Sahib; Producer: Ravi, General Pictures; Cinematography: Mankad Ravi Varma; Music: M.B. Srinivasan; Sound: P. Devadas; Art Direction: Sivan; Editing: M. Mani

Cast: P. Gangadharan Nair (Sreedharan), Kaviyoor Ponnamma (Savitri), Karamana Janardhanan Nair (trade unionist), Viswanathan (Sudhakaran Junior), Ashokan (Sudhakaran Senior)

Prizes: National Awards for Best Direction, Best Screenplay, Best Audiography and Best Regional Film; Kerala State Awards for Best Film, Best Direction, Best Cinematography, Best Audiography and Best Editing; FIPRESCI (International Critics) Prize for the Best Film, International Film Festival of India, New Delhi, 1985

Festivals: New York, Washington, London, Locarno, Brussels, Antwerp, Munich, Fribourg, Manosque, Paris, Nantes, La Rochelle, Pesaro, Helsinki, Ljubljana, Alexandria, Hong Kong, New Delhi among others

1987

ANANTARAM (Monologue)

Colour; Malayalam; 125 minutes

Credits: Story, Screenplay and Direction: Adoor Gopalakrishnan; Chief Assistant: Meera Sahib; Producer: Ravi, General Pictures; Cinematography: Mankada Ravi Varma; Music: M.B. Srinivasan; Sound: P. Devadas, Krishnanunni and N. Harikumar; Art Direction: Sivan; Editing: M. Mani

Cast: Ashokan (Ajayan Senior), Sudheesh (Ajayan Junior), Mammootty (Balu), Shobana (Suma/Nalini), N.B. Thampi (doctor, Ajayan's foster-father), Kaviyoor Ponnamma (Mother at the ashram)

Prizes: National Awards for Best Direction, Best Screenplay and Best Audiography; Kerala State Award for Best Direction; FIPRESCI (International Critics) Prize for the Best Film at the Karlovy Vary Film Festival, 1988

Festivals: Venice, Pesaro, Karlovy Vary, La Rochelle, Nantes, Amiens, Riga, Munich, Fribourg, Ljubljana, Helsinki, London, Washington DC, New York, San Francisco, Toronto, Hawaii, Alexandria among others

1989

MATHILUKAL (The Walls)

Colour; Malayalam; 117 minutes

Credits: Story: Vaikom Muhammad Basheer; Screenplay and Direction: Adoor Gopalakrishnan; Chief Assistant: Meera Sahib; Producer: Adoor Gopalakrishnan Productions; Sponsor: Doordarshan; Cinematography: Mankada Ravi Varma; Music: Vijaya Bhaskar; Sound: N. Harikumar; Art Direction: Sivan; Costumes: Sivan; Editing: M. Mani

Cast: Mammootty (Basheer), Ravi Vallathol (Razak), Thilakan (head warder), Karamana Janardhdanan Nair (political leader), P.C. Soman (head constable), Lalitha (Narayani's voice)

Prizes : National Awards for Best Direction, Best Actor (Mammootty), Best Audiography and Best Malayalam Film; FIPRESCI (International Critics) Prize at Venice, 1990; UNICEF Film Prize at Venice, 1990; Ecumenical Prize at Amiens; Awards for Best Film and Best Direction at the 2003 Auberville Film Festival for Youth

Festivals: Venice, Pesaro, Milan, Nantes, Manosque, Amiens, Munich, Fribourg, Rotterdam, Vienna, London, Ljubljana, Toronto, Los Angeles, Washington DC, New York, Hawaii, Istanbul, Haifa among others

1993

VIDHEYAN (The Servile)

Colour; Malayalam and Kannada; 112 minutes

Credits: Story: Paul Zacharia; Screenplay and Direction: Adoor Gopalakrishnan; Chief Assistant: Meera Sahib; Producer: Ravi, General Pictures; Cinematography: Mankada Ravi Varma; Music: Vijaya Bhaskar; Sound: P. Devadas and T. Krishnanunni; Art Direction: Sivan; Costumes: Sivan; Editing: M. Mani

Cast: Mammootty (Bhaskara Patelar), M.R. Gopakumar (Thommi), Sabitha Anand (Omana), Tanvi Azmi (Saroja)

Prizes: National Awards for Best Actor (Mammootty) and Best Regional Film; Kerala State Awards for Best Film, Best Director, Best Actor (Mammootty) and Best Story; FIPRESCI (International Critics) Prize at Singapore, 1994; Inter-film Prize, Mannheim, 1994

Festivals: London, Pesaro, Nantes, Brussels, San Sebastian, Fribourg, Munich, Mannheim, Rotterdam, Ljubljana, Singapore, Hong Kong, Fukuoka, Brisbane, Durban, Teheran, Toronto, New York, San Francisco, Chicago, Hawaii, Sao Paulo among others.

1995

KATHAPURUSHAN (Man of the Story)

Colour; Malayalam; 107 minutes

Credits: Story, Screenplay and Direction: Adoor Gopalakrishnan; Producer: Adoor Gopalakrishnan Productions and Japan Broadcasting Corporation (NHK); Cinematography: Mankada Ravi Varma; Music: Vijaya Bhaskar; Sound: N. Harikumar; Art Direction: Sivan; Make-up: P.N. Mani; Editing: M. Mani

Cast: Viswanathan (Kunjunni), Mini Nair (Meenakshi), Arnamula Ponnamma (Kunjunni's grandmother), Urmila Unni (Kunjunni's mother), Narendra Prasad (Vasu), Babu Namboothiri (Veluchar), Lalitha

(Janamma), Oduvil Unnikrishnan (Pachupillai), P.C. Soman (Ayurvedic physician)

Prizes: National Awards for Best Film and Best Supporting Actress (Arnamula Ponnamma); FIPRESCI (International Critics) Prize at MAMI, Mumbai, 1997; Special Jury Award at Singapore, 1996

Festivals: Toronto, London, Nantes, Pesaro, Rotterdam, Göteborg, Ljubljana, Munich, Vienna, Fribourg, Washington DC, New York, Denver, Hawaii, Paris, Tokyo, Fukuoka among others

2002

NIZHALKKUTHU (SHADOW KILL)

Colour; Malayalam and Tamil; 90 minutes

Credits: Story, Screenplay and Direction: Adoor Gopalakrishnan; Chief Assistant: Sajeev Pillai; Producer: Adoor Gopalakrishnan Productions and Artcam International; Cinematography: Mankada Ravi Varma and Sunny Joseph; Music: Ilayaraja; Sound Recording: N. Harikumar; Sound Editing and Mixing: Dominique Vieillard; Art Direction: Ratheesh S.B.; Make-up: P. N. Mani; Editing: Ajith Kumar

Cast: Oduvil Unnikrishnan (Kaliyappan), Sunil (Muthu), Reeja (Mallika), Sivakumar (Mallika's lover), Murali (Vasu)

Prizes: National Awards for Best Regional Film; FIPRESCI (International Critics) Prize at Mumbai, 2003

Festivals: Venice, Rotterdam, Göteborg, Vienna, Paris, Manosque, Nantes, Fribourg, Ljubljana, Munich, London, New York, Washington DC, Toronto, Shanghai, Fukuoka, Jerusalem among others

2007

NAALU PENNUNGAL (FOUR WOMEN)

Colour; Malayalam; 105 minutes

Credits: Screenplay and Direction: Adoor Gopalakrishnan; Story: Thakazhi Sivasankara Pillai; Chief Assistant: Meera Sahib; Producer: Adoor Gopalakrishnan; Co-producer: Benzy Martin; Cinematography: M. J. Radhakrishnan; Music: Isaac Thomas; Sound: N. Harikumar; Art Direction: Rajasekharan; Costumes: S. B. Satheesh; Make-up: P. N. Mani; Editing: Ajith Kumar

Cast: Padmapriya (Kunju Pennu), Sreejith (Papu Kutty), Geetu Mohandas (Kumari), Nandulal (Narayanan), Manju Pillai (Chinnu Amma), Murali (Raman Pillai), Mukesh (Nara Pillai), Nandita Das (Kamakshi), Kavya Madhavan (Subhadra), Ravi Vallathol (Subhadra's husband)

Prizes: National Award for Best Director

Festivals: Toronto, New York, New Jersey, Washington DC, Los Angeles, Seattle, Miami, Palm Springs, Vancouver, Trinidad, London, Warsaw, Madrid, Barcelona, Nantes, Deauville, Manosque, Rotterdam, Munich, Hamburg, Göteborg, Ljubljana, Brussels, Vienna, Jerusalem, Dubai, Cairo, Brisbane, Hong Kong, Dhaka among others

ORU PENNUM RANDAANUM (A CLIMATE FOR CRIME)

Colour; Malayalam; 115 minutes

Credits: Screenplay and Direction: Adoor Gopalakrishnan; Story: Thakazhi Sivasankara Pillai; Chief Assistant: Meera Sahib; Producer: Adoor Gopalakrishnan; Co-producer: Benzy Martin; Production: Partly supported by Doordarshan; Cinematography: M. J. Radhakrishnan; Music: Isaac Thomas; Sound: Krishnanunni and N. Harikumar; Art Direction: Rajasekharan; Costumes: S. B. Satheesh; Make-up: P. N. Mani; Editing: Ajith Kumar

Cast: M. R. Gopakumar (Neelantan), Seema G. Nair (Neelantan's wife), Master Amal Jose (Kunjunni), Indran (Mathai), Nedumudi Venu

(Mathu), Jagannathan (Kuttan Pillai), Vijayaraghavan (police inspector), Krishnakumar (rickshaw puller), Praveena (Pankiamma), Ravi Vallathol (Rama Kurup), Manoj K. Jayan (Kittu Kurup), Sudheesh (Krishnankutty), Jagadeesh (advocate), P. C. Soman (quack)

Prizes: Kerala State Awards for Best Film, Best Director, Best Script, Best Sound (Krishnanunni and N. Harikumar) and Best Supporting Actress (Praveena)

Festivals: New Jersey, Houston, Washington DC, Rotterdam, Fribourg, Madrid, Rome, Split, Dubai, Tampa, Mumbai, Goa among others

Index

Acknowledgements

For his thought-provoking work, Adoor Gopalakrishnan has been the source of inspiration for many film-makers and film critics. I too did not remain untouched by his work, and the aim of my book is to reveal some new aspects of the master film-maker. I started researching his cinema, his writings and the socio-political history of Kerala while I was a student at Fergusson College, Pune, one of the places where good cinema is appreciated and understood. The late Prof. Neela Karnik had always encouraged students towards a deeper understanding of the art form.

My special thanks go to Adoor Gopalakrishnan for believing that I could do proper justice to his films, for sparing time for me from his busy schedule and also providing some of the stills from personal collections. I also thank his wife, Sunanda Gopalakrishnan, for her support. She passed away on 22 September 2015, at the age of sixty-six.

I would like to express my gratitude to Rani Day Burra, a renowned editor of India, and alumni of FTII, Pune, who took a microscopic look at my book. The editing process was very hard. I am specially thankful to the internationally reputed film critic Jean-Michel Frodon for writing the preface to my book; Nandita Das, for sharing her experience of working with Adoor Gopalakrishnan in his film *Four Women*; Derek Malcolm, internationally acclaimed film critic, for sending me some of his views on Adoor; and P.K. Nair, the founder and director of the National Film Archive of India (NFAI) for guiding me in my study of the socio-political history of Kerala.

I am grateful to the national-award-winning film-maker Jahnu Barua; Shaji A. Karun; Beena Paul, artistic director of the International Film Festival of Kerala (IFFK); award-winning film-maker Dr Biju; and the young film-maker Sherry for sharing with me their valuable time, discussing and analysing Adoor's works.

I am indebted to Anil Zankar, the film scholar and my teacher at FTII, Pune, for sharing with me his perspectives on Adoor Gopalakrishnan as a film-maker. I would like to thank Madhu, the veteran and legendary actor, and another brilliant actor M.R. Gopakumar, for sharing some interesting anecdotes about Adoor. My sincere thanks to Padmapriya Janakiraman, N. Harikumar, Sunny Joseph and S. Sivaraman, for sharing their experience with Adoor. I am grateful to my friend Jayadeva Rentala, a journalist and film critic from Hyderabad for his encouragement.

I would like to express my gratitude to Shantanu Ray Chaudhuri, managing editor, HarperCollins *Publishers* India, for understanding the stature of Adoor Gopalakrishnan in world cinema, for coming forward to publish the book and for his suggestions throughout the process of publication which were very valuable to me.

My gratitude also goes to my friend and writer K.A. Beena, who provided me with some of Adoor's films which were not available until I viewed them at the NFAI. I am indebted to Paul Zacharia, well-known writer and winner of the Sahitya Akademi Award, for giving me a long interview; Lalit Mohan Joshi, London-based film critic and editor of *A Door to Adoor*, for arranging some books and journals in Mumbai; and C.S. Venkiteswaran, well-known film critic, for sharing with me some of the critical aspects of Adoor's cinema.

Prashant Pathrabe, director of NFAI, Pune, was kind enough to allow me to view all of Adoor's films. Kiron Dhiwar, film preservation officer, NFAI, was very helpful in facilitating a conducive atmosphere for me at NFAI. Arti V. Karkhanis of NFAI provided me with research-oriented documents. Urmila Joshi arranged all the library material at NFAI. I am thankful to all the members of NFAI, Pune.

I am also indebted to Krishna Dulal Barua and my elder brother Rupjyoti Baruah for going through the first draft of my book. I am thankful to Manoj Barpujari, Prof. Jyotirmoi Jana, Dr Dwijen Sharma, Bijit Borthakur, Dr Sanjib Sahoo, Babu Philips, Girin Borah and Bhaskar Jyoti Saikia for their support. I thank my students Rimjim Baruah, Monalisha Chetry and my brother Protush Ranjan Bhagawati for the initial motivation to do this book. I am thankful to Hillol Kumar Pathok, senior journalist at *Sadin Weekly*, for providing me space to write on cinema. I thank my uncle Mukut Ch. Bhuyan, batchmate of Adoor Gopalakrishnan at FTII, Pune, for his encouragement.

I thank my wife Ananya, my sole financier, who apart from bearing all my travelling expenses, went through my first draft. I thank all the members of my family, particularly Dr Pori Hiloidari, Dr Arup Borah and poet Prayag Saikia for their support.

Finally, I wish to thank the Kerala State Chalachitra Academy for giving me the posters of Adoor's films.